Snowdrops for a Soldier

KAREN J. YATES

A Second World War memoir about a soldier and his family who made the ultimate sacrifice at the end of the North Africa campaign.

Matador
9 Priory Business Park,
Wistow Road, Kibworth Beauchamp,
Leicestershire. LE8 0RX
Tel: 0116 279 2299
Email: books@troubador.co.uk
Web: www.troubador.co.uk/matador
Twitter: @matadorbooks

ISBN 978 1785890 000

British Library Cataloguing in Publication Data.
A catalogue record for this book is available from the British Library.

Printed and bound by CPI Group (UK) Ltd, Croydon, CR0 4YY
Typeset in 11pt Aldine401 BT by Troubador Publishing Ltd, Leicester, UK

Matador is an imprint of Troubador Publishing Ltd

For my grandchildren: Thomas, Jack, Daniel, Faye, Eve, Samuel, Matthew, and last but not least a special dedication to Charlie, who recently made his entrance into the world and is the great great nephew of Charlie Robinson, the subject of this book. Young Charlie's birth has given me the confidence, impetus and conviction I needed to get my work published.

Stay with me, God.
The night is dark,
The night is cold:
My little spark
Of courage dies.
The night is long;
Be with me God,
And make me strong.

Anon.

Contents

Tunisia – Enfidaville War Cemetery

In two steps I leave behind a frenetic, speeded-up-street – like a film on fast forward – in which every car, van and bicycle hurriedly (and noisily) makes its presence felt. Two steps is all it takes to pass through an iron gate, and by so doing I enter an oasis of peace. The view from inside the gate is majestic: the profound simplicity of a wide expanse of lush grass, a marble memorial stone in the middle and in the background a marble base waiting for the cross of sacrifice which is about to be replaced.

In this tranquil world, the predominant colours are green and white. The lush, well cut, grassy areas are wide, uncluttered spaces of soothing green. A row of young olive trees have recently been planted, adding a different shade of green; while the mature trees on the perimeter gracefully present their version. The large white memorial stone shines brightly in the sunshine. On either side of the wide green avenue, almost one thousand five hundred perfectly spaced white marble head stones stand like sentinels guarding the precious remains beneath. The complete picture is one of a well-planned, dignified, beautiful aspect that calls for – and receives – a respectful silence from all who enter: even the sparrows, I notice, defer to the peaceful atmosphere by ceasing all chatter.

Until this day, I have seen only photographs and television film of war cemeteries; yet even taking into account the second hand nature of film and photograph, the significance of the final resting place of young servicemen who have died in the line of duty is still affecting, But to stand in this quiet place breathing in its peace and ordered stillness, is to feel a powerful emotion.

The cemetery keeper walks over to me and my husband. We are looking at a plan of the cemetery and he is here to help. He finds the grave we are looking for three rows down (I didn't count the number across) – and there it is. If I felt emotional as I walked through the gate, it was nothing compared to the mixture of feelings that passed through me as I looked down at the headstone for which I had been searching. I felt deeply moved and not a little awe-struck, touched by the closeness, so many years after his death and honoured to be the first family member to stand in front of the final resting place of: "C. Robinson, Signalman – 3454037, Royal Corps of Signals, died 12th May, 1943, age 25." The inscription at the base of the headstone read: "Of such is the kingdom of heaven."

It is seventy years to the day since my uncle was laid to rest in this very place. I thought about the intervening years and wondered how many people had passed through those cemetery gates. Certainly no-one from our family came here. In the months and years following his death, to an ordinary family living in the north of England, visiting Charlie's final resting place in Tunisia was about as achievable as visiting the moon. But I wondered if by chance, during those seven long decades, someone by the name of Robinson had stood in front of my uncle's grave and felt empathy in the sharing of a name.

I knew my uncle would be in a peaceful place, laid to rest with his combat companions, in the safe keeping of the Commonwealth War Graves Commission, which, without their care and attention, these beautiful cemeteries would go to rack and ruin: overrun with weeds and creeping brambles – slowly but relentlessly hidden like Sleeping Beauty's Castle: unseen, uncared for and abandoned. But as long as these cemeteries are so lovingly maintained, the servicemen within them and the sacrifice each one made will never be forgotten.

My uncle's headstone is no different in size, shape or colour from all the others: no-one is distinguished above another. Squaddie may lie next to Sergeant, Sikh lies next to Christian. Each sacrifice makes rank irrelevant. Only the words engraved on the marble say something different: name, rank, service number, Corps. Section or Division, age and date of death, with personalised words inscribed near the base of the stone, nearest the earth. My uncle lay next to 2nd Lieutenant Cassell and beside him the Commanding Officer of the regiment Lieutenant Colonel W.P. Hobbs. Adding to the emotion of the visit, and answering the question of how my uncle met his death, I noted their proximity and the 12th May, 1943 engraved on each one. The three had died together.

I knelt on the grass in front of his headstone, and read out a letter I had written to my uncle (not knowing what else to take him) and yes, I did manage to read it, despite the intense emotion of a very large lump in my throat. (See App. D) Terry, my husband, left me in peace, strolling over to examine other headstones nearby. Growing beside, or in front of, each headstone, a flower or small bush had been planted, (not so tall as to obscure the words) but making its own little statement of individuality. Two rows above my uncle's grave, three headstones were standing closer together – almost, but not quite, touching. They contained the remains of six airmen, all travelling in the same plane, when it was shot down. To symbolize this, they were buried closer together. It is the many thoughtful actions like these that are the most touching. Within the cemetery are eighty eight graves of unknown soldiers. These are so poignant in their simplicity, merely inscribed with the words: "A British Soldier of the 1939-1945 War, and underneath the cross the words: "Known unto God."

The gardener/keeper of the cemetery melts away, thoughtfully allowing us to pay our respects in peace. Then my husband read out a poem to Uncle Charlie. The words were in the form of a prayer written on a piece of paper, by an unknown British soldier, which had been found in a slit trench in Tunisia. (See App. C) Coincidentally, the poem was included towards the end of a book of fiction he had brought on holiday, and the poem was part of the story. (Found in "The Husband" by Dean Koontz, p431) Its aptness was uncanny in both words and timing, coming to light only two days before we were due to visit the cemetery.

The gardener/cemetery keeper, seeing we were ready to leave, kindly walked over to hand me a posy of plastic poppies – those bright red symbols of sacrifice – which I tearfully pushed into the soil of my uncle's grave, before bidding him goodbye. I left the cemetery feeling comforted that his final resting place was in such a profoundly peaceful place: a place where every single man buried there was cared for as a precious symbol of sacrifice.

The emotional visit to my uncle's final resting place is a fitting climax to two years' work. Two years in which I have been amazed, informed, frustrated, amused, sad, touched and inspired. On this day I am physically closer to him, completing the story that began with inheriting his letters and diary; slowly uncovering the personality of the man: enabling me to understand, and form a bond with, the person behind the writing. At the same time I experienced a growing knowledge, awareness and respect for the sacrifices both he his family made during the 2nd World War. These first pages merely tell the end of his story, hinting at a long, long journey across North Africa to his final resting place so very far from home. Now for the beginning of his story…

CHAPTER ONE

Snowdrops On The Sideboard

I never met my Uncle Charlie. He died over two years before I was born. From an early age I was aware of a large photograph which sat on the sideboard of my grandparents' house. Dressed in his army uniform, Uncle Charlie smiled at me from behind the frame. He wore glasses with old fashioned, thick, dark rims. In my early years, the significance of this photograph was lost on me. Uncle Charlie always had a vase of fresh flowers beside him, containing the current season's blooms. In those days fresh flowers were strictly seasonal – virtually unobtainable in winter. The task of keeping the appropriately sized vases filled permanently with fresh flowers – even during the difficult winter season – was taken on by my grandma. She solved the problem of the scarcity of fresh flowers in February by picking snowdrops – the very first flowers of the year – from her tiny front garden. It must have been quite a challenge for Grandma to purchase, find or pick a permanent year-round supply of flowers; but I think she managed it (unless my memory is playing tricks on me) because I don't remember a vase ever being absent or empty.

In my early childhood innocence, the things on the sideboard were just part of my grandparents' front room: no more meaningful to me than the chairs or the fireplace. I didn't fully understand the significance of the photograph and the flowers until, approaching maturity myself, I realised that the carefully placed fresh flowers next to his photograph represented a living tribute to a never-to-be-forgotten son; a shrine to his memory. In the absence of a funeral, and a tangible, touchable grave to visit, my grandparents had to mourn their son the best way they could, so grandma picked snowdrops from her tiny front garden as a living memorial.

As I grew I was told that Uncle Charlie had been killed in the war, and with my limited understanding failed to comprehend the profound loss of a son, brother, cousin and friend that must have been felt at the time. Therefore I just accepted it in the way that children do. Later, I was aware that my mother would cry on Remembrance Sunday, and she would talk, through her tears, about how she could not have wished for a kinder, more loving, more protective older brother. It was only then that I began to understand something of her loss. I don't remember my grandmother ever talking about her son, and, to my shame, I can't recall whether I asked her about him either. At first, when their grief was raw and still sharply painful, I was too young to understand. Later, when I *was* old enough, his death, though still hurting, had been blunted by the passage of Time.

From my mother I learnt that he had been travelling in a truck, somewhere in the desert, when it received a direct hit. There was no mention of what had happened to his body, so I just assumed he didn't have a final resting place. When my grandmother died Mum inherited lots of old photographs and Uncle Charlie's precious diary. She told me about the diary, but I didn't read it until recently, after both my parents had gone into a nursing home, and I was sorting out their possessions. I read his diary with a mixture of sadness and a sense of loss, despite the fact that I had never known him. Beside the diary, I found his letters, which I knew nothing about, and later, when I was looking through my parents' photographs to my astonishment I found an image of a grave, depicting a simple wooden cross. Written on the cross member was my Uncle's name, rank, service number and date of death. The back of the photograph revealed the words: "Enfidaville War Cemetery, Tunisia." What a sad irony. A few years before, my husband and I had been enjoying a holiday in Tunisia, unaware we were only kilometers away from his grave.

I felt Uncle's diary was vulnerable to the passage of time, and my first thought was that I should make some attempt to preserve it by recording its contents; this then led to a giant leap in thought that, due to its historical and military value, perhaps I should attempt to write a book So here it is – a personal account of one soldier's experiences of war before he made the ultimate sacrifice. For myself, I am keen to discover more about the 8th Army, the desert campaign, the possible circumstances of his death, and researching the words and expressions he uses. I am starting out with virtually no knowledge of these things, but have a great desire to learn and understand. After some thought I have decided to include Uncle's letters, as they reflect, via his words, the sacrifices made by friends and family who were fighting the war from their home town. This feels like the start of a long journey of discovery.

Charles was the eldest of three children born to Andrew and Nora Robinson, who lived in Hyde, a small town eight miles from Manchester. Marjorie, (my mother) was the second child, and my Uncle Norman was the youngest. They lived in a modest terraced house, and my Grandfather worked at Slack Mills, the local cotton mill for over fifty years. He was a process worker: a "stripper and grinder." in the carding room. But Granddad didn't let his manual employment stand in the way of his journey to a good education. I remember classic books sitting on top of the piano: "The Man in the Iron Mask" and "The Mill on the Floss" and "Silas Marner." just to name the ones I can remember. I think there were others by William Shakespeare. He would sit up reading to the early hours, retiring to bed for just a few hours' sleep, before rising to face a day's work at the Mill. Obviously self-improvement was important to my granddad, so he would have been particularly proud of Uncle Charlie when he managed to gain entry to the local County School, later re-named the grammar school.

Granddad sang the bass in Slack Mills Male Voice Choir, and he wrote short stories which were printed in the local paper. Amongst the photographs I found one of his original handwritten stories in pristine condition, perfectly formed in neat, elegant letters, dating back to December, 1920; beside it was the fragile, yellowed, printed version from the local paper. I have three clear memories of my granddad: having a shave in front of a cracked mirror balanced on a dining chair in front of the fire, in which he had placed a small pan of water to boil on the coals. I remember watching as he carefully (and far too slowly for my liking) dipped the shaving brush into the scalding hot water, rubbed the brush round the circular shaving soap with its silver wrapping and worked the soap round and round his face before shaving. It took him ages to have a shave (or so I thought) while I was waiting to play Ludo with him (which is my second memory of him). My third clear memory is of him sitting on a dining chair at the back door, thoughtfully watching the sunset. I can now recall his patience and love, which I took for granted then.

My Grandmother was a homemaker, as was usual in those days. She was in charge of all the household tasks: cooking, cleaning, washing, and shopping: a full time job in the absence of today's labour saving devices. The washing for instance, was always done on Monday, and it took all day. The clothes had to go through several processes, resulting in spotlessly clean clothes. They were washed, rinsed, put through a mangle, (squashed between two rollers), starched, dried, ironed and aired. I can remember when I was very young, in the late forties and early fifties, on wet days, there would be clothes arranged on a wooden dryer.

Because grandma possessed neither fridge nor freezer, the shopping had to be done every other day. The positive side to this chore was the close proximity of different sorts of shops (before supermarkets and out of town retail outlets had been thought up). Not far along the same street there were butchers, grocers, greengrocers, chemists, and bakers. It meant that when I was a little older, and sent to the shops to buy something, I didn't have far to walk. There was home baking to be done on another day, and the net curtains had to be soaked in a substance that was supposed to whiten them: a virtually impossible task, as Grandma lived on the main road between Sheffield and Manchester with the constant fumes from traffic, factory and house chimneys to contend with. There were dense fogs in winter which caused blackened clothes, lungs and, of course, the net curtains.

My memories of Grandma are: pieces of chocolate, mint imperials (not as good as the chocolate, I thought!) jelly and custard, her big wrap-around apron, singing hymns whilst doing her housework (an important part of her faith, which gave her strength and bestowed great comfort on her) and best of all sitting on her knee while she read "Christopher Robin" to me, serialised in "Woman's Realm" magazine. Her knee was warm and comfortable and very safe.

The aforementioned memories were all garnered in the late forties and early to late fifties as I was growing up. But when Uncle Charlie was born in 1917, the world would have been a very different place, compared to the one I knew. The end of the first world war was just in sight, electricity and wireless sets were still in their infancy, only businesses had telephones, men and women worked long hours, at work and in the home, there was no health service, and, just one of the many arduous chores involved in keeping a house clean in those days, was lugging the carpet squares outside, hanging them over the washing line and beating them to eliminate the dust.

The history of that time has been well documented, and doesn't need me to go over it again in detail. However, it does help me to imagine a time, nearly one hundred years ago, when Charles Robinson was born into a vastly different world from the one we experience today. Although the history of that time helps me to have some inkling of daily life in general, to personalise it by understanding the family of which he was a member, and to actually communicate with people who knew him, helps me to take a step closer, and begin to get to know the person behind the photograph. I have been fortunate to access some memories from my mother and her cousin, Hilda, who has written several letters to me describing an extended family of brothers, sisters, cousins, aunties and uncles, who made a point of spending time together during high days and holidays – outdoors, as well as in their respective homes. Hilda has written to me in great detail about trips on the top deck of open-topped trams, when they were all riding high, excitedly singing and swaying, looking forward to a day out and a picnic in Vernon Park, Stockport.

Uncle Charlie was the eldest child born into this close-knit extended family. He was not only the eldest brother to my Mum and Uncle Norman; he was also the eldest cousin to Hilda and Edwin, who were the children of my Grandma's sister, Edith. Both Hilda and my Mum have testified to: "singing and swaying" on the opened-topped tram until it felt like it would topple over. There were Christmas parties, to which everyone was invited. They were given a "tiny present" and the food was "cold meats and home-made pickles." As the years passed, and as he was older than the other children, Charlie would not always be present at the family gatherings. But Hilda, when writing of Uncle Charlie said: "I loved him. I thought he was wonderful."

My Grandparents were both Methodists, and strictly tee-total all their lives. However, this didn't prevent the whole family from having fun. There were sing-songs round the piano, (not always hymns) followed by a game called, "The Coachman" which Hilda tells me she loved as a child. My Grandfather, who was a great story teller of course, told the story, and each person had to be a part of the coach, for example the wheels, the coachman, the whip, the seats, and when Granddad mentioned a particular part of the coach, that person had to stand up and turn around, and when he mentioned the coach, everybody had to stand up and turn around. To us, in our computerised, fast-paced, social networking world, this game seems silly and tame; but in those far-off times, it was invaluable for building secure loving relationships and family fun. A few weeks ago whilst driving along the road I recall passing four teenagers, all sat in a line with their backs against a wall, eight thumbs working furiously; every teen gazing at a screen. I thought: modern social interaction means staring at a variety of screens, differing only in size and function. Whatever happened to the simple pleasure of conducting a face-to-face conversation with a friend, using facial expressions and animated speech, adding life to a conversation?

CHAPTER TWO

Life Before The War

CHARLES ROBINSON
BORN 25th JULY, 1917
PARENTS:
ANDREW & NORA

Charlie is standing on the left of the photograph holding the flag. The writing on the bottom of the photograph can just be made out.

The church played a large part in the life of the Robinson family. Charlie also was involved in the many clubs and activities attached to it. The church offered members not only a chance to worship, but also friendship, opportunities to socialise, activities, outings, the choir, the drama group and the Scout movement. It seems that my Uncle was in just about every club, group and activity the church had to offer. He was also church secretary: I found his signature in a book prize awarded to my mum after she raised the most money for work overseas. In my possession are numerous photographs – with place names helpfully written on the back – depicting a smiling Charlie Robinson standing or sitting in the middle of a group of friends. Judging by the many photographs, there were lots of happy occasions: days out, holidays, rambling outings and cycling trips.

His life was full: of friends, family, days out, clubs and

groups. It's almost as if he sensed he had a limited time to pack as much activity into his young life as he could manage – garnering so much friendship and love along the way. I hope these positive aspects of his early life sustained him when he was so far from home.

In the following pages there are photographs of some of the outings and activities in which he participated.

Pott Shrigley 1937. (Charles Robinson on left.)
Pott Shrigley – A small hamlet near Macclesfield, Cheshire

Hyde Chapel, Gee Cross, 1936 (Charles Robinson on left)

Port St. Mary, Isle of Man, Aug. 1938. (Charles Robinson far left.)

Pott Shrigley 1937. (Charles Robinson far left)

Written on back of photo card:
"Full cast of "None So Blind." 3 Act Play, Water Street, April, 1939.
"Left to right: Gladys Collinson, Harry Fisher, Tam Morris, Phyllis
Booth, Doris Carr, Chas. Robinson, Dora Downing, Jessie Morton, Arthur
Barton, Marjorie Milnes"

The above image is my final peacetime photograph, showing a carefree Charles Robinson enjoying his pre-war life to the full.

The above photograph, taken in April, 1939, shows a relaxed and confident Uncle Charlie, obviously enjoying his part in the local play. When the photograph was taken, he could not have known that his life was about to change so dramatically. Five months later Britain would declare war on Germany, and a further five months would see my uncle donning his army uniform ready to go to war.

I have wondered how Uncle Charlie adjusted to his new life: learning to get along with other lads from very different backgrounds, being far away from friends and family and absorbing a different sort of discipline and new skills. According to my mother, father and mother's cousin, Hilda, he was a very friendly, outgoing person: testified by the many photographs taken with friends and family on outings and activities. Charlie's personality would be a big advantage when making new friends. But I do hope that the broad smile and relaxed stance in many of his photographs shield an inner strength and stoicism which would help him face up to the many challenges that lay ahead.

★★★

N.B. Before I start to record Uncle Charlie's letters I thought it might be a good idea to explain the currency in use at the time, as he refers to money in many of his letters. The basic units were pounds, shillings and pence. There were also fractions of pennies e.g. a half penny and a farthing which was one quarter of a penny.

Pounds, shillings and pence were written as: £ s d (the 'd' was originally a Roman coin, a denarius, which later became known as a penny) There were 12 pennies in one shilling, and twenty shillings in one pound; so for example one pound five shillings and six pence would have been written as: £1.5s 6d, or 5/6d if just referring to the shillings and pence alone.

CHAPTER THREE

The Letters

I have no way of knowing if the twenty three letters I have in my possession are complete. The first letter is dated 17th February, 1940, and the last one is dated 16th April, 1943. Some letters were written within a day or two; sometimes there were gaps of several months. Perhaps some were lost, or Uncle Charlie did not have an opportunity to write. I have decided to present them in chronological order and to introduce his diary in the appropriate time frame.

As Uncle's diary does not begin until 1st January, 1943, there are sixteen letters to come first. They do provide a valuable insight into both army and civilian life, as he writes of his life in the army, and comments on civilian life back home. Because Uncle's writing is small, but completely legible, the letters are easy to read and copy. I present them in their entirety, without editing.

No. 3454037 Fus.C Robinson,
No. 6 Platoon,
No. 1 Rec. Coy,
310 I.T.C. M5,
Hadrian's Camp,[1]
Carlisle.
17-2-40

Dear All,

Now I've got some writing paper I can tell you a bit more. This is a new camp, we're only the second lot of recruits in. It's a pretty big place, holding 1200 men and when we go to the cookhouse for meals there's always a pretty big queue. We're all in big wooden huts with 18 in each one, and every hut is warmed by pipes and radiators. There's a Naafi place here where we can get practically everything we want – hair cream, razor blades, boot polish, etc. as well as cups of tea and cakes.

The men in my hut are a very decent lot, mostly from Manchester, but one from Hull and one from Leeds, we've also a Stockport lad here. The N.C.O. in charge of us is Sergeant Steele, and he's a right good fellow. The other chaps all say he's the best Serg. in camp. Under him is Corporal Brookes, who will be instructing us in Physical Training. I arrived at Carlisle station at 12.30 and then we were lined up on the platform, counted and taken in groups of 20 to motor lorries. We all piled in the back and were taken 2 miles out of the town to camp. Then we had to show our calling up papers to a corporal who typed our names against a number.

After this we went to another hut and received a kit bag and 4 blankets. In the kit bag was a knife, fork, spoon, razor, cup, 3 khaki union shirts, 2 pairs woollen underpants (a bit itchy but very warm) 3 pairs woollen socks, woollen pullover, scarf, pair of mittens, 7 brushes, (boot, clothes, hair, tooth and I don't know what else) and two towels.

I shall settle down alright here because the lads are O.K. and the camp is a bit more comfortable than I expected. We haven't done anything yet but fill forms in and draw wages: 4/- (4 shillings) (what a wage, but of course it's only for Thursday and Friday). I've filled a form in to send you 7/- (7 shillings) per week. We've all done it because if anything happens to us you'll get a pension – what a thought. I think you'll get a book like a pension book and tear a page out every week and take it to the Post Office. I've made it out to be collected from the General P.O. Hyde.

I went to Carlisle last night with 6 or 7 fellows and we went to the pictures. Carlisle isn't a bad place, it's like a cross between Southport and Chester. It's rather old in places and all the streets are tree lined. It's very different than Hyde. No tram lines or sets in the road, all macadam and very clean. There's a sort of castle called the Citadel near the station. The air is very good and I bet I'll feel like 10 men in a month.

The food is different than it is at home, and there's not quite so much of it, but it's not bad. It's comical, you know, we have to put our knife, fork and spoon in our pockets when we've finished a meal. At first I put mine on my plate, but I'm getting used to carting them about now.

We get up at 6-15a.m., have a wash and shave, make our beds and sweep under them. Lights out is 10-15p.m. but you can come in anytime up to 12-00 midnight if you get in bed in the dark.

I've just come back from dinner now and we're going out for a game of football. I was issued with my boots and overall uniform this morning. This uniform consists of tunic and trousers, and is what is known as a battle dress. It is of canvas and worn inside the barracks only. We shall be measured for the walking out cloth uniform later.

I shan't be able to have any leave just yet. I have to be here a month and then if I want to I can come home from Sat. dinner until Sun. night, but I have to be in for reveille at 6-15 on the Monday. I may get a long weekend at Easter, but I don't know for sure yet. After I've been here for 3 months I can apply for 7 days leave.

The sergeant says I shall be in Carlisle for 4 months and then 2 months at some army Centre like Aldershot or Catterick. That is, of course, if nothing happens in France.

You will notice that I've written a lot of W's and then crossed them out. That is because I was going to write "we". We are all in the same boat and the same uniform, so think of ourselves as we.

I hope you are all well in Hyde and that the burst is mended. If anybody asks, tell them I'm O.K. and settling down champion.

Don't worry,

Yours, Charlie

The above copy of Uncle Charlie's first letter dated 17th February, 1940, written only two days after entering the army training camp at Carlisle, (when he managed to acquire some writing paper) recalls in fascinating detail his induction into the Army. A smooth transition from the train to Hadrian's Camp, the registering of personal details, getting settled in, receiving his uniform and meeting other men, mainly from the Manchester area. But I believe that, although he has travelled many miles from home, friends, family and familiar routines, he also leaves behind the role of esteemed eldest son within a loving family as he enters an alien world of square bashing, rules, regulations, officers and obeying orders: a world where he is not only physically, but also spiritually, absent from all that is familiar and loved. He will be mixing with lads from very different backgrounds and experiences of life; some would perhaps be rough round the edges and not always supported by family, or cocooned by Church society, as Charlie was. In some ways his life experiences at this stage would possibly have led to a naive, unworldly, young man with a restricted outlook on life. His background would provide faith, love and support, but would his naivety prepare him for the new life on which he is about to embark? By looking carefully at the old photographs taken before he was called up, I can see he looks relaxed, happy and self-assured, standing beside friends and family. I see someone who is easy amongst people, and most importantly comfortable in his own skin. Charlie, like every other lad in Hadrian's camp, in February, 1940, was in the same situation as the next man: thrust into Army training, frequently accompanied by periods of home sickness, not to mention Army food, requiring knives and forks to be stowed away inside a top pocket after use, instead of laying them aside to be picked up later by a mother or a wife. Uncle Charlie may be naïve and unworldly but I think his faith and his solid start in life would give him strength.

Charlie uses many words and expressions that reflect the language of the 1940's. He uses the words "fellows" and "chaps" and makes reference to the old pounds, shillings and pence currency. The detail he puts into his letter paints a fascinating picture of his new life, and the way he was received into the army. He also attempts to put worried minds at rest by emphasising the clean air: "I shall feel like ten men soon" the tree-lined streets, the "best" sergeant in camp, roads without tram lines, and the fact that he is already beginning to settle down.

(Postmarked, 1st June, 1940)

Carlisle,
Saturday

Dear Mother,

It's weekend now and I've just realised that I haven't written this week. As a matter of fact I'm so busy that the weeks go like wildfire. Anyway, I've quite a bit to tell you. At the beginning of the week everything was quite normal, but since Thursday, it's been far from normal. To begin with, I was inoculated again on Thursday afternoon and was then supposed to have 48 hrs. off duty. That 48 hours was up at 3-00 o'clock today. Now listen what I've done since Thursday. On Friday morning at 10-0 o'clock the order came "Outside for pay parade". I went out and we were marched to the Coy. Office and halted as usual in the road outside. Two or three minutes after Sgt. Dockerty came down and said "Tullock, Copeland, Barratt and Robinson, go and draw your pay first." The first three are in the squad above us and have had a month's longer training.

When we had drawn our pay we were told to pick up lamps, flags, telescopes, Helios and message forms and Barratt and I were told to take half of these and our rifle, tin hat, groundsheet and great coat to a field on the outskirts of the camp. Soon after we got settled we saw the other two signalling from Kingstown aerodrome and replied to them. Then the Sgt. Major and the Quartermaster Sgt. came up in a car and unloaded, of all things, a bell tent.

We were told to keep in touch with Kingstown and deliver any messages we get to the Coy. Office. At 9-0 p.m. Corporal Burkhill and John Smith came up with all our bedding in a car, and we had to do 2 hrs. duty in two's alternately through the night. It appears they were expecting an air-raid at 1 or 2 A.M. but it didn't come off. We were relieved at 7-30 this morning. I had my breakfast and when I got back to the barrack room was ordered to report with Harold Wilson to No. 1 I.T. Coy. I think I told you I was to be with the Coy. in case of air raid. I'm writing this letter from No. 1 I.T. Coy now. We have just been ordered to parade at 5-0 o'clock, and I believe we're going to Silloth. What for I don't know. Our training, for the time being, seems to have been interrupted. Well, it's half-past four now and I have to have my tea, so I'd better finish. I'll write again tomorrow or Monday and tell you the latest.

So long,

    Yours,

    Charlie

In the first line of his letter Uncle Charlie mentions the fact that it is Saturday with the week almost gone before he has had a chance to write home. This suggests that he wrote a regular weekly letter. As I only have twenty three letters in total spanning over three years, this would indicate there are many missing. I can only speculate as to what has happened to these. Nevertheless, I am very grateful for the ones I do have.

Uncle Charlie has written this letter during a very difficult time for Britain: she was in the middle of a huge evacuation of British, French and Belgian troops, who had been cut off by the German army after the battle of Dunkirk. The only way out of this perilous situation was to evacuate the servicemen across the channel back to England. What a marvellous piece of organization: a pulling together of possibly the biggest range and size of floating vessels that could be combined in a huge rescue attempt which managed to save an incredible total of 338,226 allied troops, between the 26th May and the 3rd June. Winston Churchill, speaking in the House of Commons at the time, described the situation as: "a colossal military disaster." [of] "The whole root and core and brain of the British Army." He was describing a grave situation in very frank terms, and added that "wars are not won by evacuation" in case anyone thought that the brilliant rescue of so many service men was in any way a victory for the armed forces. Nevertheless, the coordinated effort to rescue so many marooned men was, under the circumstances, very successful, when the outcome could have been so much worse. [2]

Uncle Charlie was not having the rest and relaxation he was expecting. Instead of having an easy time, in fact, he was setting up communications equipment ready to spend an uncomfortable, long, cold, night in a field, taking turns on watch, and recording and sending messages back to the company.

(Postmarked 3rd June, 1940)

Carlisle,
Monday.

Dear Mother,

Just a short note to tell you I'm O.K., but just a bit fed up at the moment. On Saturday night we paraded at 9-0p.m. (No. 1I.T. Coy) but were not sent anywhere out of camp. We were ordered to "stand to" until 5-0 A.M. Sunday morning. This means that we had to be ready to fall in on the Barrack square at 10 mins. notice any time during the night. It was the second night in succession I had spent the night with my trousers on. On Sunday we were free to go out from 4-0p.m. to 9-30p.m. and, thank goodness, were allowed to sleep without trousers in an ordinary manner. The big noises in the camp seem to be scared to death of something or someone and a company is ready to move out all the time. The four infantry coys take it in turns to stand to, but the poor old signallers are on duty nearly all the time. Also on duty all the time is the M.T. (Motor Transport) section with all the cars and lorries out on the barrack square.

In addition there are 8 "Cumberland" motor buses standing by. The reason I am fed up is because nobody seems to know just what is happening and what to do when and if it does. The Specialist Coy is not allowed out of barracks, because it supplies signallers and drivers, and taken all round everybody in the camp is fed up to the teeth. I wish they could forget their scare, and let the life of the camp return to normal. After all it is a training camp, and not a holding camp for trained soldiers. Anyway, I suppose it will settle down again in time. What sort of weather are you having in Hyde? It's great here. In fact, it's too hot for soldiering, but it doesn't half make you sunburned. We have no hot water here now because it's summer time. It's nice to have a cold shower after a sweaty day's work, but it isn't so nice having a cold shower before a day's work.

I received Dad's letter this morning, thanks for the envelopes and stamps, and he's working from 6-0a.m. now is he? Work for victory eh! Well, he's getting up before the army now. By the way, I'm hard up again (4½d left now) could you do the usual and put me on 'till weekend. I don't want to borrow because when I pay back on Friday I am short again by Sunday. Will you please give Jessie Morton Eric's address. I had a letter from her and she wants to send him his P.O. from the fund. I haven't room here so I'll put it on the other side. And so for the present, ----

Yours,

P.S No signs of leave yet Charlie

At this early stage in the war, the United Kingdom's fear of invasion was tangible, as Hitler's forces were spreading rapidly across Europe. Would the U.K. be next? Following the evacuation of Dunkirk would Germany continue across the Channel? This concern may account for the tension within Charlie's Camp, and why there was a heightened state of readiness. On the 3rd June (the date of Charlie's letter) Germany bombed Paris heavily, resulting in the death of hundreds of civilians, and the U.K. could breathe a temporary sigh of relief, as Hitler turned his attention to France.

Things were becoming more difficult at home, particularly for Charlie's father. Granddad was now starting work at 6.00 a.m. "before the Army" as Charlie points out. It is an example of how those at home were doing their bit for the war effort. Also Charlie refers to a "Postal Order from the Fund" suggesting there was some sort of local or church fund, set up to give financial assistance to service men.

The above letter was postmarked 3rd June. 1940, and it is on the following day that Winston Churchill made this famous speech; its purpose was to inspire and motivate the British people to do their utmost for the war effort.

We shall go on to the end, we shall fight in France, we shall fight on the Seas and oceans, we shall fight with growing confidence and growing Strength in the air. We shall defend our Island whatever the costs may be. We shall fight on the beaches; we shall fight on the landing grounds; We shall fight in the fields and in the streets; we shall fight in the hills. We shall never surrender.

(Postmarked 30th June 1940)

Monday
Carlisle

Dear Mother,

I am writing this from the Battalion Orderly Office – on duty again until 8-0a.m. tomorrow morning. Still, it's not so bad. The other poor blighters have to put full kit on and "stand to" every other night. They usually go out of camp for tactical training, that is learning, as fighting platoons, how to deal with parachute troops, and they say it is hard work. Our squad has to supply 2 men each day and night for telephone duty here. It works out one night in five or six. In case of air raid the others would go out to deal with the enemy, but we have to go to an air-raid shelter and await orders for signalling duties. Compared with the others we haven't a great deal to do. We haven't had an air-raid warning yet, and you have had a few from all accounts. The Germans must think Carlisle isn't worth bombing, and they are quite right, it isn't.

I enjoyed myself very much last Sunday. It was nice to have a good tea with plenty of cake and sweet things and sugar in my tea (4 lumps). After tea we played cards and had some supper. We left about 10-15.

On Friday morning at 1-30 there was a practice air-raid. I slept peacefully through it all. Next morning the Sgt. Major said only half of the company got up, and there would be another practice early Sat.

morning. Well, about 1-30, John Smith came and woke me up. I said "Go away, I'm asleep" and he laughed and left me. Nearly everybody went out and only four of us were left in our room. After ¾ hr. they came back and were told to sit on their beds. Then the Sgt. Major came and told them to get in bed. I was certain he would tell us who had never been up to report to him at 9-0 a.m., but he didn't and nothing has been said.

There's a touch of the old soldier don't you think? If the real thing happens and the siren goes, I think I shall hear it alright.

Thank you for the stamps. Now here is another little order. Could you send envelopes, razor blades and a shilling or two please? I got my P.O. from Jessie M. and Auntie Edith sent me 1/- but that's all gone and I know I shall be broke by Tuesday night unless, as usual, you rescue me. In another month or so I shall get 6d (6 pennies) a day proficiency pay, if I pass my signallers exams, so perhaps I shan't have to write so often for money then. By the way, just as a sort of reassurance I'm still O.K. and fit as a fiddle. There is no talk of drafts now that France has thrown in the sponge, because there is nowhere to send us. Whether I shall stay here after I've classified, or be transferred somewhere else I don't know. I wouldn't mind a move to another part of the country; Carlisle's getting a bit stale now. I can't say "see you soon" because I don't think it will be soon, but I hope so. Until then,
Cheerio,
Charlie

Uncle Charlie mentions the fact that the camp has not yet had an air raid warning, but in his home town of Hyde, he suggests, they have had a few. I suppose that as Paris has been bombed quite heavily the U.K. is expecting the same treatment sometime soon.

Charlie writes about having an enjoyable tea out, somewhere unspecified, with plenty of cakes and "sweet things": obviously satisfying his sweet tooth. This was followed by a game of cards and a good supper. For Charlie, it was a very pleasant change of routine and company.

Back at camp Charlie missed two air-raid practices: preferring to stay in his comfy bed and simply turn over. He was very lucky that his non-attendance had gone unnoticed. Charlie is looking forward to an increase in proficiency pay of 6d a day, (dependent on passing the signallers'exam.), which he believes will ease his money situation. He always seems to be running out of cash and asking for a loan, or purchase of some essential item like stamps or razor blades. If 6d a day were to ease his financial situation, it shows how little he earns.

On the back of this photograph Uncle Charlie has written:
"Signalling Class, Carlisle, 1940"

From left to right: Back row: R. Williams, J. Smith, C. Golding, W. Long.
Middle row: R.G. Jones, H. Withington, C.W. Harpin, Hamilton,
Front row: H. Wilson, G. Porter, A. Dean, C. Robinson, J. Strongman.

Moreover, viewed from a modern perspective, the amount is minuscule. But in 1940s values sixpence is sixpence and it *will* make a difference to him.

Charlie knows there is less chance of being drafted: "now that France has thrown in the sponge." (France surrendered to Germany before signing the Armistice on 22nd June, 1940.) Pondering on his immediate future, my Uncle wonders: will he stay put in camp, or will he (hopefully) move to another part of the country into a regiment or Corps. (Signals Corp.)?

3454037 Fus. C. Robinson (Sig.)
"E" Section Signals,
Att. 111 Fld. Reg. R.A.
Great Bentley,
Nr. Colchester,
Essex.
25/4/41

Dear Dad,

Thanks for P.O. I suppose you've already read the above address. I was going to write the usual Thursday letter yesterday when Sgt. Larkin said to Harry Withington and myself "You're going to 111 Field Regiment tomorrow" We were brought here this afternoon, and believe it or not I'm in a "Civvy" billet. Yes, in a private house, a very nice and clean one too. I'm in Chelmsford now, but it's no use giving you the Chelmsford address because we're moving to Great Bentley on Monday or Tuesday, and I understand that next weekend we are moving again. I'm sure that you won't receive this until Monday so that you will have sent my letter to 125 Bde. I'm expecting that it will be sent on. I'll let you know the next address as soon as possible. It seems a nice easy going section here, and the Serg. is O.K. It will be a change being with the Artillery after 14 months in the infantry. This signal section is renowned in the Division as the best one to get in. I'm glad that Harry has come with me though.

I never thought I should be lucky enough to land a "civvy billet". However, I've done it, and the billets at Great Bentley are going to be civvy too. So I shall get at least a week in. I think I'm in for an easy time with this section.

You can stop sending the P.O.'s now. I cleared my debt off this weekend and I should draw 15/9 next week, Whoopee! Jessie Morton says "I hope you received the 5/- P.O." Unfortunately I didn't. I suppose it would be from the comforts fund. That's the first letter I've known not reach me. It would contain 5/- wouldn't it? It was a peculiar thing. I got your letter on Tuesday as usual and you said that I could expect 5/- from Jessie. I was looking forward to her letter arriving, and on Wednesday there it was. But in it she asks whether I received the 5/- no, I'm afraid I didn't.

Well, Dad, May 14th draws nearer. I've only about three weeks to go and then "Home Again." That will be a perfect "Civvy Billet" for a week. There's just a chance that I shall get home before then, since I have joined a new section, but it's doubtful and I shouldn't bank on it.

I've just been invited to go downstairs where there is a fire, so I think I will take advantage.

See you soon,
Cheerio,
Charlie

There is a ten month gap between this letter and the previous one. Obviously the letters in-between have been lost, which is a great pity as this creates a hole in my knowledge of Uncle Charlie's army career, where he has been stationed, his experiences, and what he has to say about his life in the army. I am hoping that his service records will provide some answers when I receive them. (Post Script see Appendix B). But for now Charlie is quite happy with his "Civvy Billet", meaning that for a time he can enjoy the luxury of staying in a civilian home. In the final sentence of his letter he writes that he has been invited "to go downstairs where there is a fire" He can take advantage of some home comforts, which, no doubt would be much appreciated. Charlie is now looking forward to some real home comforts, the best kind – those in his own home, as he is due to take some leave for one week from the 14th May. I am trying to imagine how it must feel to be away from home for weeks and months at a time, and how the thought of going home to see family and friends must give rise to a very warm, comfortable feeling of anticipation. To sit by your own fireside, with your family around you, to be yourself, to get out of bed when you feel like it, to enjoy home-cooked food, to chat with your old friends – not having to consider sergeants or soldiers – must be a perfect way to 'get away from it all.'

I have just been researching "the comforts fund" as referred to by Uncle Charlie to find out exactly what it was all about. (The Internet can be a mine of information. It is certainly invaluable to my research, and saves me so much time in reading and trawling through many books.)

I have found an article by Ian Durrant, on the subject of "Comforts for the Troops." Until I read this I assumed that a "comforts fund" meant individuals and groups would send money and useful items to make life more comfortable for service men and women, as well as reminding the troops they were not forgotten, or taken for granted. But I was completely taken aback by the sheer scale and magnitude of the efforts made by the civilian population to help ease the pain of being away from home for those in uniform.

There was an army of knitters, not only in Great Britain, but in Commonwealth countries like Australia, Canada and New

Zealand – even the U.S.A. was involved – with a campaign called "Bundles for Britain." Thousands and thousands of enthusiastic knitters produced socks, helmets, balaclavas, gloves, scarves, pullovers, cardigans and wrist warmers.[3] And what an industrious army they were! Knitting was a popular pastime for housewives, producing clothing for their families. But during the war they really pulled out all the stops to produce a veritable mountain of knitted items for the troops. It was, according to Ian Durrant "beyond calculation" but the WVS (Women's Voluntary Service) had been sorting an unbelievable five tons of knitted clothing per month! And didn't it come in handy for the evacuees from Dunkirk, when the demand soared as tired, bedraggled soldiers were offered some comfortable, warm clothing on their return to England. The WVS was a force to be reckoned with. During the evacuation the women of the WVS were out in droves, meeting the trains packed with soldiers as they entered the stations of Britain, offering the men tea, tobacco, replacement shirts, and many other items of comfortable hand-made clothing. In some cases the women went without sleep for days as the trains just kept on coming.

3454037 Fus. C. Robinson (Sig)
"E" Section Signals,
Att. 111 Fld. Reg. R.A.,
Euston Park
Thetford,
Norfolk
7 – 5 – 41

Dear Mother,

I'm not quite sure when I last wrote home, so if I write anything you've heard before, excuse me won't you. We left Gt. Bentley on Sunday afternoon and started a three days scheme after which we came straight here. I am in a tent here but it's not too bad. One good thing is that it doesn't rain a great deal. It's a big change after a civvy billet. I was well looked after at Gt. Bentley. I used to get a supper from Mrs. Garner every night, and a cup of tea first thing every morning. It was alright while it lasted, but it didn't last long enough. Still, I'm very comfortable here, and I sleep like a log in a tent. It reminds me of my scouting days.

I got the 5/- from the Comforts Fund last Friday. Jessie had put 12 Inf. Bde. on the envelope by mistake, and it looked as if it had been all over the country. On the same day I had a packet of cream crackers and some chocolate from Dorothy Cooper. I don't know whether you posted the usual letter on Saturday, but I haven't had it yet – Wednesday night.

Did you have a good do last Sunday? It was a lovely warm day here, I hope you had the same sort of weather. How did Norman get on? I wish I had been there. I think it is the first Anniversary I have missed for donkey's years. I had a weekend leave from Carlisle last year if you remember. I was thinking about you all day.

I shall be coming home again very soon now. I'm not certain of the exact date, but I think it will be Friday the 16th May or Friday the 23rd. I will let you know for certain if I can later on. In any case I have to pay my own fare this time. I think it is about 36/- so could you send me £2 in your next letter – and register it please. I thang yew! I hope I'm a bit nearer home next time. How's Dad for cigarettes? If he can't get them I'll bring some home with me. I'm writing this in bed and it's going dark now so I think I'll get some shut-eye. Am I looking forward to coming home? You bet I am,

So long,
Charlie

After being so well looked after by Mrs. Garner in his "Civvy Billet" when, every night, she made him supper, and had a cup of tea ready for him first thing every morning, Uncle Charlie now finds himself sleeping in a tent again, reminding him of his "scouting days." He writes that he is sleeping well, "like a log", but his carefree time in the scout movement must feel like a fading memory of the dim and distant past.

At long last, after much anxiety, Uncle Charlie received his 5/- from the Comforts Fund, via his friend Jessie Morton, just when he had given up all hope of ever seeing it! He also received a packet of cream crackers and some chocolate from another friend. I believe that the value is not so much in the items themselves (except for Charlie's five shillings!) but in the caring thoughts that are wrapped within them – an unspoken message, but a very clear one – that a soldier is not forgotten.

The Anniversary Charlie mentions is Sunday 4th May, but I cannot discover what it signifies: not a birthday, or a wedding anniversary, but quite clearly it has some kind of family significance. The happy celebration takes place annually, and Uncle Charlie asks how Norman got on, suggesting there was some connection with his brother. He remembers taking a weekend leave from Carlisle the previous year, so it has to be meaningful. I sense sadness in his words: "I was thinking about you all day." Not only has Charlie missed out on the celebration, but he has also missed out on spending time with his loved ones.

Uncle Charlie has communicated a great sense of anticipation in thinking about going home, but it is a long way from Norfolk, and his fare of thirty six shillings (36/-) must have been a big expense for him, considering the fact that a mere five shillings was then seen as a substantial sum. As usual he asks for some assistance from Mother and Father, and to make sure he will be certain to receive the money, he asks for the £2 to be sent by registered post.

Euston Park,
22-8-41

Dear Mother,

Well, here I am, back in camp. I arrived at 10-15 last night after a fairly good journey. That 12-25 from M/cr. (Manchester) does connect with the 2-0 at Sheffield. I'm glad I didn't go to Guide Bridge. Everyone who got on there had to stand all the way to Sheffield. It's still the same here, nothing much to do, although I hear there's a scheme on for four days next week. Harry Withington went on leave yesterday.

One of the lads was at Division last week and says that I got my B3, although it has not appeared officially on Part II orders yet. When it does, though, I shall draw back pay from the day I passed the test.

Eric Holmes was here this morning and I passed on the message from his wife and family. He says we're moving to Doncaster when the time comes. I hope he's right. It will be very handy for coming home, won't it?

I did enjoy my leave, Mother, and I'm going to settle down now and it won't seem very long to my next one. I have to go for my pay now, so I'd better finish. I'll write more next time, but I thought I'd let you know I'm O.K.

Cheerio
Charlie

The photograph below is the only one I have showing Uncle Charlie with family during his home leave from the Army. It was obviously taken during the winter, as I notice my mother is wearing gloves. In the absence of a date written on the back by Uncle Charlie, as have many of the other photographs, there is no indication when it was taken. Also, the three people I can't identify were either family members or close friends. However, there is something about this photograph I really like. Perhaps it's because everyone looks relaxed and

*In the middle of the photograph is Uncle Charlie. On his right is my Uncle
Norman, and next to him is Charlie's friend Jessie Morton. On the far right
of the picture is my mother, Marjorie. I cannot name the others, although I
recognise their faces. Because these were close friends, and/or family members
Charlie did not identify them on the back of the photograph.*

comfortable with each other; or possibly it's the thought
that this may be the last photograph of Andrew and Nora
Robinson's three children, and therefore it assumes an added
poignancy.

Uncle Charlie has had a fairly uneventful journey back to
camp, but taking almost ten hours from Manchester to Thetford,
Norfolk. He was pleased he didn't board the train at Guide Bridge,
as those passengers could not find a seat until they reached Sheffield.
The Guide Bridge station is roughly midway between Hyde and
Manchester Piccadilly station on the Glossop line, and originally
had four platforms. Situated on the main line from Manchester
to Sheffield, via Woodhead, I was surprised to learn that the line is
still in operation today, but reduced in size to two platforms.

It is good news for Uncle Charlie when he learns that he has passed the B3 Signallers test. The qualification is known as an OWL (Operator, Wireless, and Line) and the B3 grade is the first level of trade qualification on completion of training.[4]

There has been talk of Charlie's unit moving to Doncaster, which would make travelling home to Hyde much easier and cheaper than his present placement in Norfolk. I feel sure that Charlie will appreciate the fact he has less to pay out in respect of train fares, as money always seems to be a significant factor to him. But for now, he is back in Norfolk, determined to settle down again, after a good, enjoyable leave.

Euston Park,
28-8-41

Dear Dad,

Thanks for letter, paper and stamps. I was out on a scheme when they came and as I was feeling a bit fed up at the time, they were more welcome than usual. We went out on Monday morning and returned yesterday dinner time. It was a good exercise as far as exercises go, we had a few good laughs amongst the swearing.

You will, no doubt, be pleased to know that I have got my B3. The names of successful operators appeared on Divisional Signals orders last weekend. Am I pleased with myself? If all goes well, I shall draw 18/- on Friday and leave 1/3 for my credit.

Last Saturday I went to see a film called "Old Bill and Son". It was alright as far as interest went, but pretty feeble from a film goer's point of view. It was about Old Bill (the better 'ole) and his son in the modern army. There were several things in it which amused us, but civilians did not seem to find it very funny. I think I shall go to see "Spring Parade" with Deanna Durbin tonight. It came round when I was in Colchester, but I didn't go.

How did Mr. Raby's last service go on Sunday evening. I'll bet it was alright. I wish I could have been there to sing Cwm Rhondda for the last hymn. I hope there was a good crowd there.

So I've another £5-10-0 in the bank now, have I? Good. If things go on as they are doing I should have a respectable amount by the end of the war. If, as some people say, it won't be over until 1943, I shall be a millionaire. Still, I think I'd rather have the war over now and stay as I am.

How is Marjorie getting through the gas capes? Has she drawn £5 in a week yet? I bet she will before long.

Well, dad, I'm coming to the end of my rope now. It doesn't take much to stump us, does it? Things are still as usual here. No work, no excitement, no worry and no nice fireside. See you in nine weeks, I hope.

Cheerio,
Charlie

Now Uncle Charlie has proudly written to my grandfather: "am I pleased with myself?" on hearing confirmation of passing the signalling test. He knows his father will be proud of his son's success, and probably just as important to Charlie, it means he will be drawing more pay!

To pass the time, Charlie goes to the cinema. He mentions possibly going to see Deanna Durbin that night in a film called: 'Spring Parade.' It was a romantic comedy musical, made in 1940 and shot in black and white. It won an Oscar in 1941 for the song "Waltzing in the Clouds." At the age of fourteen Deanna's fine singing voice was discovered; she was subsequently signed up by MGM, and started on a fast track to fame and fortune, thanks to her voice, her beauty and her glamour. She made a total of twenty two films from 1936 to 1948 and was one of the biggest film stars of the time.

It is difficult to overestimate the importance of the cinema in the 1940s. Music, entertainment and news programmes were provided by radio broadcasts, which most families listened to daily. But for the sheer thrill of not just hearing – but actually to see – glamorous, handsome and instantly recognisable film stars (the celebrities of their day): the Deanna Durbin's and the Clark Gables, captivated audiences. Additionally, cinema-goers could follow all the action on a large screen. This pastime was understandably very popular with many people, and a regular visit to the local cinema (there was more than one in each town) was commonplace.

I have just had one of those serendipity moments when looking up the Cwm Rhondda hymn Uncle Charlie writes about. In my ignorance I had not realised this hymn is also named "Guide Me O Thou Great Jehovah" or "Bread of Heaven" – either title I would have recognised immediately. It features in the Methodist Hymn Book, and has a rousing, ascending, spine-tingling tune, written by Welshman John Hughes, Dowlais. It tells the Bible story of the forty year journey of "God's People" escaping from the slavery of Egypt to find the Promised Land. During their long, arduous journey they were fed by manna (bread) from heaven; a cloud to guide their way by day and a fire to light the way at night. The words, by William Williams, can also be interpreted as an allegory of a Christian's journey through life. This hymn is a favourite amongst Methodists, but it has also featured as a fitting choice during the state funerals of Diana Princess of Wales and the Queen Mother and featured during the wedding ceremony of Prince William and Catherine Middleton.

The hymn invites people to sing heartily, with great feeling, and whenever I hear its inspirational tune, it always produces the same emotional effect as the hairs on the back of my neck stand to attention. It is not simply the tune, wonderful though it is, but accompanying the tune I have a vivid picture in my mind, of Grandma, duster in hand, singing the hymn I most associate with her: her housework hymn. Now I have a second image of Uncle Charlie standing in the choir, his voice blending with others to swell the glorious sound.

Here are the words of Cwm Rhondda:

Guide me O thou great Jehovah,
Pilgrim through this barren land;
I am weak, but though art mighty,
Hold me with thy powerful hand;
Bread of Heaven! Bread of Heaven,
Feed me now and evermore, evermore,
Feed me now and evermore.

Open though the crystal fountain
Whence the healing stream shall flow;
Let the fiery, cloudy pillar,
Lead me all my journey through;
Strong Deliverer! Strong Deliverer
Be thou still my help and shield, help and shield,
Be thou still my help and shield.

When I tread the verge of Jordan,
Bid my anxious fears subside,
Death of death and hell's destruction,
Land me safe on Canaan's side;
Songs of praises, songs of praises,
I will ever give to thee, give to thee,
I will ever give to thee.

The first paragraph on the second page of his letter is a significant and a sad one. Charlie now has £5-10-0 in his bank at home, a significant amount, considering the many items £5 could buy in 1941. Although he values money, it doesn't come close to the value of having an end to the war, and his life getting back to normal. It is ironic when he writes that people were saying the war would not be over until 1943. Sadly, that year would be the one when *his* war and *his* life would end. Meanwhile, he has "no work, no excitement, no worry and no nice fireside."

For the first time in the letters I have, Uncle Charlie mentions Marjorie (my Mum) and asks how she is getting on with the "gas capes"[5] I assume she was contributing to the war effort as well as earning a living by making these items. (My mum has told me that she decided not to join the forces as my father was in the navy and she wanted to be at home when he came back on leave.)

Notes

1 Hadrian's Camp, opened on 1st July, 1939, was built on the line of Hadrian's Wall. It could house almost 3,000 men, and was the size of a small town, with similar facilities. It was built in just 18 weeks.

2 Such was the seriousness of the situation at Dunkirk, that there was an official complete news blackout which was not lifted until the evening of the 30th May. "Listening to Britain. Home Intelligence reports on Britain's finest hour- May – September, 1940."

3 These items were much sought after as they were softer and warmer than the services' regular issue. And they had been hand made with care – offering real comfort and warmth, (particularly welcome in North Africa during cold desert nights.) I am reminded of Charlie's first letter of 17th February 1940 and his comment about receiving

his uniform and the regular issue of underpants which he describes as "a bit itchy".

4   Thank you to Martin Skipworth of the Royal Signals Museum for the above information.

5   A gas cape fits into a gas cap pouch. The cape was used to drape over a soldier's head during a gas attack to create a safe bubble under the cape, allowing the soldier to put on his gas mask without being contaminated.

CHAPTER FOUR

The Royal Corps Of Signals

Now Uncle Charlie has proudly passed the Signallers exam, I would like to explain a little about the Royal Corp of Signals.

Throughout its history the army has had a vital need to communicate orders and information, swiftly and accurately, during military and combat situations. Coloured smoke, torches, beacons, flags, drums, runners and messengers on horseback have all been employed in the past. Heliographs, utilising the sun's rays to flash messages from reflective objects, mentioned previously and practiced by Uncle Charlie during his training, were used as far back in time as the native American Indians. During the Crimean War, (between 1835 – 1837) Morse code and the electric telegraph were used for the first time. Then in 1884 the Telegraph Battalion Royal Engineers was formed.

This was followed in 1908 by the formation of the Royal Engineers Signal Service which played a vital role in signals communications during World War One. On 28th June, 1920 a Royal Warrant was signed by the Secretary of State for War, the Rt. Hon. Winston Churchill, requesting the Sovereign's approval for the formation of a 'Corps of Signals'. Six weeks later, His Majesty the King officially conferred the title 'Royal Corps of Signals'. As methods of communication became more sophisticated and the wireless set became a vital piece of equipment in its own right, soldiers needed to have specialist training in the 'Operation of Wireless and Line' (OWL), Uncle Charlie's recent qualification.

During the 2nd World War, members of the Corps served in every theatre of war, and at the end of the War the Corps had over 140,000 serving soldiers. It's motto is 'Certa Cito' translated as "Swift Sure."

The Corps' cap badge depicts the figure of Mercury, messenger of the gods. It is believed that the inspiration for the depiction of Mercury came from a Major Beresford, a Commanding Officer of C Telegraph Troop, Royal Engineers, who had inherited a statue of Mercury from his father. In 1891 the Major presented a mace or band stick to the Band of the Battalion; on the top of the mace was the figure of Mercury. The badge is nicknamed "Jimmy" by all in the Corps. and has two possible explanations for this name. The first is that the figure of Mercury is a copy of a bronze statue by the Italian sculptor Giambologna, which, over time was shortened to "Jimmy"

The second explanation of "Jimmy" comes from a Royal Signals boxer called Jimmy Emblem who was the British Army champion in 1924, and represented the Royal Signals from 1921 to 1924.

3454037 Sgm. C. Robinson,
Royal Signals,
Att. 111 Fld. Reg. R.A.,
Halkirk,
Caithness,
Scotland.
3-12-41

Dear Dad,

I received your letter, paper and stamps yesterday. I can't remember omitting to put a stamp on any envelope to you, but I suppose I must have done. As a matter of fact, in this case anyway, Jack Taylor is wrong; from this area we have to place a stamp on an active service envelope. From the Orkneys, Shetlands or anywhere abroad they do not need a stamp. The only difference between a green envelope and an ordinary one is that the ordinary one must be censored here, whilst a green one _may_ be censored at the base. In most cases, I think the authorities trust us and do not censor green active service envelopes. They may open say one or two from each batch.

I'm sorry you're having to work so hard. It will probably be worse still when the other grinder goes won't it? I heard on the wireless last night that an inquiry is going to be made into the importance or otherwise of everyone's job. They might make the number of grinders up to normal afterwards.

We have a wireless set now. The receiving set is in No. 1 hut and in No. 2 and No. 3 (ours) we have extension speakers. Believe me, it's working in fine style. I waken up to music (about 8-0a.m.) and go to sleep to music. It's a grand life. We keep up with the news now, too.

I like this place much better than Norfolk. It really is lovely sometimes. The sun does not rise very high, and consequently the sunrise and sunset creates lovely effects. The moon on the "Loch" is worth seeing too. And, of course, I must not forget the "Purple hue of the highland hills."

I notice that Hyde is having a "Warships" week. I hope you realise the £150,000 you have set as your target. I think you will somehow. Hyde never lags behind in efforts of this sort. By the way, whilst I'm on the subject of money, I've got a Scotch pound note. I've never seen one before and shall bring it home when I come on leave. It's issued by the Clydesdale Bank of Glasgow. I never realised that "Bank of England" means England and not Scotland did you? That sounds crazy, but you know what I mean, I hope.

Your news about Stan Cross surprises me. Is he marrying Joan

Carr? All my friends will be married before the war is over, if they aren't now.

> *That's just about all this time dad, so*
> *Cheerio,*
> *Charlie*

Uncle Charlie is now stationed at Caithness, Scotland, and seems to be enjoying himself, surrounded by beautiful scenery and spectacular sunrises and sunsets, in this the most northerly county of Great Britain. He is awakened by the radio and goes to sleep by the radio, and generally seems more contented than in his previous letters. As with most of his letters, this particular one does have a censor's stamp on the front: "passed by censor No. 442.[1]

Uncle Charlie has stated in an earlier letter that Granddad is having to start work at 6 o'clock in the morning, and I assume the reason for this would be that as so many men are now in uniform, those left behind are being stretched in order to cover production demands. Cotton, as well as wool, was a vital natural commodity; far more important than today, with so many synthetic fibres used in the manufacture of fabrics.

I have discovered my Granddad's marriage certificate on which it states his occupation as "stripper and grinder" and his father's occupation as "stripper and grinder" also. So he did follow his father into the same line of work. I wonder how many combined years they both served in this demanding job. (I know my Granddad retired after over fifty years of service) and only enjoyed three years of retirement before he passed away.

Uncle Charlie is sympathetic in respect of his father's increased work load at Slack Mills. And it seems as though his work is about to become even more demanding when the other "grinder" goes. But what exactly did a stripper and grinder do in a cotton mill?

After the raw cotton arrived in tightly packed bales, it was unpacked and partially cleaned by a pressure blowing process before passing into the carding room where the cotton fibres were further cleaned, and at the same time drawn out into parallel lines by a carding engine. It was the job of the strippers and grinders to strip the dust and cotton fibres sticking to the teeth of the carding engine, and then to "grind " or sharpen the wire teeth of the machine by using revolving rollers covered with emery. The process of stripping the machine resulted in thick clouds of fine dust which frequently led to a lung disease known as byssinosis, which had similar symptoms to asthma. As the workers in the carding room were exposed to more dust than any other employees in the mill, they suffered from the highest incidence of death due to respiratory diseases. This amounted to 24% of all mill workers. From 1917 after the gradual introduction of a special exhaust ventilation system, locally applied to the stripping brush, as well as a vacuum air cleaning system, the unhealthy dust was virtually eliminated and the incidence of respiratory deaths was in marked decline.[2]

These were the conditions in which my Grandfather worked for five decades, and his father before him, who, before the introduction of efficient ventilation systems, would have had greater exposure to cotton dust. My Grandfather died of cancer at the age of 68, which may or may not have been the result of the conditions in which he had worked for so long. Uncle Charlie is concerned about Granddad's increasing work load, and longer hours. Hopefully, the proposed review of civilian jobs will find in favour of employing more grinders.

Between 1941 and 1942 the Government introduced National Savings, in which individuals and groups were encouraged to save. Each city and town was given a target sum to aim for, based on the size of its population. This would enable the purchase of a warship, (smaller ones, like corvettes for towns and villages, and battleships and aircraft carriers for cities) and the amount of money Hyde was expected to raise was a huge £150,000! This ambitious money raising venture was known as "Warship Week". Towns and cities throughout the country would raise money to purchase a Royal Navy ship, and once the ship was purchased, the local community would adopt the ship and its crew. Women would knit woollens for the crew, and when possible the sailors would visit the sponsoring town or city; sometimes to take part in a parade, or just to exchange plaques, objects and photographs. The Royal Navy had lost so many ships at this stage in the war that it was vitally important these ships were replaced as soon as possible. The solution was certainly an ingenious one, motivating the civilian population to help fund a fighting ship, giving them a purpose, involvement, some control, and thereby boosting morale.[3]

Finally, Uncle Charlie is the proud possessor of a "Scotch" one pound note, something he has never seen before, and intends to take it home on his next leave for everyone to see.

3454037 Sgm. C. Robinson,
Royal Signals,
Att. 111 Fld. Reg. R.A.,
Halkirk,
Caithness,
Scotland,
10-12-41

Dear Dad,

Thanks for letter and paper. I'm sorry that the weather was so bad for the Warship Week parade. The start seems to have been a wash-out.

I've no doubt, though, that Hyde will provide the £150,000 required for a corvette.

Since I last wrote, things have been happening in the Far East, haven't they? I keep wondering whether America will be able to provide us and Russia with supplies now that she is at war herself. Aren't the Japanese dirty, treacherous blighters. I hope America wipes them off the face of the earth. I was glad we had a wireless set on Monday night when Mr. Churchill's and Roosevelt's speeches were on. Did you hear them?

Is Marjorie working at Dickenson's? Where is the place, I don't seem to know it. There's one thing about it, she won't have to join the women's forces will she. That is, if she doesn't want to. Hasn't Jim been called up yet?

I'm pleased to hear that you are having a look at the concert. They don't seem to have any producer or anybody at all to criticize. I think you'll be a great help to Jessie. I should like to have a look at them myself and see the concert when the time comes.

It's a lovely day here. The sun is shining brilliantly and there's a nice fresh sea-breeze blowing. I'm sure you're not getting sun in Hyde like we are here. I'm out for a walk on the hills this afternoon (it's a half day holiday). I'll bet you wish you were coming with me.

See you soon,
Cheerio
Charlie

Oh dear, the start of Warship Week was a "wash-out" for the town of Hyde. I can just imagine all the work that went into preparations for a big parade, only to be ruined by the weather. However, knowing the determination of the people, it was probably just a minor setback before starting the fund-raising effort again. Uncle Charlie has no doubt that Hyde will raise the money to buy a corvette. What confidence he shows in a small town raising such an enormous amount of money as £150,000![4]

And, despite the war, The-Show-Must-Go-On response to the proposed concert, desperately in need of a producer, as Granddad offers to come to the rescue.

Uncle Charlie's letter was written three days after the Japanese bombed Pearl Harbour. In less than two hours after the surprise attack began, a total of 21 ships of the United States Pacific fleet were either damaged or sunk. At the same time the Japanese attacked military airfields before the American aeroplanes could get off the ground to defend their ships in Pearl Harbour.

The next day the President of the United States Theodore Roosevelt made a stirring speech to the people of America, describing Japan's unprovoked attack on Pearl Harbour as a deliberate act, despite Japan deceptively talking of peace and making false statements of hope, they were, he said, simultaneously, planning the attack, designed to inflict as much damage as possible on the American fleet based at Pearl Harbour. Japan also attacked Malaya, Hong Kong, Guam, Philippines, and the islands of Wake and Midway. President Roosevelt said: "I ask that the Congress declare that since the unprovoked and dastardly attack by Japan on Sunday, December 7th 1941, a state of war has existed between the United States and the Japanese empire."

The destruction of much of the American fleet in the Pacific, as well as many lives lost, was a massive blow to the American people, and their anger and outrage turned to determination – a determination to enter the conflict, and contribute to the overthrow of their enemy, Japan. Three days later, Japan's allies Germany and Italy declared war on the United States, and Congress replied immediately to the effect that America was at war with them.

On the 8th December, 1941, Winston Churchill informed a hastily convened Parliament that in addition to Pearl Harbour the British territories of Malaya, Singapore and Hong Kong had also been attacked, and therefore a state of war existed between Great Britain and the Japanese empire. The conflict had become a global one.

Uncle Charlie has used some uncharacteristically strong words of condemnation on hearing the news of Pearl Harbour, calling the Japanese "dirty treacherous blighters", blighters being a word rarely used today, but probably a common choice in 1941. The words "dirty and "treacherous" is quite strong language from Charlie, and must reflect his feelings on the matter. I suppose the sudden, unprovoked severity of the attack created shockwaves throughout the allied countries – not just in America. Now that the United States has joined the conflict, Charlie is wondering if she will help out with sending much needed supplies and equipment to assist the United Kingdom and Russia. I think Winston Churchill must have been feeling Britain was now in a stronger position with the financial and moral support of the United States. I can visualise Uncle Charlie and his fellow soldiers crowding round the radio on that Monday night, listening intently to Roosevelt's and Churchill's significant historic speeches.

In his final paragraph Uncle Charlie writes he is planning to go out for a walk on this "free afternoon" amongst the beautiful countryside in which he is now stationed. An added bonus is the brilliant sunshine, which is incentive enough for him to venture outside. When he writes to his Dad: "I'll bet you wish you were coming with me" he is referring to the fact that my Granddad was a great walker, and used to walk the eight miles from Hyde to Manchester every Saturday afternoon, before catching the bus back home. What wouldn't my Granddad have given to walk beside his eldest son amongst the majestic, beautiful, awe-inspiring hills of Scotland?

3454037 Sgm. C. Robinson,
Royal Signals,
Att. 111 Fld. Reg. R.A.,
Halkirk,
Caithness,
Scotland,
8-3-42

Dear Dad,

Before I forget (I did last week) I must say that I can't remember any firm in Leicester from which I got an electric cooker for Mrs. Taylor. I can only just remember getting one at all. I should think the manufacturers name would be on it somewhere. Sorry.

You will remember that last week I told you what lovely weather we were having. There's four inches of snow now and it's still falling, and we're going out at seven o'clock on Tuesday morning on a scheme. That means I have to get up about five – brrr!

How's the coal situation at home, I hope you've got plenty by this time. Do you remember the January just before I was called up? We had no coal for one day and we were all taking home wood from work. I went to see a British film called "Cottage to Let" on Thursday. Have you seen it? Alastair Sim is in it. I liked it very much.

I'm blowed if I know what to write about. I don't want to bore you by describing what I have for meals, how many books I've read and what cakes I buy in the canteen and consequently I can hardly fill two sides. Still if I let you know I'm still alive every week, it's something isn't it? After two years, I've no new training to write about or anything like that. Oh! There is a little bit of news, I'm drawing 3d. per day extra now (second year pay) making my total pay 28/-. See you about April 10th I hope.

Cheerio
Charlie

Uncle Charlie's first paragraph, where he writes about supplying an electric cooker for a Mrs. Taylor, suggests that at some point in the past he may have worked in retail sales, possibly selling electrical items. However, I have now received my Uncle's Army Service Records stating that his employment on being called up was working for an accumulator manufacturer.

Given the cold, snowy conditions they are experiencing in Caithness, the prospect of rising from a nice warm bed at five o' clock in the morning to venture into several inches of snow less than two hours later, is not something Uncle Charlie is looking forward to.

He asks about the coal situation at home, and if they have enough, remembering a time two years ago, just before he was called up, when the family had run out of coal, and they were forced to bring wood home from work.

I have discovered a report from Hansard,[5] dated January 1941, (a year before Charlie's letter was written) when the House of Lords were discussing the problems of the previous winter's serious coal shortages. Twelve months on, they claim, there has been very little improvement, and they are meeting to discuss the possible solution to a long-standing problem. There were calls for the Government to improve the distribution of coal, the general agreement being that as there was more than enough coal for the entire country's needs lying in the coalfields, then the shortages must stem from the methods of distribution. After some discussion about using different transportation systems: roads, railways, canals, ships, it was agreed that with better co-ordination and co-operation between different transportation systems, all methods could be utilised to ensure sufficient deliveries of coal to where it was needed for both industrial and domestic use.

Lord Addison suggested that the problem lay in poor

management which resulted in coal dumps less than 25% full, when there were huge stocks of coal held up in the coal fields. He called for co-operation between the Ministry of Transport and the Ministry of Mines: instead of each blaming the other, they needed to work together to achieve greater efficiency in the movement of stock. He also asked the Government to consider the obvious step of estimating how much coal would be needed over a given period, thereby enabling efficient forward planning to be made.

It seems strange to me that the whole country could pull together so successfully to help the war effort, yet the distribution of a vital fuel source was seemingly stuck in the mire of poorly managed Government departments, who seemed intent on passing the buck, instead of working together for the common good. Hopefully, by March 1942, the date of Charlie's letter, the coal situation has improved and the family will be enjoying a warm welcoming fireside.

"Cottage to Let" starring Alastair Sim and John Mills, both famous actors at the time, went on general release in 1941. It was a spy film concerning attempts by Nazi spies to kidnap an inventor. Uncle Charlie, after enjoying the film, asks my Granddad if he has seen it. I wonder if he did and what he thought of it. Charlie is now enjoying a pay rise of 3d. and his two years in the army have earned him the grand total of 28/- per week. He can now afford to buy extra cakes, and other sweet things he loves so much; and he is hopefully looking forward to leave on April 10th, when he can savour some of Grandma's home-made cakes.

Notes

1 All letters from service personnel were censored and any sensitive information which could possibly be passed to an enemy was

either crossed or cut out. Also films, newsreels, news broadcasts and newspapers were censored for containing any information deemed to be bad for morale, or too gruesome to report. A new Government department called the Ministry of Information took on the task of censorship on the outbreak of the war.

2 "Cardio-Vascular Disease in Cotton Workers." By Richard Schilling & Nancy Goodman from the Nuffield Dept. of Occupational Health, Manchester University. Published in the British Journal of Industrial Medicine 1951.

3 1,178 Warship Weeks were held in Britain. An incredible total of 8 battleships, 4 carriers, 301 destroyers, 25 submarines, 164 corvettes and frigates, and 288 minesweepers were adopted by local communities.

4 Following a successful "Warship Week" in December, 1941, the destroyer "HMS Wrestler" was adopted by the town of Hyde. Exactly how much money was raised is not known. Thanks to http://hydonian.blogspot.co.uk

5 Hansard (Lords Sitting) "Coal Distribution" dated 29th January, 1941. Vol. 118. 263-76

CHAPTER FIVE

Cruising To Egypt & El-Alamein

3454037 Sgm. C. Robinson,
Royal Corps of Signals,
Att. 111 Fld. Reg. 1915,
C/o A.P.O. 1915.
12-7-42.

Dear Mother and Dad,

Here I am again, and still as fit as the proverbial fiddle. I'd like you to see me just now, I think I'm browner than I've ever been in my life before. You can't beat fresh sea air and sunshine, can you? It's Sunday afternoon now and as we expect to reach the second port of call sometime next week, I thought I would write one or two letters to be sent ashore there.

I understand that I shall get some shore leave when the ship arrives. I'm looking forward to it very much because I like the prospect of seeing a strange town in a strange country of which I have read and heard so much. In addition I shall be able to stretch my legs a little. After a week or two at sea you feel that a good walk would be just the thing. I'll bet Dad would give a lot to come with me. You do understand why it's impossible to tell you where I shall be, don't you?

I've still no idea of where my terminus is going to be. I wish I *knew, not only out of curiosity , but to help me to prepare myself a little. I may be able to tell you when I get there; we shall have to wait and see.*

We have a library on board now and I've taken a book by Hugh Walpole[1] called "The Sea Tower". I don't know whether you've read it or not, Dad, but I'm enjoying it very much. Between the library and my bridge duties I'm passing the time very nicely.

I was having a wash and shave the other night and we were having the common slanging game about the places we all come from. I had made a remark about Glasgow and MacFarlane said "Quiet, Hyde". A voice from the back said "Who comes from Hyde". I said I did and it turned out that the owner of the voice lives in Mottram and works at the Rexine. We then had a chat about the district and chaps we both know who work in Newton. He didn't know Stanley Jackson but knew a lot of the fellows who went to the Rexine from the County School. We spent a pleasant half-hour talking about Hyde and district, and decided that we seem and indeed are a long way from home now.

I hope you, Norman and Marjorie are all O.K. Has Jim Tighe been called up yet? I am anticipating keenly the first letter I get from you, although I don't expect it for a long time yet.

I expect to be able to send a cablegram from this unnamed port I keep talking about and hope you will get it quickly, before this letter. Don't worry about me, I am quite O.K. and enjoying my free cruise.

All the best.

Love,

Charlie

The invisible, yet powerfully strong, even unbreakable, cord connecting Uncle Charlie to his homeland and loved ones is being stretched now like the carding machine at Slack Mills as it pulls and elongates the cotton fibres. He is on a troop ship travelling to an unknown port of call in an unknown country. He writes "I like the prospect of seeing a strange town in a strange country of which I have read and heard so much." which hints he knows where he is headed, but then writes: "I have still no idea where my terminus is going to be". There may be rumours flying round the ship regarding their destination. But one thing is for sure, every man knows he is heading for a theatre of war. The training is behind them now and this war is for real. They all know that life will become more precarious: for the first time they will face the enemy. Reading his letter, I felt a seemingly illogical fear for Uncle Charlie. Perhaps that same silken thread binds me to him nearly seven decades later; and if *I* was afraid for him, I wonder at the depth of my grandparents' worries for their son and the dangers he must surely have to face. Significantly, he would like to know where he is headed, so he can prepare himself. For now Uncle Charlie is suntanned, enjoying his "cruise", his book, his duties on the bridge, and the company of a fellow soldier from Hyde, who had presented a surprising and invaluable link with home. Uncle Charlie discusses the Rexine factory in Hyde with his new-found friend and discovers that they both know some of the people who work there. Charlie is looking forward to walking out to stretch his legs a little and to see the sights and sounds of a foreign country.[2]

On the final page of his letter Uncle Charlie mentions his younger brother Norman and his sister Marjorie who is not yet married to my father Jim Tighe. I know my Uncle Norman joined the army, but the details of his service are unknown to me, and unfortunately he died many years ago, alongside his wife, due to a tragic accident. It sounds, from the tone of his letter, that Charlie is having a little dig at the absence of a letter from my mother and father: "keenly anticipating it" but not expecting it for "a long time yet." I know my father was called up in 1942, but he cannot recall which month it was.

The above photograph of the 'Awatea' shows her neat lines and attractive appearance. Transformed in 1942 from cruise ship to troop carrier, she transported Charlie from the Clyde to Durban, South Africa. Reproduced with kind permission of The Dock Museum, Barrow-in-Furness.

3454037 Sgm. C. Robinson,
Royal Corps of Signals,
Att. 111 Field Reg., R.A.
M.E.F.
26-9-42

Dear Mother and Dad,

Since I last wrote to you I have moved. Now I'm in a pretty big camp. There are several canteens quite near and, in the camp, everything I want. I can get a nice shower-bath anytime, and that counts for a lot in this part of the world. Here, too, is an open-air camp cinema. I have been and what a laugh I had. I first went on Tuesday. Now, when there's an air-raid they put all the lights out (there's no permanent black-out here) and naturally the open-air cinema show has to stop as well. I saw all the supporting films and the big film had been showing about ten minutes when the siren went. The film faded out and we were told to return, with our tickets on the following night. I went again on Wednesday and believe it or not exactly the same thing happened. I left the place and had only got about ten minutes' walk away when the "All Clear" went. It was one of the funniest things I've ever seen to watch everybody dashing back to the cinema to see the continuation of the film – they start again if the "All Clear" goes within an hour. I suppose I missed about ten minutes of the film all told. There is a lot of French spoken here and the films have the French words printed on the film like the old silent days. I ought to be able to brush up my French a little whilst I'm here.

This camp is very close to a big city and although I haven't been yet I'm expecting to go in tomorrow night. I shall probably be able to tell you more about the place in my next letter. I'm keen to see it because I've heard such a lot about it.

27-9-42

Well, I don't need to wait until my next letter. I was in the city last night, and what a mixture of a place it is – East and West all jumbled up together. You pass a fine building and then find yourself amongst squalid little open-air native shops. And there are street hawkers selling everything you could imagine – razor blades, fountain pens, cheap toys and I even saw an old bird with a tank of coffee strapped to his back. In addition there are literally thousands of boot-blacks, and they are the most persistent people I've ever seen. If you stand for long looking into a shop window you find your boots cleaned – whether they needed it or not – and a hand held out for the money. One of our chaps had one boot done in the street and the other in the tramcar. They follow you everywhere – even in café's. French seems to be the usual language amongst Europeans. All the shops have French signs outside Chemiste, Dentiste, Cadeaux (Presents) and all the rest. The newspapers are *printed in French and the directions outside the trams also. I shall definitely have to brush up on my French. The traffic is on the right-hand side of the street too, a fact which is a bit bewildering at first. And the smells – you get the most awful smells possible sometimes in the side streets. What a place! I think I'd rather be in Manchester now that I've seen this over-rated place.*

Still, as I've said before, I wouldn't have missed it. You always wanted to sample a low-down dive in these foreign places didn't you, dad? My advice after seeing one is – don't. I sampled one and talk about rough. There was a dance floor about the size of a pocket handkerchief in the middle, and tables all round. We hadn't been in more than quarter of an hour before there were two fights going on, and bottles and tables being thrown about. Lord, what a place.

I haven't had any more mail after the ones you posted on July 18th. I suppose there will be more on the way. Please write often because we live on letters from home. I hope you are getting mine through alright now. After the first wait, we should get each other's' mail quite regularly.

I expect you are all working hard still. By the way is Jim in the R.A.F. yet? Are Norman and Marjorie doing their stuff? Mother, I know will be doing hers. I'm perfectly O.K. and happy. Cheerio for now.

Yours
Charlie

I am encouraged that Uncle Charlie has not lost his sense of humour as he describes the scene at the open-air cinema during an air-raid warning, when the film started, stopped, started, stopped, then started again the following night. The soldiers, as they hurried from the cinema, must have looked like extras in a dark, grainy, silent film as they scattered in all directions, before repeating the same sequence again and then again.

Uncle Charlie is now further away from home than he has

ever been before; not just physically, but also culturally and sensorially, with sights, sounds and smells, competing with hands held out for money in payment for unwanted shoe-shining. The noise, the heat, the dust, the hustle and bustle, a foreign language being shouted, traffic driving on the other side of the road, a man carrying a tank of coffee on his back, and the general mayhem paint a vivid picture of life in this foreign city, making even the rougher areas of Manchester seem more attractive to Charlie.

I laughed when I read the story of a soldier having one boot shined when he stopped to look in a shop window: the determined local, not to be thwarted, followed the soldier onto a tram to finish the job and receive his money. Not only is this foreign city in a foreign country with its alien sounds, sights and smells, it is also a world away from life before the army.

At the time of writing this letter Uncle Charlie has been in the army for two and a half years. On joining up, he would have been a naive, protected young man of twenty two years. A young man committed to his family, his church, his friends, his activities, outings and excursions. I imagine that that length of time in the army would have changed him into a more rounded, worldly-wise individual, and yielded some memorably colourful experiences like the one above.

I thought Uncle Charlie's description of two fights, with bottles and tables flying and the tiny dance floor, suggested he was in a bar; although he did not say this in so many words. I wonder if he had tried a beer whilst in there. I'm sure my Granddad, a life-long teetotaller, would not have approved. But then under the same circumstances as those Uncle Charlie found himself in, would Granddad have been tempted I wonder? What is certain, this experience will have contributed greatly to Charlie's education, and I think my

Granddad would have enjoyed reading such a descriptive paragraph from his son.

Thanks to the War Diaries, I have deduced that the foreign city Charlie describes so vividly is, in fact, Cairo, as it is the closest city to his camp at Almaza. Having been to Cairo, even many years after my Uncle, I have experienced for myself the same noise, colour and chaos that still reign supreme. I didn't see a man carrying a tank of coffee on his back, but I do remember seeing a man peddling a bike with a large tray of freshly baked bread balanced on his head, held there with one hand, leaving the other free to steer the bike, as it wove its dangerous way around the blaring horns of the traffic! These strange sights would have been similar for me as for Uncle Charlie, but *his* eyes would have witnessed many allied soldiers from different countries and regiments, as well as the trams and persistent boot-blacks on the street.

The large army camp of Almaza, near Cairo, held hundreds of soldiers from New Zealand and Australia as well as those from Britain. No wonder there was trouble when so many young soldiers were thrust together on a night out in Cairo.

Uncle Charlie requests as many letters as possible from friends and family, as they all "live on letters from home" The further away from home they are, the more important letters become. They are the home-spun silken thread making a connection to loved ones and helping to reduce the distance. Finally, he asks if my father has joined the R.A.F. yet, and the answer I can give is: 'no' because he joined the Royal Navy. Uncle Charlie asks about my Mum, Uncle Norman and Grandma; I wonder how they are coping with the worry of not knowing the exact whereabouts of their loved one, what danger he may be in, how his health is holding up and whether he has the mental strength to stay as positive as his letters suggest.

The War Diaries have helped to fill the gaps between letters.

Charlie stayed in Durban from the 20th July until the 16th August when his Regiment embarked on the "Kosciuszko" and set sail for Egypt, and the Red Sea port of Tewfik, by the entrance to the Suez Canal, docking on the 7th September. On the 9th September the Regiment reached Kabrit, a large R.A.F .base, where they took part in training exercises. On the 20th September the Regiment left Kabrit by road and arrived at Almaza later that day, where 111 Field Regiment assumed the duties of Depot Regiment at the Middle Eastern School of Artillery. Their days were full, consisting of large amounts of training with field guns and ammunition. Undertaking such vast amounts of training is preparation for one outcome: to win the battle for North Africa, which would begin with El-Alamein, the optimum place to make a stand as it was situated close by the Mediterranean Sea. Thirty miles to the south was the Qattara Depression, a vast sea of shifting, unstable sand; impassable to heavy tanks and vehicles. Therefore with the Mediterranean to the north and the Qattara Depression to the south, an enemy outflanking manoeuvre was out of the question. The fighting had to take place on that thirty mile line.

Both Allied and Axis armies were determined to win this strategically crucial battle for different reasons. The Allies saw the winning of El-Alamein as a first step on the long road to gain entry into Europe via the Mediterranean or: "the back door." Once in Europe they would begin to advance, with the aim of freeing the countries Germany had occupied by force, and restoring Europe to its former order. As for the Axis armies of Germany and Italy, their objectives were to break through the Allied lines and take control of the Middle East oil fields, thereby cutting off Britain's main oil supply, and disabling the transportation of food, fuel and equipment to and from the U.K. The anticipated outcome would be to starve Britain into submission. The enemy also aimed to seize control of the Suez Canal, preventing ships from passing through with raw materials. This would be a double blow to the United Kingdom, as, by blocking the Suez Canal, ships on their way to Britain would have to travel right round the horn of Africa, not only taking longer, but using more precious fuel, and risking poor weather conditions as they transported essential supplies. Both sides of the conflict had a great deal to lose, but a tremendous amount to gain by winning the forthcoming battle of El-Alamein. For several weeks, under the cover of convincing camouflage, the British had been stockpiling equipment: guns, tanks and ammunition, amassing a total of 1,351 tanks and 1,900 artillery pieces. They also gathered together a large force of 200,000 soldiers. A major weapon in their armoury was when 300 American Sherman tanks arrived. These powerful tanks could fire a six pound shell capable of penetrating an enemy tank from 2,000 metres away.

Suddenly, on the evening of the 23rd October 1942, as the BBC pips announced the time of 9-00p.m. a massive total concentration of the fire power of 592 guns opened up simultaneously along a thirty mile front from the Mediterranean to the Qattara Depression. This conclusive action, lasting for an unimaginable six hours, combined with air support from the R.A.F., superior tanks and artillery guns, better fuel supplies and a greater number of soldiers, began the battle which, twelve days later, would result in overwhelming the German and Italian armies. Decisively beaten they were forced to retreat. El-Alamein was, for the allies, the first victory of the second world war and Churchill, with his uncanny ability to supply a pithy comment said later: "Before Alamein we never had a victory, after Alamein we never had a defeat." This first victory was so complete and so important to the allies that Churchill, mightily relieved, ordered every church bell in the country to ring out its announcement of the victory.

The hard-fought battle of El-Alamein stretched from the 23rd October to the 4th November. For both sides the deafening noise, the intensity, the apprehension and the lack of rest, must have felt like twelve months instead of twelve days. At the end of that time 25,000 German and Italian troops had been killed or wounded and many thousands taken prisoner. The Allies lost 13,500 men, of which 4,610 were killed or missing.

Uncle Charlie was somewhere in all this fighting. Where was one soldier amongst 200,000 others? The War Diaries informed me that 111 Field Regiment was commanded by the 50th (Northumberland) Division, situated just below the half way point of the line and opposite the Italian 27th Brescia Division.

On the evening of the 23rd October, 1942, in the quiet before the storm of artillery fire, Charles Robinson, weighing 57kg., standing 162cm tall, with a chest measurement of 86.4cm^3 was waiting: A small signalman attached to 111 Field Regiment, Royal Artillery, he was waiting nervously to begin playing his part in the drama that was to follow. It was to be his first taste of real fighting with a real enemy, intent on destruction. I suppose each soldier has his own way of dealing with pre-battle tension. How was Charlie coping at this time? Was he praying? Was he nervously smoking a cigarette? Was he talking quietly to his comrades? Was he thinking of his family, and trying to relax before the firing started, or was he reflecting on the carefree days of many moons ago, when he cycled to the quiet little hamlet of Pott Shrigley? Every soldier knows that the peace and quiet is about to be shattered. My father who lost 70 per cent of his hearing when he was in the Royal Navy due to gunfire noise, (officially a blast injury) has told me that the firing of guns during battle is earth-shatteringly loud, and seems unceasingly relentless, drilling into the brains of anyone standing close enough.

There is, of course, the added apprehension and uncertainty related to the question: "Will I survive this night? That this question should be asked by young men, many of whom are still in their teenage years, is too cruel to contemplate when applied to a generation whose peace time thoughts would never turn to their own mortality.

Of course, Uncle Charlie did survive that first night, and many more nights to follow. His Regiment's casualties were light; three men killed in action, one wounded and one wounded and evacuated. It is recorded in the Regimental War Diaries that on the following day (24th October) the Regiment (thankfully) had a quiet day. However, they do record a noteworthy entry: a certain resourceful, (one could describe him as swashbuckling) Captain Mellor, who was initially suspected of being wounded and missing, actually turned up later that day, having first been captured, then later escaped, from the Italians! But in the language of the Regimental War Diaries, written by an officer, formally stating facts, orders, incidents and information, Captain Mellor's adventure, like all events, had to be recorded in a professional, unemotional, uncritical manner. The Regimental War Diaries' daily reports are reproduced in italics.

SATURDAY, 24th OCTOBER:
0810hrs. Casualty report from 212 Bty. Killed in action: 3. Wounded and evacuated:1. Superficially wounded: 2. Capt. K.W. Mellor, R.A. suspected wounded and missing.
1300hrs. Capt. Mellor reported safe having been prisoner in Italian hands and escaped.
1545hrs. Regiment fired 432 rds. on 300 M.E.T. and tanks in ALINDA DEPRESSION. Result cannot be seen from R.3.
1546hrs. 476 Battery under mortar fire.

2230hrs. 124 Fld. Regt. Group (111 & 124) fired concentrations for
80 minutes on areas in Squares.
2400hrs. A very quiet day for the Regt.

SUNDAY, 25th OCTOBER:
If an officer is killed or wounded he is always named by the
War Diaries. But all O.R's (other ranks) are counted but not
named. The Allied plan is to fool the enemy into believing
that the main thrust of the attack will be in the south, where
the 44th Infantry and 7th Armoured are positioned, with
Charlie's Regiment, as part of the 50th Brigade, situated above
them. In fact the real plan is to concentrate the attack in the
north, where there is a railway line and the only paved road
running parallel to the Mediterranean (which offers a much
better surface for the movement of vehicles than the soft
desert sand and tracks found further south). This road also
provides near-access to the Mediterranean Sea which would
be the ultimate aim of the Allies. However, up there the 9th
Australian Division is in trouble, suffering heavy losses, as
the enemy relentlessly attacks them. The Allied bluff has not
fooled the enemy at all.

MONDAY, 26th OCTOBER:
The 9th Australian Division is attacked by the Italian
Bersaglieri Regiment. Starting just after midnight on this day,
111 Field Regiment, fighting most of the night, put down
large concentrations of fire, causing heavy enemy casualties.
But they did not have it all their own way, as 6GH (Gordon
Highlanders) were held up by heavy enemy artillery fire.

TUESDAY 27th OCTOBER:
Again, in the north, the Bersaglieri Regiment tries unsuccessfully
to dislodge the Australian 9th Division, and the 7th Armoured

Division (the Desert Rats) move north in support. The Allies are creeping inexorably closer, or actually pushing through the enemy lines. The War Diaries record a warning order for the Regiment to also move north. Two Regimental Batteries have moved across to support the Free French.

WEDNESDAY & THURSDAY 28th & 29th OCTOBER:
Two German Panzer Divisions and the Italian 7th Bersaglieri Regiment suffered heavy losses. The 26th Australian Brigade also suffered with 27 soldiers killed and 290 wounded. The Italian anti-tank gunners fought bravely, fiercely defending their positions; all were killed or died from wounds, apart from 20 wounded men who were captured the next day. Rommel, Commander in Chief of the German desert army, magnanimously paid tribute to those brave Italian soldiers who had fought, almost to the last man. After two days of fierce fighting, the British still had 800 tanks in operation, while the Axis had only 148 German and 187 Italian tanks left. To make matters worse, the Axis armies were desperately short of fuel. On the 28th October, as part of the 50th Brigade, Charlie's 111 Field Regiment prepared to move north. The plan was to support the 1st Armoured, while they pursued Rommel as he retreated. But before they were able to move 212 battery experienced heavy shelling, and R.H.Q. was also shelled and had to be moved to another location. One soldier was killed and one artillery battery destroyed. That night the Division staged a mock attack, aimed at diverting the enemy.

FRIDAY & SATURDAY 30th & 31st OCTOBER:
The Australians gained ground once more and reached their objective in the north, (the railway line and road) but on the 31st Rommel brought up a battle group from the 21st Panzer Division, resulting in heavy, sometimes hand-to-hand

fighting; but the Axis forces could not gain the upper hand. The War Diaries reported: *476 Battery engaged enemy with harassing fire from temporary position.*

SUNDAY, 1st & MONDAY, 2nd NOVEMBER.
The War Diaries report that the R.A.F. leant their considerable weight to the fierce fighting in the North by conducting heavy bombing raids on the enemy for seven long hours during the night. This offensive was part of code name "Operation Supercharge" and the R.A.F. attack was followed up by a four and a half hour barrage of gun fire from troops on the ground – designed to break through the enemy lines where the greatest concentration of men and equipment, and also the fiercest fighting had been taking place. The objective was to destroy the armoured forces of the enemy and force them into the open where they would use more of their precious fuel. A further objective was to block the enemy supply line to prevent the movement of supplies.

These objectives were achieved, and Uncle Charlie's Regiment, commanded by the 50th Infantry Division, taking part in the action with concentrations of fire, was involved in the advance into enemy territory. Rommel's Afrika Korps was in retreat.

Due to the successful intensive bombardment of the enemy more and more Allied forces burst through the German lines; but the 9th Armoured Brigade suffered heavy casualties: attempting to destroy German tanks, it had sacrificed itself on the gun line, and of the initial 400 tank crews, 230 were killed, wounded or captured. Whilst the Allies were successful in their overall objectives, it was a very high price to pay for the 9th Armoured Brigade.

TUESDAY, 3rd NOVEMBER:

On this night Rommel's Afrika Korps retreated a distance of six miles, but the Italian Corps and the 90th Light Division stood firm. Also, British forces launched three Infantry Brigade attacks in an attempt to capture the strategically important Tel El Aqqaqir At seven o'clock in the morning, Charlie's 111 Field Regiment encountered mortar and machine gun fire, but later that day, tellingly they report: *Enemy have withdrawn from foremost positions. Patrols encountered no immediate opposition other than mines and booby traps. Front quiet.* The enemy have gone; the lads just had to be very careful where they trod!

WEDNESDAY, 4th NOVEMBER:

The British X Corps has succeeded in capturing Tel El Aqqaqir – a major victory – as this place runs straight through the Axis lines. X Corp's successful action has led to the fracture of the German army, which is now in full retreat, ending the battle of El-Alamein in favour of the Allies. Charlie's 111 Field Regiment has been busy this day advancing generally, but encountering isolated pockets of resistance during foot patrols. Orders have been received from 50th Division that the primary role of the Regiment is to support South East Yorks in holding Ruweisat Ridge against a possible counter-attack from the north.

So this hard-fought, sometimes brutal, battle has been won. Not only was it a battle of guns, tanks, bombs, bullets, shells and grenades, it has also been a battle against the elements: the heat of the day, the cold nights, the flies, the dust and the sand storms. It has been bravely fought by British, German and especially Italian soldiers, and I am not ashamed to say I feel a sense of pride that my Uncle has come through this battle, despite the many privations he must have endured.

The battle of El-Alamein has been won, and the German

army is in retreat; but by no means is this the end of the North Africa campaign. In his famous Mansion House speech, just days after the Allied victory, Winston Churchill suggested that on the road to winning the war there would be more battles to face:

Now this is not the end. It is not even the beginning of the end. But it is, perhaps, the end of the beginning.

THURSDAY, 5th NOVEMBER:
The 50th Division was ordered to begin mopping-up operations, during which time five thousand prisoners of war were captured. I imagine there must have been a very long line of depressed and defeated German and Italian soldiers. I wonder if the Allied soldiers experienced a heightened sense of victory on seeing their defeated and captured enemy, or if they were just too weary to feel like true victors after nearly two weeks of fighting. The War Diaries tell me that Charlie's Regiment took no part in this particular operation with prisoners, but were involved in other areas of mopping up post battle. The 7th Armoured moved across country to intercept the coastal road at Sidi Haneish, while the 1st Armoured were ordered to make a wide detour deep into the desert, ultimately to swing up to cut off the retreating enemy on the road at Mersa Matruh. These excursions were not a complete success as there were fuel shortages, and the R.A.F., tasked with undertaking bombing raids, was hampered by identification problems which compromised accurate targeting. The long chase across North Africa has begun.

FRIDAY, 6th NOVEMBER:
The British 7th Armoured Division had come upon the German 21st Panzer Division and the Voss Reconnaissance Group early in the day, resulting in several clashes, during

which the 21st Panzer lost sixteen tanks and numerous guns, and also narrowly missed being surrounded by the Allies. Yet somehow the Germans managed to escape by the skin of their teeth. Meanwhile, 50th Division is now confined to the less prestigious task of clearing the battlefield. Charlie's Regiment has been sent out to collect salvage, particularly guns and ammunition, left behind by the retreating enemy.

SATURDAY, 7th – THURSDAY 12th NOVEMBER:
The 1st and 7th Armoured Divisions continue to make steady progress in following the enemy's retreat, but are then slowed by the boggy conditions caused by heavy rain the previous night. To add frustration to their slow progress, they also had to wait for fuel which was still on its way along the coastal road. For 111 Field Regiment the salvage drive continued, with several enemy guns and much ammunition retrieved. The War Diaries also made reference to the Regiment and 476 Battery:

Submitting to an inspection by the Commanding Officer. Permission was granted for certain officers and OR's to visit Alexandria. It was noted that the Adjutant was one of the first to avail himself of this privilege.

Initially, I thought Uncle Charlie had managed to obtain permission to visit the city, as his diary which begins on the 1st January, 1943, contains the hand stamp of a shop in Alexandria, so it was obviously purchased there. However, in his letter dated 9th January, he tells the family he disappointingly didn't get the chance to see the city. Someone, (perhaps the Adjutant) brought the diary back for him.

On the 8th November, "Operation Torch" began, when American, British and Commonwealth troops landed at the western end of the North African shore in Vichy held Morocco, Algeria and Tunisia.[4] These were all French speaking colonies, administered by the puppet government of Vichy France. Algiers was easily taken by the Allies, but Tunisia was much more difficult to overcome, and took a further six months of fighting before it succumbed, as Rommel decisively moved crack Panzer Divisions up to meet them. But by the 11th November,[5] following the decisive naval victory of Casablanca by the Americans, the Vichy army did change sides and joined the Allies in North Africa. As the Eighth Army advanced westward from Egypt the American, British and Commonwealth armies advanced eastward to meet them from the north.

FRIDAY, 13th NOVEMBER:
The War Diaries record that the Adjutant returned from Alexandria refreshed. The salvage drive came to an end and 111 Field Regiment was cited as: *having contributed not less than its fair share to the 50th Division total.*

SATURDAY, 14th NOVEMBER:
The Commanding Officer of 111 Field Regiment inspected 212 Battery and pronounced: "Unsatisfactory results". However, there was some light sporting relief and a bit of fun for the men as the War Diaries put it: *the business of fighting being temporarily at an end, recreational training was inaugurated with a football match which ended when the ball burst!* I wonder if Uncle Charlie joined in the game.

Later in the day a Captain Jenkins came to inspect the men from a hygiene aspect which I find a little amusing, as here they were, in the desert heat, with water in short supply, having just run around with a football. I hope the captain wasn't expecting neatly combed hair and the pleasant aroma of aftershave! Apparently he was regarded with some suspicion, as he came without his identity card; but, nevertheless, the men did manage to persuade him to agree to build some latrine seats.

SUNDAY, 15th NOVEMBER:
A quiet day. About one hundred men attended a church service.
I expect Uncle Charlie was one of them.

16th & 17th NOVEMBER:
The War Diaries record some training duties for Signallers. The Commanding Office of 111 Field Regiment inspected the guns and found them to be dirty. They will have to be cleaned and re-inspected. I wondered aloud to my husband how they could possibly expect guns to stay bright and shiny in the desert. He gave me one of those condescending looks, like he does when I ask him a question about the car engine, and patiently explained that a dirty gun is inefficient, and therefore may not fire properly. Oh! I see.

Some unwelcome news has been received by Charlie's Regiment in the form of a movement order. They will not only be moving location, but they will also have a new role as Corps Artillery, under the command of 30 Corps (XXX Corps). In the words of the War Diary:

This order was received with regret as the Regiment has been trained mainly as Division Artillery, and as cordial relations had been established with H.Q.R.A. 50 Division.

The Regiment did not actually move until the 27th November, and in the intervening ten days they had collected some more serviceable salvage left behind by their hurriedly retreating enemy.

They received a final inspection by 50th Division Commander, and sent out a reconnoitering party to recce. the new regimental area. At 0800hrs. 111 Field Regiment moved out in two stages, ready to begin their new duties within XXX

Corps, and to push forward to meet their final North African destiny in Libya and Tunisia.

On the last three days of November there was little to report, apart from one day of cleaning and maintenance for equipment, and one day of cleaning and maintenance for soldiers – bathing parties were sent to sea! The Regiment moved out on the 30th November, at 0800 Hrs.

Notes

1 Walpole, Hugh 13th March, 1884 – 1st June, 1941. Prolific English writer. He was a bestselling author in the 1920's and 1930's, but his works fell out of favour after his death. He wrote 36 novels, short stories, plays and 3 volumes of his memoirs.

2 From information contained in the Regimental War Dairies of 111 Field Regiment, Royal Artillery June – December, 1942) I learnt that Charlie was on board H.M.T "Awatea" (coincidentally built in 1936 at Barrow-in-Furness where I now live) when he wrote the above letter dated 12th July, 1942. The previous month, from the 11th to the 17th June his Regiment had been taking part in gun practice at Redesdale military firing range in Northumbria. On the 18th June the main body of the Regiment left for Glasgow and on the 21st June "Awatea" sailed from the Clyde to arrive in Durban, South Africa, on the 20th July. Thank you to Lee Richards of Arcre document copying service for kindly providing me with the Regimental War Diaries.

3 Data received from Charlie's service records: His statistics were taken on enlistment.

4 The Government of France which collaborated with the Axis powers during the German occupation of France. The Vichy Government was virtually a puppet regime, and was headed by Marshall Petain who proclaimed the Government, following the military defeat of France by Germany.

5   It was on this day that the "Awatea", the ship which had transported
Uncle Charlie from The Clyde to Durban four months previously,
was sunk by enemy aircraft. Transporting commandos, she was
taking part in the "Operation Torch" landings, and proudly featured
in the vanguard of the multi-national fleet landing in Vichy-held
North Africa. She had discharged her cargo at Bougie harbour in
Algiers, started to make her way out to sea when she was attacked by
enemy bombers and torpedo planes. She was hit by two bombs and
two torpedoes and sank a few hours later, with a fierce fire raging
on her bridge. However, the crew were rescued, there was no loss
of life, and the captain and crew received citations for bravery. The
"Awatea" was a beautiful ship, a cruise ship, not meant for a combat
role, but now armed with guns, she stuck to her task and went
down fighting to the last, bringing down one enemy plane with her
A.A. guns. The Captain claimed: "She fought the fight of a battle
ship."

CHAPTER SIX

The Chase

It is December now. XXX Corps and Charlie's 111 Field Regiment is seriously on the move, as the following details show:

TUESDAY, 1ˢᵗ DECEMBER:
Regiment left Hageet-el-Inhaba and moved to Sidi-Suleiman – distance 73 miles.

WEDNESDAY, 2nd DECEMBER – THURSDAY 3rd DECEMBER:
Regiment left Sidi-Suleiman, and marched to El-Adem. Distance 84 miles. Spent the day in El-Adem maintaining vehicles and equipment.

FRIDAY, 4th DECEMBER – SUNDAY 6th DECEMBER:
Regiment left El-Adem and marched to Si-Mansur. Distance travelled 81 miles due to Regiment having to go south beyond Bir Viakeim, to by-pass mine fields of Gazala. The Regiment travelled from Si-Mansur to El-Meddar – distance marched 63 miles.

The next day they left El-Meddar and marched to a point 21 miles north of Antelat.

MONDAY, 7ᵗʰ DECEMBER:
The Regiment is progressing smartly and is now located 15 miles north of Jedabaya on the Benghazi – Jedabaya road.

TUESDAY 8th DECEMBER:
Recce. party sent out to choose regimental position.

WEDNESDAY 9th DECEMBER:
Regiment massed. Recce. party rejoined main body.

THURSDAY 10th DECEMBER:
Digging parties were sent out. Some shelling of digging parties. One man was killed in 212 Battery.

FRIDAY 11th DECEMBER:
Digging parties returned to Regiment at 1500. Shelling less acute.

SATURDAY, 12TH DECEMBER:
The day was spent in preparation for action. Some vehicles evacuated for repair at El-Adem were returned. Enemy was reported to be thinning out in Mersa Brega.

SUNDAY, 13th DECEMBER:
Digging parties went out to complete Northern Position, followed by Command Post and Signal Section parties to establish Regiment and Battery H.Q. (That would be Uncle Charlie helping to prepare the communications needed ready for action.) *Guns must be ready for action on the night of 13/14th December. Regiment reported to be in action at 17.30 hours.*

Montgomery and his troops are ready to do battle again with Rommel. Although the Axis armies were in retreat they did not stop fighting as they went, which meant the Allies had to maintain pressure on the enemy.

MONDAY, 14TH DECEMBER:
Although there are three pages of the War Diaries devoted to this day, I have found it doubly difficult to read them, as they

seem to have been written hurriedly, and with a blunt pencil! From the words I can make out it looks like the Regiment is required to build a firm base at Mersa Bresa. It appears there have been visits by the Seaforth Highlanders and the Black Watch. The words I could make out clearly were: …each man was issued with one gallon of water, and a happy time was had by all…the Division's first proper wash for a while. How the lads must have enjoyed their gallon of water!

TUESDAY & WEDNESDAY 15th & 16th DECEMBER:
Nothing of note was written on these days.
17th, 18th, 19th DECEMBER:
Training started. Training continues. Training continues.
20th DECEMBER:
Church parade and recreation.

The following letter from Uncle Charlie was written on this day.

3454037 Sgm. C. Robinson,
Royal Corps of Signals,
Att. 111 Fld. Reg. R.A.,
M.E.F.
20-12-42

Dear Mother and Dad,

I suppose that today you are recovering from the momentous happenings of yesterday. How did it all go? When you write telling me about it, please write in detail, won't you? I should like to know everything from A to Z. Wouldn't it be alright if I could see a newsreel of it all! Yesterday in the afternoon I was swimming in the Mediterranean and thinking of Marjorie all the time. I came out of the water, dried myself, and when I put on my watch it was 4-0p.m. That means 2-0p.m. in England.

Honestly, I stood still and thought about Norfolk St. Chapel and Marjorie, Jim and you all. Then I looked round and saw the deep blue Med., the white sand and the cloudless blue sky and thought "It means nothing to me compared to Hyde at the moment." Then common sense came to my aid, and I realised that in order to enjoy home life again, I, and thousands of others must endure this exile, which does not always mean swimming in the Med. as you will realise, I don't doubt. The harder we work and fight out here, the sooner we shall be back home again. I think everyone gets these periods of home-sickness occasionally. Especially when some outstanding event takes place.

I received your air graph of Nov. 14th today. Thanks very much. I'm sorry if I've caused any anxiety at home by not writing often enough. I do realise the fact that every letter you get from me eases your minds even before you open it, and I will definitely write more often from now on.

But I have some excuse, you know. Sometimes the position is such that it would take a braver man than me to calmly sit down and write a letter. However, it is not always like that and I will write more frequently. I know you must worry a little.

I am still without any N.C.H.'s, but am expecting them any time now and looking forward to their arrival very keenly. We are short of reading matter just now.

The letter which Mr. Oldham gets from you, Dad, will, I am sure, please him. He keeps all the letters he receives from soldiers' parents in Hyde, and treasures them. I can count on you to pen a letter which will not let us down. He will appreciate it, I know. Did I tell you that he keeps a record, in a book set aside for that purpose, of all the Hyde boys who have called on him, their addresses and their parents' names? He is a most interesting man, and a wonderful talker.

I can understand Norman's feeling just now – waiting and wondering when. I felt just the same three years ago. Three years – ye gods! It doesn't seem so long ago. I'm certain that when Norman joins the Army he will settle down quickly and enjoy the life. But I can't help a little undercurrent of thought cropping up and saying "I hope Norman manages to keep out of it." It's since coming out here that I've had the thought. Soldiering in England is a fine life.

My air graphs and letter cards seem to be finding their mark alright. I'm glad because I sometimes doubt whether all my mail gets home. I think is does, though, in time.

I suppose you will get this about Dec. 31st so I'll finish by wishing you all a very Happy and Prosperous New Year, and may I be with you for the next one.

    Cheerio,

    Charlie

P.S. So you have dodged the dentist again, Dad. I really am surprised at you.

My Granddad was famous for avoiding the dentist's chair. I can remember that he had lots of spaces between the remaining few teeth arranged at random in his upper and lower jaw. His fear of the dentist overcame any thoughts of possessing a dazzling smile. He refused to smile on photographs, but he did smile at me regularly. If you love your Granddad, it doesn't really matter what he looks like – for after all, love is not always the preserve of the beautiful. I think, reading between the lines, Uncle Charlie found it hard to be sympathetic, and would prefer his father to overcome his fear and visit the dentist to improve his appearance.

It must be at those times when "momentous happenings" are taking place at home when, for a soldier, home and family are missed most of all. There will be a deep longing to be part of a celebration that is so precious: the gathering together of all those people who are cared most about in the world; the photographs, the laughter, the conversations, the jokes, the "sweet things" that Charlie loves so much. And not forgetting the feelings of sadness for a family when a brother is not present at the wedding of his sister. The celebration Charlie is referring to is the marriage of my mother and father. For some reason their wedding was postponed until the 22nd December, so I must assume that Charlie wasn't aware of the delay when he wrote this letter. No matter. His thoughts were with them, and that's what counts. A marriage is a time to make solemn vows: a commitment to life-long fidelity and love. It has certainly been the case for my parents who are, as I write this, both 90 and 89 years respectively; and their marriage that took place nearly 70 years ago, despite illness and advancing years, continues to this day. I think of my mother and father and how sad they would feel that a key family member was missing on their special day.

Uncle Charlie did his best to take his mind off the "momentous happenings" at home. He tried swimming in the Mediterranean. He tried to appreciate his lovely surroundings: the clear blue sky, the soft white sand, the turquoise water, but he failed miserably. Feeling very homesick, his thoughts were on his family, and particularly focused on his sister. He pictured her walking down the aisle with their father, ready to make her life-long commitment to my father.

He even made allowances for the time difference, and thought about her making her vows when it was 2.00p.m in England, as he walked out of the sea and put his watch back on. Much has been written about the "ultimate sacrifice" but that just comes at the end of so many smaller sacrifices along the way.

Trying to look on the bright side, he casts aside his sorrow and with an increased resolve decides to work hard and get the job done that he has been sent out to do. He always seems able to gather some positive thoughts (at least in his letters) and looks forward to the day when he can be home for good. He fervently wishes to be back home next year for the family Christmas and New Year celebrations, not knowing that he would never see his home and family again. The thought strikes me with some force that the Robinson family will, with thousands of others, pay dearly for their contribution to the defeat of Nazi Germany. I do not state this with any political, humanitarian, or pacifistic axe to grind. I am just stating a sad fact.

At the time most of the population seemed to pull together, making personal sacrifices for the common good. This was evidenced by their tremendous efforts in working longer hours, joining the W.V.S. raising money for warships, and sending parcels to servicemen they didn't know.

They lost homes and loved ones during the blitz, they spent long hours in bomb shelters, put up with food and fuel shortages, and coped with rationing. City dwellers sent their children to live in the countryside for their safety. The country was united in fighting a just war against a dictatorship which they believed would – if the nation did not stand fast – overrun the United Kingdom, as it had with most of Europe.

Uncle Charlie also realises that his younger brother is likely to be caught up in the war, and feels some concern, knowing how dangerous and uncertain a soldier's life can be. He thinks soldiering in Britain is a "fine life" but knows it is a very different story under fire in a foreign country. Charlie hopes in his heart of hearts, that Norman can "keep out of it" somehow.

Uncle Charlie promises to write more often, but reading between the lines I get a sense that the quiet times are few and far between, and during these times the last thing he feels like doing is writing a letter. He doesn't want to paint a bleak picture brought on by fatigue and the stress of battle. But, on the other hand, he realises that when his family receive a letter from him they know he is alright; so he will try to write more often, and keep the details of his situation to himself so as not to worry them any more than necessary.

Charlie is eagerly awaiting an 'N.C.H. parcel', which appears to be one containing reading matter, as he states he is running short of something to read. After much pondering and unproductive forays onto the internet, wondering what on earth N.C.H meant, I had one of those 'moments' again, when I suddenly became aware of a thought rising from the morass of my memory banks. When I lived in Hyde about forty years ago, the local paper was called the "The North Cheshire Herald". Problem solved.

However, I have had no luck in discovering the details of the mysterious Mr. Oldham of Hyde, who so meticulously recorded the details of soldiers and their families. I have been in contact with the local archivist, who, with very little to go on, has not managed to find out who he was. I hope the many names Mr. Oldham so carefully recorded have not been lost, and are still in existence somewhere.

I notice that Uncle Charlie quite formally refers to him as 'Mr' and that reflects the formality of the time. Anyone older or not so well known would be respectfully addressed as Mr. or Mrs. Only friends and younger family members would be spoken to using their first names. Aunties and Uncles would always be addressed as: "Auntie Doris or Uncle Bill." Even if a mature adult nephew or niece addressed either of them as Doris or Bill it would be frowned upon and considered to be a mark of disrespect, resulting in a severe reprimand. I remember this formality also applied when I was growing up.

In those days, mothers had sole responsibility for raising the children, with fathers taking more of a back seat, perhaps taking on a disciplinary role, or playing games, rather than changing nappies or feeding, Also, the females of the family had quite strict, (if arbitrary), rules for certain words they had decided could not be voiced in front of children. For example my Grandma's next door neighbour was called Mrs. Smith. I never knew her first name, perhaps because it was not used in my hearing. When we went next door to visit, I was puzzled by lots of whispering, soundless mouthing of words and furtive looks in my direction.

It wasn't until years later that I found out the poor lady was suffering from a condition that could only be whispered in fearful awe, suitable only for voicing amongst adults, and certainly not in front of children; as if by speaking the word, they would become contaminated by its name: that word was "cancer". In those days it instilled even more fear and dread than today, as sixty years ago that dreaded word was received as a death sentence. In Mrs. Smith's house, round a green tablecloth, edged with large tassels, I remember other words were whispered (while the tea was being poured) which were not considered suitable for my young ears. When I was aged five or six years all this secrecy puzzled me, and sometimes I would ask for an explanation; but I never received one – only a severe look and the words "never you mind." Over decades, the attitude to children has completely changed: in those days, on the one hand, children were protected from what were thought to be undesirable words, and yet on the other, they had complete freedom to play and explore, frequently being shooed outside to "go out and play" No-one believed that children were in danger from undesirable adults, and as there was much less traffic on the roads, anyway, if children had been taught to; "look both ways" what else could harm them?

Uncle Charlie and I both shared Grandma, not at the same

time of course, and in a different relationship, but we did share the essence of her. When her son was killed, and I, as her first grandchild, was born two years later, she transferred her lost love and affection to me and taught me her social values in the same way she had taught them to Charlie.

DECEMBER 21st – 24th
The War Diaries record the continuation of training for the Regiment, and on the 22nd December two officers went to collect some Christmas fare. Exactly what type of seasonal treat would be on offer was not recorded. On the 23rd the Corps Commander sent a letter of appreciation for the work carried out by all units.

CHAPTER SEVEN

"We Know You Are Alright Charlie."

Charlie took a break from training to write the next letter on Christmas Eve.

> *3454037 Sgm. C. Robinson,*
> *Royal Corps of Signals,*
> *Att. 111 Fld. Reg. R.A.*
> *M.E.F.,*
> *24-12-42*

Dear Mother and Dad,

Tomorrow is Christmas Day. I don't know exactly what we are getting out of the ordinary, but I understand there's one or two items of Yuletide good-things to be had. I shall be able to let you know next time I write. What are you having this year? I know one thing, and that is that you will have a fine time with your nuts Mother.

It's nice of Mrs. Allgood to send a present every year isn't it? I'm going to have a swim in the Mediterranean tomorrow, if possible. Just so that I can say that I've been in the sea on Christmas Day. I don't suppose there's anything special taking place in Hyde is there? No carol singing or anything like that. There is one certain thing, we here, shall not see a "White" Christmas this year.

Now I come on to the subject of money. Here I am drawing 26/8 each week in the desert where money is of no use at all. I propose, therefore, to send 10/6 of it each week home to be put in my bank, and here's how it is done. You know, Mother, that I allot you 1/- per day, or 7/- per week. I've filled in another voluntary allotment form which increases my allotment from 1/- to 2/6 per day or from 7/- to 17/6 per week. Out of the 17/6, you will still get your 7/- whilst the remaining 10/6 will be mine. Got it? You will get a new book, like the one you have now, to take to the post office each week. There is, however, one thing to watch. I have increased my allotment from Jan. 1st 1943. You may not get the new book until the middle of February or even March.

Now at this end, my pay will be 10/6 less from Jan. 1st so you will have to draw back pay to January 1st for me, when the book comes through. I think that's pretty clear and you will understand it, but if you don't, ask me about it when you write. The important thing to remember is that if the book comes at the end of February you will have two months or 8 weeks ten and sixpences to draw for me because I have not drawn them here. I've done this because I thought my money would be better in the bank than hanging about here in my wallet where it can be easily lost. I could, of course, have left it in credit, but I don't trust Army pay offices. It's far better in my own bank.

In the camp, Mother, we've just found one of your nightmares – a snake. He was a fine specimen, about five feet four inches long and an inch and a half thick. First of all, a truck was run over him, but that didn't make any impression, so one of the boys got a bayonet and cut off his head. That, of course, did the trick. The peculiar part of it all, though, was that nearly an hour afterwards his body was still coiling and wriggling. I couldn't understand it at all. I know that after a thing is killed sometimes it's nerves twitch for a while, but in this case it was a slow, long move all along it's body.

You remember, some time ago, I drew your attention to a sentence in one of your air graphs "We know you are alright, Charlie" and asked you to remember it as I would tell you a story about it when I came home? Well, I'm now in a position to relate the story. When I *got that letter we were in a valley, which because of the attention paid to it by the Luftwaffe, had been nick-named "…"* (the name has been obliterated by the censor) *I had just been handed your air graph and had just read that sentence when a Stuka flashed down and machine-gunned us. A bullet lashed into the sand not more than a foot away from my feet. We dived under a truck.*

As I lay under the truck and the plane passed overhead, I said to myself "We know you are alright, Charlie" and had a good laugh at myself. Afterwards I told the boys who had been under the truck and we all had a good laugh. Anyhow, as the saying goes "a miss is as good as a mile" and "all's well that ends well." I've had more hair-raising experiences too, which I'll tell all in good time. The important thing is that I'm still O.K. and as fit as ever. As my pen is running dry and the paper is running out, I'd better finish. A Happy New Year to you all.

Cheerio,

Charlie

Along with his fellow soldiers, Uncle Charlie is looking forward to a little treat of some sort on Christmas Day, just to mark the special day with something out of the ordinary. I cannot imagine what it will be: perhaps a different meal from army fare, possibly some sweet thing, (Uncle Charlie would like that!) Could it be a little memento, or token present? It may cheer the men up a bit, but nothing significantly alters the fact that none of them are really where they want to be on Christmas Day. Hopefully they will all enjoy a day of peace. Uncle Charlie might manage a swim in the Mediterranean on Christmas Day which would be a novelty as well as a pleasant interlude for him. Back in England, Grandma, who likes her food, will be tucking into the nuts she obviously enjoys so much.

The next two paragraphs on the subject of money would have challenged the superior brains of the code-breakers at Bletchley

Park, who, during the war, managed to decipher the German Enigma machine, the toughest code to crack involving the most complicated letter sequences imaginable. What they would make of Uncle Charlie's request to his mother would probably have them baffled for days! A thought occurs to me that the two paragraphs would be useful for exercising young minds in mathematics, logic and computing skills! They would also test any G.C.S.E. student of today studying the old monetary system of pounds, shillings and pence.

What on earth my poor Grandma made of those two paragraphs I have no idea. I can imagine her puzzling and puzzling away, until finally, unable to make any sense of it, she asks my Grandfather what he thought, and he, in turn, might have puzzled and puzzled away before asking my Uncle Norman what he thought. I hope this complicated equation was solved to Uncle Charlie's satisfaction and his earnings were placed in the correct account at the right time. As well as having a highly developed monetary sense which told him that his money was safest in the bank at home, not in his wallet, or written down as a credit in some Army accounts book, he also had the ability to work it all out in the first place. I wonder how long it took him.

There was some excitement in the camp when a large snake was discovered and finally dispatched with a bayonet after being run over by a truck had no effect. Uncle Charlie writes so well; his description of the snake and its long slow death must have caused a repulsive sort of fascination for his mother when she read the letter.

The over-riding feeling my Grandparents would have felt was one of relief when he wrote back quoting from an earlier letter of theirs: "We know you are alright Charlie" He nearly wasn't. He relates so well the attack by the Stuka[1] letting loose a hail of bullets, one of which narrowly missed his foot as he and his fellow soldiers dived under a truck. Releasing their fear and tension after the attack, the "boys" laughed about the incident when Charlie described reading his parents' letter earlier, and then thinking to himself as he lay under the truck, with bullets lashing the sand around him: "We know you are alright Charlie". Charlie ends the letter with his usual optimism quoting "All's well that ends well." and: "A miss is as good as a mile." And he wishes everyone a happy New Year.

DECEMBER 25th:
Uncle Charlie did have a quiet Christmas Day, as it is recorded in the War Diaries that a Regimental holiday had been declared. What a welcome relief for the lads. Merry Christmas!

DECEMBER 26th:
The Regiment has received word that it will be moving to the 22nd Armoured Brigade.

DECEMBER 27th:
Regiment moved at 2100 hrs.

DECEMBER 28th:
Regiment arrived MARBLE ARCH at 0700 hrs. and reached concentration area of 22nd Armd. Bde.

Marble Arch is the name of a large camp, well inside Libya.

DECEMBER 29th:
During week Regiment has received reinforcements: 11 officers, 56 O/R's.

There follows a list of named officers who have joined the Regiment.

DECEMBER 30th:

Training with 22nd Armoured Brigade started. Exercises in manoeuvre and firing with "A" Division. 212 and 476 Batteries had individual training, practising manoeuvers with tanks. All officers attended lecture on battle …? by C.O. of 5R Tank Regiment.

DECEMBER 31st:

G.O.C. 8th Army visited Rgt. 1200hrs. He saw 24 Battery on manoeuvre with tanks. C.O., C.O.2, Adj. & R.S.M. at R.H.Q. 212. Seemed satisfied with what he saw. The C.O. & Adj. went to 1R.B'.s and arranged training for following day.

The important visitor to 111 Field Regiment was Montgomery himself, the man in charge, the man with full responsibility for the 8th Army. Bernard Law Montgomery, 1st Viscount Montgomery of Alamein, KG, GCB, DSO, PC. affectionately known as "Monty" had seen action in the First World War, when he was seriously wounded. In April 1941 he became Commander of X11, responsible for the defence of Kent. Believing that thorough training of troops was essential, he instigated a tough training regime and insisted on high levels of fitness for all soldiers.

Montgomery took command of the 8th Army on 13th August 1942, creating X Corps which contained all armoured divisions, to fight alongside XXX Corps – containing all infantry divisions.

Montgomery was convinced that employing the combined operations of Army, Air Force and Navy, would result in a more efficient, unified and focused operation, and very importantly, he believed that when soldiers on the ground could see the Royal Air Force attacking the enemy from above, morale, which was critically important to any regiment, was improved no end. Montgomery also liked to appear before his troops as often as possible, often giving out cigarettes to the men. In this way he became a familiar figure, always on their side, a fellow soldier – not some remote leader with whom they could not identify. He inspired unquestionable loyalty from his 8th Army soldiers.

3454037 Sgm. C. Robinson,
Royal Corps of Signals,
Att. 111 Fld. Reg. R.A.
M.E.F.
31-12-42

Dear Mother and Dad,

Today is the last day of 1942. It's been a very full year for me. From the North of Scotland to the North of Africa, via South Africa and Egypt. Not to mention 11,000 miles on board a ship. What a year! I sincerely hope that I shall make the return journey during 1943. Do you think there's much chance? The chaps here are very optimistic. One thinks the war will be over in March! Another is more steady and plumps for June! I think it's the great Russian show that's put the finishing touch to this optimism. In my opinion there's a pretty good chance of me being home this time next year. Just imagine it. Honestly, you know, I find it a bit difficult to imagine myself back at home for good. It will be a job to settle down in Civvy St. again. However, I'm letting my imagination run away with me. We've a lot of hard work to put in before the happy day arrives.

Since my last letter-card I've received a post card written on Nov. 25th from mother and an air graph 5/12/42 from dad. Thank you both. Glad to hear that Mr. Oldham had his usual Xmas letter in the paper – and I got a mention, nice work. If chance does take me his way I shall certainly look him up again, but between you and me I'm hoping not to go back that way, but to go straight home from here. Jessie Morton informs me that Norman passed grade 1. Good. But I sincerely hope I wasn't wrong when I imagined Norman to be playing for Marjorie's wedding.

Just think, I may have a young brother in the Army at this moment. I'm glad Marjorie got my telegram; was it in time? And did you give her the pound, Dad? By the way, when you tell me that you have received mail from me, could you also let me know the date on which I wrote it? It will help me to know exactly where I'm up to.

We are having a change of money here. Our Egyptian money is being withdrawn and changed for British Military money and in future we shall be paid in British Military Money. We all welcome the change. There will be pound notes and, I understand notes for smaller amounts down to 1/- They are different in pattern but of the same paper as ordinary British notes. It will be nice to be able to count up in £. S. D. again.

There's still no sign of any N.C.H.'s here. The first one ought to be through any time now. Did you ever get the snaps I sent from South Africa? I hope you did because they were very interesting.

Please excuse me if I cut this one short, and scribble a bit, but I want to get it in tonight's mail. I'll write again soon.

Cheerio

Charlie

Uncle Charlie begins his last letter of 1942 by reflecting on all the travelling he has done and the countries visited. He fervently hopes that the war will soon be over, and he believes there is a good chance he "will be home by this time next year". It is sometimes apposite that we cannot see into our future, as it would only lead to despair. As a member of a close-knit family, being away from home for months on end, having to rely completely on eagerly awaited letters as the only source of contact, Uncle Charlie cannot help but be affected by his "exile".

The mysterious Mr. Oldham pops up again, this time with

reference to his regular Christmas letter published in the local paper, in which he mentions Uncle Charlie. This has given me a clue, namely a publication date of 4th December. I contacted the local Tameside archivist[2] requesting a copy of the letter written by Mr. Oldham. He kindly obliged, and from this I discovered that Mr. Orlando Oldham was an ex pat., born in Hyde, who had moved to Durban over thirty years before. Obviously, he retained close ties with his home town, and encouraged soldiers from the Hyde area to visit him in Durban. He kept meticulous records of these lads and their families. Now I understand that Charlie's visit to Mr. Oldham, did not take place in the Hyde area, as I thought, but actually came about when Charlie was stationed in Durban, before he set sail for Egypt. Charlie impressed and inspired by this man encouraged my grandfather to write to him, which he did. I wonder how many service men en route to the Middle East visited Orlando Oldham to experience his hospitality and his link with their home town. How many families were listed in his books and what happened to them?

I think Charlie is referring to the siege of Stalingrad in his comment about the "Great Russian show." In the summer of 1942 Germany attacked Stalingrad, putting the city under siege. As the weeks wore on, and despite occupying 90% of the city, the German army was unable to dislodge the pockets of resistance put up by the Russian people. They would not surrender. This led to millions of deaths, often due to starvation, as there was no food to be had, and it has been said there wasn't a dog or a cat left alive! Still they would not surrender. Finally, by November, the German army became cut off and surrounded inside Stalingrad, coinciding with the onset of the deepest of Russian winters. The German soldiers were weakened by the freezing cold temperatures, lack of food and relentless Russian attacks; but Hitler, unmoved by his soldiers' plight, ordered his army to "stand fast"

Outside the city the German army was unable to break in to assist its fellow soldiers, and by the beginning of February 1943, it was all over: the Germans had either surrendered or been killed. I think in his words: "The great Russian show" Uncle Charlie is referring to the bravery of the Russian people who set a fine example to the Allies of what can be achieved with enough determination, bravery and the mental strength never to surrender.

Uncle Norman has passed the Grade 1 Exam for the Army, and Charlie hopes that when he imagined Uncle Norman playing the church organ for his sister's wedding he was not wrong. He wasn't. Mum's younger brother *did* play for her wedding. Uncle Charlie's wedding present to my mum and dad was £1. If an on-line inflation calculator is correct, one pound would be worth £38.57 in today's money.

Charlie is anticipating a change of money, from Egyptian to British Military money which is similar in feel to Sterling, but of a different colour. Charlie is pleased that the new money will be in the familiar £.S.D. format. As Uncle Charlie writes in his last letter of the year, it has been a full one, and I am sure, none more difficult than the final few months since arriving at the port of Tewfik on the Suez Canal. All his previous experiences in the Army from donning his first uniform to basic training, signalman training, staying in various camps and billets throughout the U.K, to sailing 11,000 miles by troop ship, were merely precursors to the main event: that of a soldier fighting for the principles of freedom and democracy, not only on behalf of the United Kingdom but for every country under Axis domination.

Although Charlie did not volunteer – he was called up – his commitment to the job in hand was total; summed up in his own words within his letter dated 20th December: "then common sense came to my aid and I realised that in order to enjoy home life again, I, and thousands of others must endure this exile." and "the harder we work and fight out here the sooner we shall be back home." These words were written at a time of severe homesickness, so he had to summon the mental strength to write them, when he was desperately missing his family and fervently wishing he could be back home to enjoy, and be a part of, his sister's wedding.

But I have learnt just a small part of Uncle Charlie's story of the last few months. I can only guess at the shocking things his eyes have witnessed, the hardship, the hurt of both body and soul. The ups and downs of war: the giving of thanks for surviving another day, the heat of battle, the weariness of the spirit, the quiet times, the earth-shattering times, the times when a trusted friend is lost, to confide in no more. But there have been lighter moments, too, when these good friends, with the optimism of youth, could laugh about amusing situations as they happened.

The times of irritation when grains of sand find their way into everything, eating tinned and dried foods, rarely enough water for a proper wash, let alone a bath, obeying orders instantly, and being ready to kill or be killed – in hand-to-hand fighting if necessary. When guns from both sides of this conflict are killing soldiers, how does a man come to terms with the fact that the next bullet, bomb, shell or piece of shrapnel may have his name on it? The best way of coping with this life of combat, Signalman Charles Robinson resolutely decided, as a new year beckoned, was just to get on with the job he had been given to do.

Notes

1 The Stuka was one of the most feared aircraft of the 2nd World War. Its inverted gull wings and fixed undercarriage gave it an evil

appearance, and when it came down out of the sky screaming, with its "trumpets of Jericho" screech, it spread fear amongst soldiers and civilians alike. This dive bomber was in operation with the German Luftwaffe from 1937 to 1945. To add to its fearsome reputation the aircraft allegedly sank more ships than any other plane during the war.

2 Thank you to Jacob Corbin of Tameside Local Studies and Archive Centre (www.tameside.gov.uk) for copying and forwarding Orlando Oldham's annual Christmas letter printed in the North Cheshire Herald, dated 4th December, 1942.

CHAPTER EIGHT

The Diary

Uncle Charlie's diary measures 10½ cm. by 7cm (or 4¼ inches by 2¾ inches in 1943 terms). With only enough room for recording two days on one side of each page, Uncle Charlie had to keep his writing very small to fit in what he wanted to say. He seems to have made a greater effort to write even more legibly, if that is possible, in order to ensure his tiny writing was easy to read. It is almost as if he knew that others would be reading his words, and I wonder what he would think of his niece, turning these very pages, now with worn edges, who is touched to be reading about his experiences, and inspired enough to write about them nearly seventy years later.

The diary was printed in Egypt, and on the fourth page in, under the heading "Personal Memoranda" Charles Robinson had, of course, neatly written his name. Four pages from the end Uncle Charlie had written: "ARMY ACCOUNT 1943" followed by weekly entries starting on the 1st January. On this day the credit column amounted to: £4-12-10, and at the bottom of the page, his final entry for the 7th May showed a total of £18-10-10. The debit column next to it was blank. His final entry is on the 6th May, so typically he must have calculated his earnings in advance, just before the 7th. The neat, hand-written column of 1943 figures are just as poignant to me as anything else he has written as they help to reveal the personality of the

Uncle I never knew: the neatness of the entries and the need to record and total his weekly pay, demonstrate an ordered mind. This generates a feeling in me that had he been lucky enough to survive the war, he would have carefully calculated how to put this hard-earned money to good use.

An old, worn, age-damaged diary, written in Charlie's own hand, describes his days in more detail than his letters which were written for the benefit of the family, and therefore necessarily censored by him. His personal diary, on the other hand, describes his days in action, details his many and varied experiences, the soldiers he shared his days with, and, in just a few lines of writing each day we get an insight into the daily challenges faced by one soldier during the Second World War.

JANUARY 1943

Friday, 1st Jan.
Finds me in camp at Marble Arch Att. 22 Armd. Coldest day I've seen so far out here. In evening Pommy and Len Hulse came over to our truck and with Mat. Read and Jimmy Mathews made biscuit porridge and had a brew. Russian news good.

The complete Regimental War Diaries reports from 1st January to 12th May 1943 can be found in Appendix A

Although Uncle Charlie writes he is now attached to 22 Armoured Brigade, it seems to be mainly for training purposes, and will not become official until the 10th. From the map of North Africa (on the following page) Marble Arch camp can be seen near El Agheila over half way between El-Alamein and Tunisia. The 8th Army is now well inside Libya, and on its way to the capital Tripoli. Friends are visiting Charlie's truck for some "biscuit porridge and a brew." I think this porridge is probably made from the soldiers' biscuit ration containing Arnott's hard-tack biscuits which were solidly hard, heavy and filling, only becoming palatable when mixed with either reconstituted dried milk, tea, or water. The friends, enjoying some refreshment and discussing the wider war, in particular the battle for Stalingrad, which after months of fierce fighting, starvation and now freezing weather conditions, is now turning in favour of the Russians, who will soon be claiming a desperately hard won historic victory over the Germans.

Sat. 2nd Jan.
Still dull, but warmer. Erected end-fed aerial with Ally Hay for 9 set. On duty 5 – 10 p.m. 30 Corps on air but very faint. Velieki-Luki captured by Russians.[1] Heard that Jerry is digging in up the road.

Wireless set 9 was a mobile transmitter/receiver developed in 1939. It was used for medium range (up to 35 miles) communications for AFVs and Divisional Signals in truck and ground stations. It was also the first really successful tank set. The good news is that the weather is warmer, but the bad news is that the Germans are: "digging in up the road" Is further fighting on the cards?

Sun. 3rd January
On duty 5-8a.m.. Had to waken Bert Atkinson and Mr Hugo at 6-30. Rained hard whilst I was doing it – just my luck. Went out on shoot but it was cancelled at 11-45a.m. owing to severe sandstorm. Visibility nil. Played solo in our truck in evening with Mat Read, Pommy and Len Hulse. Wrote to Jessie Morton.

The War Diaries confirm the poor weather conditions on the 3rd and 4th January: "Rgt. went to ranges to calibrate guns. However, a sandstorm blew up and it was impossible to carry out …? detail. Rgt. returned from ranges and battled against the storm in the lines."

Mon. 4th January.
Sand-storm still blowing but getting easier. Moved 9 set end-fed.
Played solo with Mat Read, Len Hulse and Pommey in our truck in evening. Made porridge and brewed up. Wrote home.
     Sandstorm continues all day.

It is hard to imagine rain falling heavily in the desert, followed by a severe sand-storm – horrible conditions to contend with – best place to be, I think, would be ensconced safely in the truck, playing cards and writing letters, as Uncle Charlie did.

Tues. 5th January.
Went out on exercise. Regiment and Armoured Bde. 8-00a.m. until 3-30p.m. Officers should be taught to use Remote Control properly. Played solo with same three. Made porridge. Heard rumour that Regiment is on half- an-hour's notice to move. Action again I suppose. Storm ended.

The exercise Uncle Charlie writes about is quite an important one, judging from the amount of detail dedicated to this event in the War Diaries. (See Appendix A)

Despite the fact that the German army is in retreat, the 8th Army doesn't rest on its laurels, but continues striving to improve via a thorough training regime. Charlie has seen so much fighting over the past few months that he seems to have become inured to a life of combat. When word goes round that the regiment is on thirty minutes notice to move, I can almost hear a sigh of resignation as he writes the following matter-of-fact statement in his diary: "Action again I suppose."

Wed. 6th January
Went out on Regimental calibration shoot. Set on gun position. Some
guns had crew of only 3 men. Shows how short-handed Regiment is.
The section is very short as well. Lovely warm, sunny day. On duty on
9 set 5-10p.m. Received long awaited letter from Elsie. Worth waiting
for! Shall be glad to see her again.

Charlie comments on the shortage of man-power on gun crews
and the regiment in general, but is cheered up when he receives
a letter from Elsie. I think she has made his day.

Thur. 7th January
Had day more or less off. Went to bed during morning to try to make
up lost sleep. Have been feeling tired for a day or two now. I think it's
the constant night duties which cause it. Heard that we move up on
Sunday. Wrote to Elsie in afternoon. Played solo in evening. Made
porridge. On duty 10-1a.m. Two "Honey" tanks arrived for R.H.Q.

The officers must have taken notice of Uncle Charlie's diary
entry of yesterday, and brought in reinforcements sharpish!!
Charlie has a welcome easy day and a chance to get his head
down in the morning to replace some lost sleep. He enjoyed the
usual evening recreational activities of card playing and making
porridge, after writing to Elsie in the afternoon.

The light M3A Stuart tank was nicknamed "Honey" by the
soldiers. This tank was supplied by the Americans to British
and Commonwealth forces during the 2nd World War, under
the "Lend-Lease" scheme whereby America shipped supplies
and equipment to the Allies between 1941 and 1945. A massive
31.4 billion dollars' worth of equipment was sent to Britain.
Amazingly, the final annual payment of the debt Britain owed
America was made on the 29th December, 2006, after more than
fifty years.

Fri. 8th January
No pay today. Canteen opened. Got some fags. Am leaving S4 after
18 months and going on C.O.'s salmon tin with Harry Withington.
Very pleased to be working with Harry again, although job might be a
dangerous one. Started a letter home but did not finish it.

Uncle Charlie is about to start a new, possibly dangerous job, working in the C.O.'s "salmon tin"[2] with Harry Withington. (Possibly the same Harry Withington who goes right back to their signaling training in 1940[3]) Harry also gets a mention in Charlie's letter dated 25th April, 1941.

Sat. 9th January
Finished my letter home but could not hand it in yet owing to move.
Packed all my kit and transferred it to salmon tin. Went back to S4
in evening and made porridge and had brew. Had silly row with Mat
Read about my milk. O.K. afterwards. Shared bivvy with new driver.

The War Diaries noted that the C.O. and the Adjutant have already left for the Army Commanders' Conferences, and Uncle Charlie is himself packed up and ready to go. The letter, mentioned in his diary, is reproduced below. For me, it means a great deal to read of a letter penned by my Uncle decades ago and then to be privileged enough to have that very same letter as a physical presence in my hand, makes it doubly meaningful.

3454037 Sgm. C. Robinson.
Royal Corps of Signals,
Att. 111 Fld. Reg. R.A.
M.E.F.
9-1-43

Dear Mother and Dad,

In the last four days I've had four communications from you. A post card from mother and one from Norman, a new letter card from mother and an airgraph from Dad. Thanks very much for them all. Norman's card was written on Dec. 1st, Mother's on Dec 2nd, your letter card Mother was Dec 9th and Dad's airgraph Nov. 28th

You tell me, Norman, about going to Stockport for your medical and passing A1. Nice work. Did you go to the Orphanage on Lancashire Hill? If I remember correctly, that's the name of the place I went to. I hope you managed to stay at home until after Marjorie's wedding. Perhaps you are still at home. And you have been fitted up with false teeth. I'll bet you are flashing a real Odol smile now! By the way, Norman, I hope you manage to get into the R.C.O.S..

In your card, mother, you say you were having potato pie on the day you wrote it, and how would I like to drop in. Well, you know me! I think if I suddenly went home and you put the whole brown dish in front of me I could shift it. Have you started your canteen work yet, mother? I'm sure when you do you'll make a jolly good job of it. Will you excuse a little laugh at the idea of you in the women's police force? I couldn't help it.

I'm very sorry to hear that the wedding had to be postponed for three days. So when I was thinking of you all, I was a little too previous, wasn't I? Still, it doesn't matter very much whether it was Saturday or Tuesday, my thoughts and good wishes were with you. I, too, think that your present to Marjorie and Jim was a handsome one. No wonder they were pleased. I'm glad to hear that Jim likes the Navy and is thriving on its grub.

Now, Dad, the news in you airgraph is very similar to that in Mother's letter card. About the wedding, Norman's medical and the addition to the W.R.N.S. of Jessie Morton. There is one question which I can answer however. The first N.C.H. has not arrived in the

M.E. yet. And I did not go to Alexandria. We had to move before I got the chance. It was a poor show, I badly wanted to see the place.

I got Elsie's letter which you redirected on Sept. 29th the other day. In it she says she would call round and get my address from you, but as I've had incorrectly addressed air-graphs since then, and you haven't mentioned it, I conclude she didn't go to see you. By this time she will have my correct address, I hope. I wish in a way she had been to see you and then you could have passed an opinion on her. I think you would have liked her.

The sand storm I told you about, died down after a couple of days. The weather has been warm and sunny again, although today there's a cold wind blowing. I understand that the heat will begin to make itself felt again towards the end of February. The shorts will have to come out again. We've been wearing battle-dress since the beginning of December. It's a short winter here, isn't it?

How does my bank account stand now Dad? Would you mind letting me know next time you write. Has the new voluntary allotment book come through yet? If the war goes on much longer I shall be a millionaire! Never mind, the more the better I say.

We are all hoping to get the war over quickly now and to return home. Everybody is keen to finish it, here at least. That's all for now. I'll soon be writing again.

Cheerio

Charlie

Uncle Charlie was very pleased to receive four letters in four days and probably read each one avidly, more than once! Uncle Norman has passed the Army medical with flying colours: pronounced A1, possibly achieving this at Pendlebury Hall, Lancashire Hill – formerly an orphanage. The same building in which Charlie believes he may have passed his own Army medical, almost three years before. The imposing Hall is now a grade two listed building. Unfortunately, these days, it's impressive, ornate interior is now closed to the public. Charlie hopes his younger brother can get into the R.C.O.S. (Royal Corps of Signals).

After existing on Army rations of bully beef, canned meat and vegetables, powdered potatoes and dried cabbage, the thought of sitting down at grandma's table with a huge dish of home-made potato pie in front of him, must have made him desire an Aladdin's lamp; and with one wish, a second later, he would be back home, with the familiar big brown dish in front of him, savouring the aroma from the escaping steam, knife and fork in hand, (like the comic hero Desperate Dan), ready to demolish a big dish full of pie. I don't know if grandma applied to enter the police force, but like Charlie, I cannot help but raise a smile when I think of her in uniform, ready to uphold the law. It seems incongruous that a woman who is carrying a little extra weight, shall I say, with gentle ways and an easy-going smile would be able to get tough on criminals, and even make an arrest! I think she has made the right choice: and the canteen will suit her very well.

In regard to the wedding, although Uncle Charlie unknowingly imagined the ceremony to be taking place on the wrong day, the right sentiment was there. He may not have been present in body, but he was there in spirit, alongside his family the whole day, and that is what counts. It seems my parents were happy with their unnamed wedding present from grandma and granddad.

Charlie's friend Jessie has joined the Royal Navy (W.R.N.S.) and he notes with some irritation that his N.C.H.'s have still not arrived in the Middle East. He was also very disappointed when he was prevented from visiting Alexandria – somewhere he really wanted to see. I feel a sense of disappointment for him that he did not manage to see such a famous city.

I think that the girl, Elsie, mentioned for the first time in his letters and diary, is quite important to him, as his diary entry on the 6th January states that he was pleased to receive a "long awaited letter from Elsie." He has encouraged her to visit his parents, and he seems keen for them to like her. I wonder where they met, what kind of relationship they have, and if it would have developed into something more serious had he lived. Charlie, always keen to find out how his finances stand, asks his dad to let him know how his bank account is faring, and signs off by saying he will be writing soon.

Sun. 10th Jan.

Regiment started to move West again. Did 63 miles. Truck on fire owing to charging leads shorting. Not serious, no damage. Set went dis. Unlucky day in general. When we reported it, Mr. Hugo asked whether we were pulling his leg! Slept in salmon tin. Very comfortable.

Uncle Charlie and Co. are not having a very good day due to a fire in the truck's engine, followed by the radio set going down. I assume "dis." means disabled, or dysfunctional. But things were not all bad; at least the "salmon tin" was comfortable.

Comments written in the War Diaries note that 111 Field Regiment is now officially under the command of 22nd Armoured Brigade.[4]

Mon. 11th Jan.

Move westward continued. Did 110 miles. Finished near Sirte. But? Mr Barnes in S4 and we got lost owing to breaking down. Tried to find the rest but when it got dark camped for night. Raid by 20 M.E.'s on nearby aerodrome about 4-0p.m. Big clouds of smoke caused. Set closed down again as it went dis.

It must have been a somewhat unnerving experience, getting lost and becoming separated from the rest of the Regiment due to the breakdown problems of both truck and wireless set. The raid on the nearby aerodrome by "20 M.E's" (Messerschmitt M.E.109) enemy aircraft probably did not help soothe the lads' nerves either, as they must have been worried about any stray bombs that might come their way. The rest of the regiment was not too far away, as the War Diaries noted: *Rgt. moved S.W. of Sirte.*

> *Tues. 12th Jan.*
> *Moved off again at 8-0a.m. Got location of Regiment from 30 Corps and found them at 9-30 a.m. Unloaded truck. Sorted out lead trouble and fixed up entirely new battery lead. In evening borrowed stove from Tommy Smith and brewed up. Had some tinned fruit. Air-raid on aerodrome at night. Were told today that General Montgomery says we are going to Tripoli. Be there on 22nd.*

Thank goodness Uncle Charlie and Co. were reunited with the rest of the Regiment an hour and a half after setting off that morning. They must have felt very relieved. Uncle Charlie sorted the problem with the battery lead and made the necessary repairs. His last sentence, written on this day, was pushed onto the top of the next page. The news about going to Tripoli was probably too important to leave to the next day.

> *Wed. 13th Jan.*
> *Static today. Began to sort out truck. Mr. Hugo came round at 8-30 to tell me my set was required for regimental scheme. Notice too short. C.O. was annoyed because I wasn't ready. Told off Mr. Hugo who in turn told me off. However, everything O.K. later. Brewed up and had fruit.*

So far over the last few days Charlie has had a row with Mat Read about milk and now he has had an argument about the lack of readiness of his wireless set when the C.O. required it for a regimental scheme. The irritated C.O., "told off" Mr. Hugo, who, passing the irritation down the chain of command, told Charlie off; but Charlie, not able to criticise anyone else, would simply have to make do by explaining his difficulties with the dysfunctional wireless set.

It sounds odd to hear a soldier addressed as 'Mr.' This is something I shall have to find out.[5]

> *Thur. 14th Jan.*
> *Moved off at 7-45a.m. C.O. and Adj. riding with us. Large number of vehicles and tanks. Got through without any air-attack. Was on the set, without a break from 7-00a.m until 10-30p.m. Not a bad day's work. Most of R.H.Q. got stuck in a Wadi and didn't come in at all. Slept beside the truck. I've never seen a vehicle as crowded as ours is with kit.*

Uncle Charlie's truck, crammed with kit, lucky not to be attacked from the air, now part of the big guns of the 22nd Armoured Brigade, is one vehicle amongst a huge convoy, moving inexorably towards yet another confrontation with the enemy.

> *Fri. 15th Jan.*
> *Moved about 10 miles west and then static all day. Battle started. Tanks went in but guns did not open fire. Large numbers of enemy transport retreating north west. At night 51st Div. put up heavy barrage. MacFarlane and McLeod are with this Div. now. Set closed down at 8-0p.m. Had good night's sleep*

After a heavy night time barrage by the 51st Division and frustrating static on the wireless set all day, Charlie was still able to relax enough to enjoy a good night's sleep. From this statement, I can only conclude that, thankfully, he is becoming battle hardened, and is able to sleep when he needs to.

> *Sat. 16th Jan.*
> *Moved off at mid-day. Were on the move until 6-30p.m. Our tank patrols were out ahead of us and reported enemy M.T. and tanks moving N.W. 93 Officers and men and a Panzer Brigadier captured by our Bde. Reached Sedada where airfield is our objective. Bombed 500 yards away about 11-00p.m.*

The Brigade has managed to pull off quite a coup in capturing such a high ranking German Officer as well as 93 enemy officers and men. I think that the bombs, dropping at11-00p.m. must have been getting a little too close for comfort at only 500 yards away.

> *Sun. 17th Jan.*
> *Moved off at 7-15a.m. Found that enemy has left the airfield. Were static after 9-0a.m. waiting for General Montgomery to arrive. He is advancing with us from now on. Moved at 1500hrs. Enemy still retreating. General Montgomery's car was next to us in convoy. Had good view.*

What excitement for Uncle Charlie and the men travelling with him, to be driving right next to the car containing the most charismatic, well-loved, respected and best known General of the Second World War – the man who was supreme Commander of the 8th Army in North Africa, the man who masterminded the Battle of El-Alamein, and the following chase across Egypt into Libya. Now, Montgomery, travelling proudly beside his men, is advancing towards the capital: Tripoli.

> *Mon. 18th Jan.*
> *Moved W and N again. Misrata taken by 51st Div. Enemy moving*

towards Tripoli. On the move all day. Reached within 5 miles of Zliten and stayed night. Reports from forward patrols say going is bad from here on. Deep Wadis. Our patrols occupied Zliten. Arabs friendly. Glad Italians have gone.

The 8th Army is making good progress, the 51st Division taking Misrata. The forward patrols report bad going from this point with deep Wadis to negotiate.

Tues. 19th Jan.
Stayed in same place all day. Our patrols in front report clear of enemy. 50 Miles from Tripoli by road. 3 Italian civilians brought in at own request. Teased the Arabs who cheered our patrol. Going bad in front. May have to wait until road is repaired. Enemy in force at Homs and Tarhuna. Bde. halted while suitable road between these places was being recc'd. 7th Armd. Div. towards Tarhuna.

It appears that the Brigade is frustratingly stuck, only fifty miles from Tripoli, waiting for the engineers to either make a road repair, or the forward patrols to find a navigable way through the rough going.

3454037 Sgm. C. Robinson,
Royal Corps of Signals,
Att. 111 Fld. Reg. R.A.
M.E.F.,
19-1-43

Dear Mother and Dad,

I'm sorry I haven't been able to keep my promise I made about writing every four days. However, by the time you get this you will know the reason why. As a matter of fact, I have been very busy and this is the first real opportunity I've had to scribble you a line or two.

Today, I received three letters. An air graph from mother, a letter-card from dad and a letter from cousin Hilda. Your letter card, dad, was full of news about the wedding. I'm very glad that everything went off alright. You seem to have got into a bit of a mess when you left, or when Marjorie left I should say, her gloves behind. I can well imagine her voice when she made the announcement in the taxi. And you had to borrow a ladder to get into the house. What a joke! No wonder that mother, sitting in Chapel, wondered where on earth you and Marjorie were.

It's good news, too, that Norman was able to oblige on the organ. It would have been a stroke of extremely bad luck if he had been called up beforehand. I am looking forward keenly to your next letter and a further description of the day's happenings. Glad to hear, as well, that you are sending some photographs of the "Do". I shall be waiting for them. I had an air-graph from Mr. & Mrs. Holmes the other day in which they said they would be at the wedding. Were Marjorie and Jim very nervous? Did you have much trifle at the feed? How I envy you. For a war-time wedding they don't seem to have done badly at all. However, I await further details.

In you air-graph, mother, you say you can always remember the age of Vera Holden's baby, because she was born just before I left England. It is now seven months within a day or two since I left. It does not seem anything like that. Up to now it is the longest period of time I have spent away from home. I'm certain that when I return it will seem strange for a day or two. But I shall certainly have a "Beefer" with the water and the bath and the grub. I think the thing I would like most of all just now is to be lying soaking in the bath, scalding hot. Oh Boy! It might not be long now.

The N.C.H.'s haven't arrived yet. That's done it! My pen has run dry and I've no more ink! (The letter continues in pencil) However, to continue. We have been told that there is some delay regarding the mail over Christmas so perhaps that accounts for it. I should like to see a N.C.H. again. I saw the last one in South Africa! Mr. Oldham had it.

Have you got my extra voluntary allotment yet? At least you will have the letter-card in which I explained about it. It should come through about the middle of February.

I think that's the lot this time. I'm sorry it's such a scribble but I haven't much time. I'll write again as soon as possible.

Cheerio,

Charlie

Uncle Charlie apologises for not writing every four days, as promised. He explains that he has been very busy, for reasons that will have become obvious by the time his parents receive the letter. He knows that, to the Allies, their vitally important progress across Libya, on the way to winning the war in North Africa, lies in the imminent liberation of the capital, Tripoli; this event will lead to banner headlines printed in the newspapers, announced with pride over the radio, and shown on newsreel footage to cinema audiences all over the country.

I have a vague recollection of my mother telling me about the incident of the mislaid gloves on the day of her wedding. She was certainly determined to be "properly" dressed, and therefore persuaded my granddad (who, being a man, probably felt that his daughter could get married perfectly well without gloves) to ask the taxi driver to turn round, take them back home, borrow a ladder from a neighbour, climb up the ladder, carefully climb through the bedroom window, (taking care not to ruin his best suit), run downstairs, find and snatch the gloves, dash out of the house and into the taxi again. Retrieving the missing gloves made granddad the hero of the day – particularly in my mother's eyes – when he went to such a great deal of trouble to ensure that nothing could spoil his daughter's special day. Meanwhile, grandma was sitting in Chapel, wondering what on earth had happened to make them so late, imagining all sorts of scenarios, and thinking of the worst possible outcomes.

I think my father would also have been experiencing some anxious moments as he waited for the arrival of his betrothed. Charlie could see the funny side to the comedy of the gloves, but he was pleased that Uncle Norman had not been called up, and therefore available to play the Chapel organ for his sister. Uncle Charlie is anticipating further details, and photographs in their following letters.

I had been wondering if Uncle Charlie had managed to enjoy some leave before departing the United Kingdom and setting sail for Durban. Charlie's letter has answered my question in the affirmative. With his usual accuracy in calculating not just money, but time and distance as well, Charlie has worked out that it has been seven months, almost to the day, since leaving his home and the country of his birth, to embark on a new and dangerous adventure, leading to the most testing, challenging time of his life. He also knows the age of Vera Holden's baby.

Seven months is the longest period of time Charlie has spent away from home, and he is missing the simple pleasures of home life: good, home cooked food and most of all a long soak in a hot bath would be so welcome after months of sweaty, dirty, sandy conditions in which a bath was out of the question and the very best he could hope for would be a wash, or better still, a cold shower (if there was enough water that is). Charlie is fervently hoping that before too long he will be back in his own home enjoying the comforts and relaxation that can only be found within one's own four walls. My uncle's hopes of a speedy end to the War keep his spirits up, and give him something positive to aim for. Thoughts of home will always be uppermost in his mind.

Uncle Charlie has not seen a local paper since he was in Durban at Mr. Oldham's house, many months ago. Apparently there has been some delay with the Christmas post, which is not surprising when one considers the mileage these soldiers have travelled since leaving El-Alamein. It would be difficult for the post to keep up with their progress. Charlie ends his letter with an apology for the "scribble". What scribble? My only comment is that the quality of this letter is no different to any other I have read.

Wed. 20th Jan.
Stayed in same place again 51st Div. at Homs. Got bags of water and had a bath. Felt grand. Had a slap-up evening meal of M & V and lovely? biscuit porridge, fried biscuit and jam. We move out tomorrow I hear.

The above diary entry is the first time I have struggled to read Uncle Charlie's writing. Perhaps he was feeling tired after feasting on such a big meal of meat and vegetables, and allowed his writing to become uncharacteristically sloppy. I hope I have deciphered it correctly because, for me, the importance of accuracy is paramount. Today Charlie has enjoyed a treat by acquiring some bags of water, enabling him to have a bath. How he must have enjoyed the luxury of a soak. When the Regiment stops for the day to refuel, refit and maintain equipment, it must feel good to have a break from being on the move, to get on with some chores, and to enjoy a much- needed bath.

Thur. 21st Jan.
Moved at 8-30. Went onto the road and travelled as far as Homs where we spent the night. The road is blown up in several places. Plenty of grass and trees. Much pleasanter than Egypt. Small children didn't know whether to salute us our way or Italian. Tried both. Changed trucks tonight.

It must have been so much easier moving by road again, even if it had been blown up in places. They are travelling through some green and pleasant countryside which is appreciated by Uncle Charlie after the dry conditions of Egypt. I can picture the scene: the regiment (minus 212 Battery) moving along the road in convoy. So many friendly soldiers with their vehicles, big guns and equipment, completely captivating the local children, particularly the boys, thrilled to see real soldiers in real military vehicles moving past them on the road. The children are trying to salute, but don't quite know how.

Fri. 22nd Jan.
Set off at 7-30. Intended entering Tripoli today. Saw several Italian families who have not left their homes. Flew a white flag from chimney pots. Got held up by mortar fire. Could not overcome obstruction on road at this point. Stayed the night. Too bad. Within 16 miles of Tripoli.

Disappointment and frustration all round as they were unable to reach Tripoli as planned. Uncle Charlie and his fellow soldiers passed several Italian houses showing white flags tied to their chimney pots.

Sat. 23rd Jan.
Moved on at 5-30a.m. Tripoli fell early this morning. But we were not first in. The 7th Armoured Div. beat us to it. We went to a farm 3½ (5 kilos.) south of the town. Two or three Italian families still living here. Very nice people. Can't understand why Italy declared war on us. People didn't want it.

As anticipated Tripoli fell to the Allies. But the 11th Hussars, part of the 7th Armoured went in first, and Uncle Charlie's Regiment had to settle for second best: a shortfall of 5 kilometres to the south. Worthy of note is Charlie's comment about the Italian families living on the farm when he stresses that they are: "very nice people" as though this is surprising, having been their enemy for so long. Perhaps the Italians have assumed the undeserved reputation of fanatics. He realises that ordinary people are caught up in wars like ordinary people the world over, and would, given the chance, want to get on with their lives in peace; not having to conform to declarations of war made by politicians.

Sun. 24th Jan.
Lovely warm day. Did my best to talk to one of the Italian chaps. Made friends with his 3 year old son Pepo. Bonny little chap. Bright too – he can speak Italian and I can't! Saw the people going to church this morning. Hope we stay here for a long time.

I feel quite sad reading this day's diary entry. In Uncle Charlie's military dominated world when he is either preparing for combat or resting from combat or moving from one military engagement to the next, this little interlude of normality must feel like manna from heaven to his soul. It is Sunday and he sees the local people on their way to church. Was he thinking back fondly to his own place of worship: Norfolk Street Methodist Chapel, Hyde, in what must seem a lifetime ago; and did he offer up a little prayer I wonder? Charlie made a sociable attempt at conversation with Pepo's father, and even managed a little joke about his little friend Pepo being able to speak better Italian than he did! This was a relaxing day, spent talking to people other than military personnel; and the innocent company of a child was in stark contrast to the male dominated world of the soldier. Little Pepo had an effect on Uncle Charlie, and he would have dearly loved to stay longer to enjoy some rest and relaxation, and to spend more time with this family, who were once the enemy, but have now become friends. Perhaps Charlie felt that this playful contact with three year old Pepo was a glimpse into fatherhood. How cruel fate can be sometimes: it snatched away his chance of ever becoming a father. Hidden in the seven short sentences of this day's diary entry is a volume full of desire for a normal, peaceful existence.

> *Mon. 25th Jan.*
> *Was put on duty guarding well all day. Not bad. Nothing to do but watch chaps drawing water. Played with Pepo again. Made porridge in evening.*

A second relaxing day for Uncle Charlie.

> *Tues. 26th Jan.*
> *Should have been on guard tonight, but it has been arranged for Batteries to send guard to R.H.Q. Just in time. Only had to fill cook-house water tins.*

A third relaxing day.

> *Wed. 27th Jan.*
> *Were paid £4 today. First pay since Jan. 1st. Wrote home and to Eric Holmes. Leave to Tripoli starts tomorrow I hear. Hope so.*

A good day for Uncle Charlie – he managed to enjoy some further relaxation – allowing him to find the time to write some letters; but what really made his day was when he received the huge sum of £4 – an accumulation of several weeks' pay!

> *Thur. 28th Jan.*
> *Had a stroke of luck. Was amongst first four from Signals to get a day in Tripoli .Got there at 10-45a.m. Not a bad place. Very much like Cairo, but smaller and cleaner. Couldn't get a bite to eat all day. Spent most of my time wandering in native quarter. Place not organised yet.*

Chosen with Sgt. Atkinson & Harry to represent Sigs. in Victory Parade on Sunday.

111 Field Regiment is now close by Libya's capital city, Tripoli, and Charlie is delighted to be granted a day's leave to visit the city. He enjoys wandering around foreign cities (when he can get the chance) to take in the unusual sights, sounds and aromas that emanate from a very different culture (at least from an Englishman's perspective) with fascinating shops and markets selling unusual spices, fruits and vegetables. These local markets are manned by traditionally dressed people, speaking an unfamiliar language. Charlie enjoys savouring the colourful aspects of a foreign country. He has a further piece of luck – as well as the honour – along with Sgt. Atkinson and his friend Harry, to be chosen to represent Royal Signals in the Victory Parade this coming Sunday.

Fri. 29th Jan.
Spent the morning cleaning up and getting ready for practice victory march. Paraded at 2-30p.m. Practiced eyes-right marching up and down the lane.

Uncle Charlie, Harry and Sgt. Atkinson are making sure they practice to perfection in order to put on a good show for the locals, the Regiment, Royal Signals, and the 8th Army, as well as to impress the Army's top brass, and last, but certainly not least, General Montgomery himself.

Sat. 30th Jan.
Went to Bde. at 8-0a.m. Whole Bde. pushed up for another practice. Have chalked my belt and gaiters pure white. Never let it be said. Were inspected by Brigadier who said we were very smart considering lack of cleaning stuff.

I found Uncle Charlie's account of 30th Jan. 1943 very touching. The pride and satisfaction he felt on achieving his "pure white" belt and gaiters: taking the trouble to ensure those parts of his uniform would stand out as white as he could possibly make them. He was one of many – true soldiers to the last – who had prepared conscientiously for the forthcoming parade. Despite all they had endured: fighting many battles – and not just with the German Army – they had also fought sand-storms, endured limited water and food rations, and finally, very harsh living conditions as they crossed the Libyan desert. Yet despite all these privations the touching thing for me was that these lads were proud to put on their very best show. The commitment made by the soldiers was acknowledged by the Brigadier, who praised them on their smart turnout, despite the paucity of cleaning materials.

Sun. 31st Jan.
The great day at last! Left the farm at 8-0a.m. in truck. Arrived in Tripoli at 8-45a.m. Lined up and marched 9 abreast through streets to Piazza Castella where thanksgiving service was held. Gen. Monty. there. March-past followed. Monty took salute. Very impressive. The Italians don't seem to be worried at all about our occupation of their town. Lined the streets to watch the parade. Wrote to Hilda and Elsie (air graph only).

Uncle Charlie was impressed by the events of this memorable day, when the men marched nine abreast through the streets of Tripoli, showing off their "pure white" belts and gaiters, with the inspirational General Montgomery taking the salute. It was a day when even the Italians – their former enemies – were lining the streets, wanting to be part of the celebration. This event would be headline news throughout the world, and my grandma and granddad would have read of this day's victory parade in the newspaper, heard it on the radio, and perhaps even have gone to the local cinema to watch it on the newsreels. They must have known there was a good chance their son would be in Tripoli with the 8th Army. If they did witness the event on the Pathe News at the cinema, they would be avidly searching for sight of their son, somewhere amongst the hundreds of proud soldiers. I can't help but feel that if a camera had rested on him for less than a second it would have been enough for instant recognition, followed by an excited spreading of their news round all the family, friends, neighbours, work places, shops, stores and passengers on the bus – in fact anyone near enough to listen to the story of Charlie's fame.

Mon. 1st Feb.
Left the farm at 11-0 a.m. in salmon tin with C.O. Called at 30 Corps. Got to new location about 5 miles W. of Tripoli at 12-15. Opened up 19 Set to CCRA 30 Corps at 4-0p.m. Still on as I write this at 12-15. We are supposed to be staying here for a month. I hope so! Might get into Tripoli now and then. Feel that word from Elsie is overdue. She wrote last on Nov. 20th.

The Regiment has once again come under the command of 30 Corps, in their familiar role as Corps artillery. Uncle Charlie is hoping he will be able to fit in more visits to Tripoli if they can stay put for a month. He is concerned that Elsie doesn't appear to be in a rush to write to him.

Tues. 2nd Feb.
Closed set down at 4-0p.m. Whitened belt, gaiters and cross-straps for parade tomorrow. Wrote home. Three short and sharp air-raids on Tripoli between 6 – 8 in the evening. Terrific A.A. Barrage. Played cards in Signal office tent.

Wireless Set 19.
(With kind permission from: Louis Meulstee: "Wireless For the Warrior.")
Primarily developed for AFV's but later used as a general purpose set.
Range up to 15 miles.

There was no account of the day's happenings in the War Diaries, which is surprising as Charlie mentions three short, sharp air-raids on Tripoli with a fierce anti-aircraft barrage in reply. I wonder if Uncle Charlie is actually beginning to enjoy smartening up in readiness for another parade, because he has now whitened his belt, gaiters *and* cross-straps! I think it would make a pleasant change for the lads to show off once in a while after all the hard work they had done.

Wed. 3rd Feb.
Held practice parade from 9-45 until 12-40. Were complimented by Corps Commander. Parade tomorrow for a M.I.G.E. (most important gentleman.). We think it is Mr. Churchill. Hope so. Had afternoon off.

Reg. War diaries: *TRIPOLI 1200hrs. – Guns and men lined Tripoli-Garian Rd. for Corps. Cmmdrs. Inspection. Under 12 hrs. notice to join 7 Armd. Div. 1500hrs. Regt. to join 7 Amd. Div. forthwith. C.O. and Adj. went fwd. to 131 Bde. H.Q. 6 reinforcements arrived.*

I like the acronym M.I.G.E. It is very helpful to me that Charlie had written down its full meaning, as I would not have had a clue what it meant. There must have been some speculation flying round the men as to whom this V.I.P. would be. Rumours always seem to fly around faster than anything else.

111 Field Regiment, with very short notice, is about to join the 7th Armoured Division. Formed in 1940, this crack Division fought in every major battle of the North Africa Campaign, before going on to distinguish itself in Italy. Again the Division took part in the D-Day landings, moving through Europe and on into Germany. In the 1950's the Division was disbanded, before becoming the 7th Armoured Brigade. The Division retained the famous nickname: desert rats – its mascot being the jerboa. During the battle of El-Alamein the Division was almost always in the vanguard, pushing up through or around the German lines, dealing with mine fields and generally being in the thick of the action. The 11th Hussars, part of the 7th Armoured Brigade were the first to liberate Tripoli. I wonder how Uncle Charlie felt about his Regiment becoming part of this respected Division. But, continuing in the thick of the action, would his job become more dangerous now?

Worthy of note for this day, 3rd February, 1943 is Winston Churchill's speech addressed to General Montgomery and the men of the Joint Headquarters of the 8th Army. Churchill knew that every soldier had given his all, and he believed that the sacrifices each one had made contributed to the Allied victory, and subsequent liberation of Tripoli. On the day before he reviewed the troops, Churchill paid tribute to the 8th Army. His speeches are worth repeating in their entirety, but as the following is quite a long one, I have just picked out the sentences which, to me, are the most meaningful.

"you have chased this hostile army and driven it from pillar to post over a distance of more than 1,400 miles as far as from London to Moscow… you have altered the face of the war in a most remarkable

way...in the tireless endurance and self-denial of the troops, and in the fearless leadership displayed in action, can be appreciated only by those who were actually on the spot. I must tell you that the fame of the desert army has spread throughout the world, and everywhere your work is spoken of with respect and admiration ...It must have been a tremendous experience driving forward day after day over this desert, which it has taken me this morning more than six hours to fly at more than 200 miles an hour...you will fight in countries which will present undoubtedly serious tactical difficulties, which, none-the-less, will not have the grim character of desert war which you have known how to endure and how to overcome."

Notes

1 VELIKIYE LUKI was a small city, south of Stalingrad and west of Moscow. The city possessed a vital railway supply line to service the German army laying siege to Stalingrad. Therefore control of the city was vital. The Russians, since August 1941 had had varying success in recapturing the city with the aim of cutting off German supplies, which would lead not only to the failure of the siege of Stalingrad, but could ultimately threaten the entire German front. So on this day, as Uncle Charlie notes, the Russian army has finally achieved its long-desired objective – that of re-taking control of their city.

2 Charlie's expression "salmon tin" does not appear to be a general slang term for a vehicle in use by the Army during the 2nd World War. The National Army Museum and the Royal Signals Museum have both drawn a blank. I can only conclude it is a term coined either by Uncle Charlie himself or his Commanding Officer.

3 See photograph: "Signalling Class, Carlisle, 1940" p.26

4 An Armoured Brigade fought in both defensive and attacking roles. When they were on the attack their role was to destroy the enemy's heavy guns, situated south of the enemy lines, thereby creating a hole in their rear defences, allowing the infantry to take advantage

of the gap and slip in. When the Brigade was used in a defensive role, its task was to protect and support its own heavy artillery and tanks.

5   A Lieutenant or a 2nd Lieutenant in the Royal Artillery is traditionally addressed as 'Mr'. Thank you to Martin Skipworth of the Royal Signals Museum.

CHAPTER NINE

On Parade For The Top Brass

Thur. 4th Feb.

Paraded at 10-30. Lined the road near our camp. Saw Mr. Churchill. He was smiling broadly and gave us the V sign. Had a good view. He passed very slowly, 6ft away. Glad I've seen him. With him were General Alexander and Monty. Moved west to join 7th Armoured Div. 60 miles

Reg. War Diaries: TRIPOLI – 1100hrs. Tripoli-Garian Rd. lined by Rgt. to cheer Rt. Hon. Winston Churchill, P.M., C.I.G.S. Gen. Sir Alan Brooke, C. in C. Middle East, Sir H. Alexander and General Montgomery as they passed. The turnout of the Regt. after crossing the Libyan desert was very favourably commented on.

1300hrs. 21 reinforcements arrived. Rgt. under Cmd. 131 Bde. and moved to 50 miles W. of Tripoli.

Uncle Charlie's diary entry on this day becomes four lines of history; his tiny writing, in its historical context, seems magnified ten times. Charlie has been standing about six feet away from the most influential leaders of the Second World War. The War Diaries, written in pencil, always factual and understated, have the effect of doubly underlining Charlie's words by repeating the names of the men who have the greatest roles and responsibilities, and are the biggest decision makers

126 SNOWDROPS FOR A SOLDIER

in the United Kingdom. These men bring a huge influence to bear on the progress of the 2nd World War.

Winston Churchill,

Prime Minister of the United Kingdom, army officer, politician, (holding various Cabinet posts) historian, writer and artist. The only British Prime Minister to win the Nobel Prize for literature, and the first person to be made an Honorary Citizen of the United States. In the 1930's Churchill was criticised for warning about the dangers of Nazi Germany, (with hindsight he was right) leading to his unsuccessful campaign for British re-armament. He became Prime Minister on the 10th May, 1940, and immediately steadfastly refused to consider defeat, surrender or compromise. This attitude, found within his uplifting, morale-boosting speeches, demonstrates a supreme skill, inspiring the nation to pull together. Churchill's speeches were vital during the early, dark days of the war, when Britain stood alone, facing a possible invasion. Charlie, in his short account of seeing the British Prime Minister, noting the "V" sign, the "broad smile" and "Glad I've seen him." says something about the effect it had on my Uncle. Despite the criticisms that have been levelled at Winston Churchill, perhaps some justified, to me the bottom line reads that he was a successful, inspiring, popular leader of a united, determined country that fought successfully to overcome its enemies.

Gen. Sir Alan Brooke, C.I.G.S. (Chief of the Imperial General Staff)

The second man to be named by the War Diaries on this day was Sir Alan Brooke, followed by his formal title which does not really give a clue to his role, which is in fact head of the British Army, a post he had held since December 1941. After leaving Woolwich Military Academy he joined the Royal

Artillery. Steadily climbing the ranks, he achieved the rank of Major General in 1935.

Following the fall of France in 1940, Brooke skilfully extracted his Corps and organised its retreat to Dunkirk He became chairman of the Chiefs of Staff Committee, and Principal Military Advisor to the War Cabinet. He was at Churchill's side at Allied conferences when all crucial military decisions were made. Brooke and Churchill had many volatile disagreements, but Brooke always told Churchill how he felt about strategy, and was true to his beliefs.

Brooke was a first class communicator: he spoke in a compelling, lucid manner – a great asset when dealing with Winston Churchill – as well as the Americans. Speed and clarity of thinking, and the ability to choose his generals wisely, as well as the loyalty with which he backed them was key. Alexander, Montgomery and Slim, all Brooke's protégés, proved to be exceptional generals.

Brooke was a keen ornithologist, often to be seen out relaxing, feeding the birds in St. James's Park – all the better to be fresh for Churchill's late night meetings. In 1944 Brooke was promoted to Field Marshall, before being awarded the grand title of Baron Alanbrooke of Brookeborough in 1945.

Sir Harold Alexander – Commander in Chief, Middle East.

Alexander, after leaving Sandhurst, where he completed his army officer training, served in the First World War, receiving various honours and decorations. It was Alexander who presided over Montgomery's victory at the second battle of El-Alamein, and the advance of the 8th Army to Tripoli. Later the American and British troops who had landed in Morocco and Algeria the previous November, as part of Operation Torch, converged in Tunisia, merging with the 8th Army. Both were brought under the command of the newly-formed 18th Army Group, commanded by Alexander, reporting directly to Dwight D. Eisenhower, the Supreme Allied Commander in the Mediterranean.

So far, we have the Prime Minister with his right hand man, Sir Alan Brooke, who is head of the Army, and the principal military advisor to the War Cabinet, followed by Sir Harold Alexander, Commander in Chief of the Middle East forces, and last, but not least, in this illustrious group of the most powerful men to orchestrate the history of the Second World War, came Montgomery, who needs no further comment. These influential decision makers all passed within a few feet of an impressed Charles Robinson. I like the fact that Uncle Charlie and his fellow soldiers were praised for their smart appearance, despite all their trials when crossing the Libyan Desert. This demonstrates to me that those in command were not immune to the difficulties faced by the lower ranks, and were prepared to give praise when it was due.

Fri. 5th Feb.
Moved on again to front at 7-0a.m. Bombed and strafed at 11-0a.m. Shelled when in Pisida village about 3-0p.m. Shrapnel went through our truck from back and through windscreen. 19 set wrecked. Nobody hurt! Strafed again by M.E. 109's at 6-0p.m. What a day! Quiet tonight.

Reg. War Diaries: *The pursuit of Rommel's remnants taken up again. 1500hrs 212 Bty. moved fwd. to 2 miles S.W. of Pisida and remainder of regiment ...? 5m E. of Pisida for night. The main road was strafed and dive-bombed twice during the day. 2 O.R's injured and two guns slightly damaged.*

After the previous day's excitement, and the novelty of seeing the top brass, it is back to business as usual – but not quite – as a very different, potentially perilous, sort of excitement happens in a flash, as they continue on their journey. What luck for everyone travelling in the truck today that only the wireless set was wrecked, as a piece of shrapnel (it must have been a big piece!) travelling like a missile, entered the rear of the truck and broke out through the windscreen. This incident was some extra good luck for Charlie who couldn't have been working on the set at the time. Then to add some ongoing tension, in the early evening they were shelled and strafed by M.E. 109's[1]

My Uncle deservedly had a quiet night after all the bombing, shelling, strafing and pieces of shrapnel he had had to endure. I hope he managed to get some sleep.

The War Diaries refer to "The pursuit of Rommel's remnants" as though they were some kind of raggle-taggle outfit, easily caught and overcome with the 8th Army's superior soldiers and equipment. This was not quite the case, as "Rommel's remnants" didn't just run away, but proved to be perfectly capable of bombing, shelling and inflicting as much damage as possible as they retreated.

Erwin Rommel – German Field Marshall – commander of the Afrika Korps, North Africa.

He was Montgomery's opposite number. Rommel had been awarded the German Iron Cross in the First World War for heroism, bravery and leadership. He was not called "the desert fox" for nothing. In his autobiography Harold Alexander described Rommel as a wizard of the battlefield, and a "fine technician."[2] Rommel was decisive: when the British and Americans invaded Algeria and Morocco in early November 1942, wasting no time, he rapidly moved his crack Panzer Divisions right up to meet them. He was fearless, driven and full of initiative. The two adversaries had completely different personalities. Whereas Rommel was quick thinking, decisive and had a keen tactical brain, Montgomery was steadier: thinking, planning, desiring the certainty of complete preparedness before acting. His were a safe pair of hands, carefully considering his options before making a move. Before El-Alamein, Montgomery spent weeks building up men and equipment under some very clever camouflage, making certain he had the man power and the fire power he needed to ensure success. During the North Africa campaign, Montgomery's personality fitted the Allied situation perfectly, as he had more troops, equipment, guns and artillery pieces as well as adequate supplies. He had the luxury of time – time enough to methodically plan the campaign, playing to his natural strengths which gave him the advantage over his adversary. Conversely, Rommel, who, despite repeated requests (denied by Hitler) for more fuel and supplies, was prevented from employing all his tactical skills.[3]

Sat. 6th Feb.

In same place all day. Two or three more shells in village. We have moved back just outside the village. South African fighter pilot reported to our car (adj.) after having been brought down by A.A. fire. Wasn't hurt. Raid by 5 ME 109's about 6-0p.m. No bombs dropped here. Quieter day than yesterday. Can expect R.A.F. support tomorrow.

Something a little different occurred today when an uninjured South African fighter pilot knocked on Uncle Charlie's car door after his plane was brought down by anti-aircraft fire. Despite an air raid at six o'clock Charlie had a much quieter day. The War Diaries report that the observation post moved up to the Tunisian border, looking out over the country to which the German army had retreated. The Tunisian terrain is favourable enough to enable the Germans to dig in and fight their final battles against the Allies. Three months on, the Axis forces will surrender, giving the Allies total victory in North Africa. Following their success in the fierce battle of El-Alamein, the 8th Army has chased the Afrika Korps from Egypt, across the vast landscape of Libya, and is now hammering on the door of Tunisia, ready to face their final clashes on this continent.

Sun. 7th Feb.
Medium battery across the road opened up this morning. Drew reply from a Jerry 7 inch gun which fired intermittently all day. Moved about a mile up the road now about 600 yards south of Pisida. Rained hard last night. Blankets wet through. Wilcock and Kay came up as reliefs – scared to death!

Still under fire most of the day, Charlie's Regiment now moves almost within sight of Pisida, their next objective. Last night it rained hard enough to thoroughly soak Charlie's blankets; wrapping oneself in a soggy blanket, is about as much fun as cuddling up to a wet Alsatian dog. The dark wet night certainly spooked the two soldiers sent to relieve them.

Mon. 8th Feb.
Same place all day. Lovely warm sunny day. Closed set down at mid-day. Sat outside in sun reading. Wrote letter-card home. 170mm still shelling. Carter of 211 Bty killed today. Wilcock and Kay came again as reliefs. I went with Pomford on line truck and laid a line to Bde Main. Lineman now.

Uncle Charlie had some welcome rest and relaxation today, (despite the continued shelling) sitting reading in the sun and writing a letter to his family. That same letter, written in the warm sunshine of a foreign land, on reaching England, would be delivered on a cold winter's day, by a shivering postman, possibly tramping through snow. I can picture the scene: everyone sitting round a warm fireside, taking it in turns to read Charlie's letter, and thinking with relief: "we know you are alright Charlie" because a letter received is a life confirmed. Unfortunately I do not have this particular letter.

Having only the newsreels and perhaps the odd picture to refer to (they did not possess a television of course) I wonder how Charlie's parents envisaged the desert lands their son was passing through. During the 1940's ordinary people like my grandparents never ventured beyond the U.K. The nearest they came to "abroad" would have been a day trip to a Welsh sea-side resort. Ireland, Scotland, the south of England would all have been out of the question for two reasons; they were too far to reach easily, and were also expensive. The photograph of Uncle Charlie with his friends on the Isle of Man (p11) after a boat trip half way across the Irish Sea meant that he had travelled further across a body of water than any other family member, even before being posted abroad! When that carefree photograph was taken in 1938, he could never have imagined how many thousands of miles he would travel by sea on two troop ships, as well as moving across a large part of the land mass of North Africa in an assortment of army vehicles.

Some bad news has come in: a fellow soldier of 211 Battery has been killed today. And Charlie has not been completely idle – he and Pomford laid a line to Brigade Main. The War Diaries report that they are holding strong positions on the Tunisian frontier. Everything is progressing nicely.

Tues. 9th Feb.
Still in same place. Terrible day. Completely different from yesterday.
It rained fairly hard practically all day. No shelling. Mat Read and

Taylor came as reliefs. We sat in Withington's dug-out and argued about the war. Received 2 air-graphs – Dad and Marjorie – 19th Dec.

Although they remained in the same place, the weather didn't stay the same, raining hard most of the day. At least the shelling had stopped, allowing the lads to enjoy some peace and quiet. I note Charlie is still not far away from Harry Withington, which is amazing after all these years. I trust it is the same soldier he completed the signalling course with.

Wed. 10th Feb.
Moved today at 2-30. Back into desert South of Zuara. I think we are being attached to another Bde. 22nd Armoured, I hope. Rained again. My blankets are wet and I had no chance of drying them today.

They seem to be experiencing some nasty weather on the border between Libya and Tunisia, with periods of heavy rainfall resulting in wet blankets again for Uncle Charlie. Not able to dry them off, I expect it will be another uncomfortable night for him, cuddling up to the wet Alsatian again.

Thur. 11th Feb.
Car was kept moving around in same locality. – main R.H.Q., C.R.A. Tac Bde etc. Finally came to rest at 6-30p.m. Still no chance to dry blankets. It's cold and miserable getting into a wet bed. Sand storm this afternoon, followed as usual, by rain. Never seen so much rain out here. Hope I can dry out tomorrow.

There seemed to be a fair amount of driving round in circles today, visiting various positions – unlucky for Charlie as it didn't give him the opportunity to get his blankets dry, and so he faces another miserable, cold night, when elusive Sleep will not pay a visit to a body shivering with cold. From the War Diaries account it looks like the regiment is back under the command of the 7th Armoured Division.

Fri. 12th Feb.

More rain and a sand-storm today. It cleared up about 3-0 and I put out my blankets. They are now fairly dry, thank goodness. Wrote an air-letter home. Am going down to R.H.Q. tomorrow for a rest from wireless. Will be very welcome. Ally Hay and I erected a first rate bivvy which shouldn't leak. Capt. Strutt told us about staying in Chatsworth House, Alnwick Castle, etc. Interesting.

The poor weather continues with more rain and a sandstorm, but to Uncle Charlie's relief the weather clears up and he is able to put his blankets out to dry. He is looking forward to a welcome rest from the wireless set, spending the next day at Regimental Headquarters. Hopefully the new bivvy will not leak, and the blankets should stay dry.

Sat. 13th Feb.

Went down to R.H.Q. Made Ronny Hobb's truck my H.Q. Lounged about during morning and as it was a hot day, put out my blankets. Completely dry at last. In the afternoon read once again "Pip" by Ian Hay. It's very good. In the evening we made some porridge. Slept in back of Ronny's car. Heard that Jerry has evacuated Ben Gardane.

Uncle Charlie, savouring a full day of rest, has finally managed to get his blankets completely dry, followed by a relaxing afternoon spent reading his book, by novelist and playwright John Hay Beith CBE, soldier and schoolmaster. (1876-1952). Published in 1917 "'Pip' – A Romance of Youth" was his first novel. Uncle Charlie enjoyed reading this book "once again" but gives no clue as to what it was about.

Notes

1 The Messerschmitt BF109 or ME109 (named by the Allies) was the most successful plane in use by the Luftwaffe. It started life during the Spanish Civil War and continued in service, with various modifications, until the end of the 2nd World War.
2 Taken from http://www.spartacus.schoolnet.co.uk/GERrommel. htm#source. Extract from: General Alexander's autobiography: "Memoirs: 1940 – 1945."
3 www.topedge.com/panels/ww2na/tacticshtml

CHAPTER TEN

Tunisia

Sun. 14th Feb.

Arrived back at Tac. H.Q. at 8-15. On set immediately. We moved west at 12-15. Crossed the Causeway into Tunisia. From Egypt to Tunisia in three not so easy stages! Had to work on set until 2-10a.m. Not a bad day's work – 18 hrs. eating on the job. Driver gets our meals ready. Good thing too. Wrote to Elsie (air letter) today. Still haven't heard from her.

At last, the regiment has crossed the border into Tunisia. The shortest distance by air, as the crow flies, from Egypt to Tunisia is 1,356 very long miles. But, taking into account the convoluted, zigzagging route the regiment has taken during the last three months: dodging mine fields and blown bridges, bypassing cratered roads and negotiating deep Wadis, has made the journey from Egypt, into Libya, across the Libyan desert and into Tunisia actually twice as far as the direct route, and, in the mix, strewn with man-made obstacles – the Afrika Korps!

After a day's much needed rest, Charlie has been concentrating hard today, back on "set" until after two a.m.- a total of eighteen hours on the job, and Elsie still hasn't written to him!

Mon. 15th Feb.

Moved on at 9-0a.m. Battle formation. Object is Ben Gardane which we reached at 3-0p.m.without opposition. Gave lift to 2 French officers. They were very spick & span. I don't know where they sprung from. Got letter from Elsie at last. Scrapped the one I wrote to her yesterday. Completed 3 years' service today.

The Regiment, expecting opposition, moves off in either battle or desert formation, depending on whether the reader believes Uncle Charlie's diary or the War Diaries' account. I don't pretend to understand the intricacies and details of the above mentioned formations, but I can appreciate the principle involved. As there is no natural cover in the desert, the movement of vehicles throwing up clouds of dust is obvious, and if these vehicles are moving in straight lines, an incoming enemy plane, carrying either bombs or machine guns, can easily get a fix on the straight line formation, enabling it to attack and knock out the vehicles. Therefore, the purpose of a desert formation, where vehicles move in several staggered columns is to make those vehicles a smaller target, and therefore more difficult to attack from the air.[1]

With little or no opposition the Regiment reached its objective of Bengardane, and stayed there for the night. Uncle Charlie's vehicle seems to lead a double life as a taxi for foreign servicemen; this time it was two "spick and span" French officers who were given a lift. Previously it was a South African airman who had been shot down. After receiving a long awaited letter from Elsie "at last" Charlie scrapped the one he had intended to send, which could possibly have been less than complimentary given the amount of time he had waited so eagerly for her to communicate with him.

Today is the 15th February, 1943, exactly three years since

Charlie, a naïve and unworldly recruit, joined the Army at the tender age of twenty two years. After being called up, Charlie would lose status as an esteemed eldest son from a close-knit family, becoming merely one of hundreds of young men, all of the same basic rank, all in basic training. Additionally there was the trauma of being away from family, friends and familiar routines. Those early weeks in the army were hard to endure for all those lads called up to serve their country, many, like Charlie, being away from home for the first time. But, I feel, for Charlie, due to his background, during those first few weeks in that alien world, he would need to summon a great deal of courage and mental strength.

Looking back over the three years from 15th February, 1940, that time span could not have been more eventful for Signalman Charles Robinson in respect to the thousands of miles of travelling he has experienced. His army career, even just in the U.K., lists a range of billets, tents and training camps: beginning with Carlisle and ending with the Clyde, from whence he set sail for the foreign shores of Durban, Egypt, across North Africa to his final resting place in Tunisia.[2] As time moved on, marching beside it has been the spectre of increasing demands on physical and mental reserves: focus, resolve, confidence, bravery and commitment. Since arriving in North Africa, his days have become ever more challenging: dealing with the demands of desert conditions, desert warfare, battles with the enemy and the inherent strain of facing up to the task of becoming a fully experienced combat soldier. The naïve young man, protected and esteemed at home, three years on, has become worldly-wise and mature; a battle-hardened soldier – but one that never sacrificed his basic humanity. Over the next few weeks as the fighting intensifies, Uncle Charlie will experience many near misses and there will be several occasions when his life, like a candle subject to the vagaries of the wind, will come closer and closer to being snuffed out, until, three months' hence he will lose the final battle.

> *Tues. 16th Feb*
> *Stayed in Ben Gardane today. The Bde. hasn't enough transport to go much further. Air-raid by 12 M.E.'s at 12-15 midday. Short and sharp, but fierce while it lasted. 3 men of 211 Bty. wounded. Heavy A.A. fire around here. Wrote again to Elsie and home. Went to pictures in middle of desert in evening! "Torrid Zone" – James Cagney.*

After being fiercely attacked by the enemy, causing some casualties, answered by anti-aircraft fire, Uncle Charlie is able to enjoy enough relaxation to write to Elsie and his family and to see an adventure film at the cinema in the desert. "Torrid Zone", starring James Cagney, was released in May 1940, almost three years previously. Nevertheless, although not new, the film still provides an opportunity for the men to lose themselves in an adventure, with the leading stars of the day: James Cagney and the glamorous Ann Sheridan, who provides some erotic interest for men who have not seen the opposite sex for many months.

> *Wed. 17ᵗʰ Feb.*
> *Moved on this morning – 20 miles. Arrived in location at 3-0p.m. and stayed the night. Reminds me very much of Mersa Brega. (Libyan city) Ops. Office erected. Sets closed down. Looks as if we might stay here a little while. Car broke down in afternoon. Transmission wires.*

I imagine there would be lots of mechanical breakdowns due to the high mileage strain on vehicles, combined with the dusty, sandy, dry desert conditions.

Thur. 18th Feb.

Stayed in same place today. Sets off. Had a good rest. Mechs. working on the car. I cooked the dinner – chips, fried onions and bully. (canned corned beef) *Not bad. Borrowed "A Tale of Two Cities"[3] from Ronny Hobbs. Will enjoy reading it again. Two M.E. 109's over this morning. No damage done.*

Uncle Charlie's writing seemed to be a little untidier than usual, so I had to find my magnifying glass to check out some of his words. He has had a quiet, restful day, and took on the role of chef while the mechanics mended the car.

Fri. 19th Feb.

In same place all day. Truck being repaired. Harry moved off in Humber and 19 set at 9-0p.m. Regiment moved off at 1-0a.m. Car repairs finished about 2-0a.m. Ray and I brewed up and listened to BBC 9 o'clock news. Lots of tanks moving up. Mat Read still insists that war with Germany will be over by June 30th

There are some advantages to being a radio operator: ready access to world news via the BBC as well as inside knowledge of incoming news and events as they happen to the regiment. I am assuming Uncle Charlie caught up with the rest of the regiment after the truck repairs had been completed. Mat Read is very optimistic that the war with Germany will be over by June 30th. He is partly right, as the war in North Africa would be over by then, following the German surrender in Mid-May, but there was still the rest of Europe to set free. Accounting for some sixty percent of all armoured cars, the British made Humber was the most numerous. Humber also manufactured the Osprey, a light reconnaissance car, and the Scout car, which was a light armoured car.

Wireless Set 11.

Sat. 20th Feb.
Salmon tin moved off at 10-0a.m. Arrived at RHQ at 12-0. Opened
up to 131 Bde. On 11 set[4] straight away. From 4-0p.m. until 6-30
was one long continuous air-raid. Dozens of Stuka's and ME's.
Bombs close, but no one of RHQ hurt. Very exciting. Wrote home. –
poor letter owing to interruptions by Luftwaffe.

Uncle Charlie's regiment has had to withstand a fierce onslaught
from the German air force, and it is fortunate that only one
soldier has been wounded and evacuated. Uncle Charlie
describes the sustained attack as "exciting" which I assume had
the adrenaline pumping round his body, perhaps dispersing any
fear he may have felt.

Also for the past four months since El-Alamein Charlie has
survived countless attacks from a variety of enemy weapons,
and has become inured to almost daily combat. However, he
states the attacks have affected his letter writing ability, so as I
am lucky enough to have his letter, (reproduced below) it will
be interesting to see if he is right.

Dear Mother and Dad,

Two more letter cards received. They are yours Dad of the 16th
and 25th Jan. Thanks very much. They came two days ago and with
them letter-cards from Rosie Glithero and Jessie Morton and air-
graphs from Mrs. Jackson (Doris) and Jack Taylor. I had a good do
didn't I? It isn't often I get six letters all at once.

It's good to hear that recruits are still going to Hadrian's Camp.
I'm sure Norman's Home Guard pal will enjoy himself there.
Norman will too, if he has to go there. It's a grand camp – home from
home – although the boys probably don't realise it. I'd give a lot to be
back there again.

I don't wonder, Dad, that you cannot play Billiards so well on
a table 4ft by 2! After playing on a full size table you will feel as if
you are tickling them. As for spin or any kind of bias, well, I should
imagine it can't be done.

And Norman has bought a violin! I should have thought he
would have been satisfied with the piano and the organ. I'm sure it
will be much more pleasant listening to him playing the piano than
attempting to play the violin. Have you had a go at it yet?

I must agree with you that Arthur Barton's arrival when
you were writing the letter-card of Jan. 25th did rather spoil it. I
agree, too, that his story of how he got the leave is rather tall. As a
rule C.O.'s don't bother their heads about men's leave, they have
more important things to think about. A section officer or platoon
commander usually arranges leave. Only in very special cases is the
C.O. consulted.

I'm so glad that Searle had a photograph of the wedding in his window. You know all this talk about the photos, makes me very impatient to receive them and I don't suppose I shall for months yet.

I was stuck for a book the other day and managed to borrow "A Tale of Two Cities." I studied it for Matric. you know, and as I read on, I can well remember the passages which, in my own copy are underlined. Still, whether it is for study or not it's a jolly fine book. By far the best of Dickens in my opinion.

There doesn't seem to be much to write about just now. I mean, there is plenty I could write about but only a little I may, so I'm afraid a little will have to do. Anyway, you have said yourself that a note proving that I'm O.K. will do. This is little more than that, I know, and must apologise for it. I'll try and pen a more interesting one next time. I may have more time and less interruption then. I hope so.

And so for the present ---

Cheerio

Charlie

Despite Uncle Charlie's comment on his "poor letter" in this day's diary entry, the only difference I can see from his usual letter, is that this latest Air Mail Letter Card is shorter, covering only two and a half sides instead of the usual completely covered three sides. I can see no difference in the quality of his handwriting and no evidence of interruptions causing disjointed thought processes, or problems with grammar or spelling. His letter is of the usual high standard, despite attempts by the Luftwaffe to thwart his attempts to write by disrupting the peace and quiet of his day. Perhaps, due to the bangs and crashes of this sustained air attack, the near misses and the high adrenaline rushes they cause, lead him to assume he has not penned a very good letter, when in fact there is no difference in quality.

Charlie is pleased to have received six letters at once from his Mother, Father, friends and neighbours. Receiving no other form of communication from home, letters truly are the most precious link – sent from a small mill town near Manchester, taking only a few weeks to arrive, they have travelled over two thousand miles to Medenine, a south eastern town in Tunisia, with its vastly different culture, climate and scenery – a world away from Hyde in Cheshire, and probably beyond his family's understanding of a foreign country. But, the most important thing from their perspective, receiving a letter from him is when, breathing a sigh of relief, they can say: "We know you are alright Charlie."

Writing about his training days at Hadrian's Camp in Carlisle three years ago, when he was a young, naïve recruit, Charlie looks back to his time there with rose-tinted lenses in his black framed glasses. Now, in hindsight, he realises that in contrast to the current stresses of combat, when life can literally hang in the balance, Hadrian's camp is a piece of cake, and communicates this fact in his letter to reassure his younger brother and his friend not to worry if they are sent there.

I wasn't aware that my granddad played billiards, a similar game to snooker, but much older – the English version dating back to the 16th Century. Perhaps my granddad acquired this small table for use at home, and possibly they had a full size billiard table at church. I certainly cannot see my granddad, given his strong aversion to alcohol, playing this game in a public house, or in a billiard hall. But Charlie's description of "spin" and "bias" suggests he has some knowledge of the game, and possibly also played billiards with his father.

Again, demonstrating his sense of humour, I notice Uncle Charlie slips in the word "attempting" when referring to Uncle Norman's mastery of the newly acquired violin, thinking he might be making a few unplanned squeaks at the high end of the musical scale. Pondering on the violin's potential to get on family nerves; this might be the one and only good reason for being away from home! And if his father gets in on the act as well it would be a doubly good reason.

If I look carefully at the bottom of the photograph of my parents' wedding, I can just make out the slightly embossed letters of "Searle, Market Place, Hyde." Searching the internet I have found several old black and white postcard views of Hyde; many taken by the then local photographer, Searle. Uncle Charlie would have known the location of the shop, but can only imagine the wedding photographs on display in Searle's window when, ironically, every friend, family member and indeed, everyone in Hyde who happened to be passing, could see his sister's wedding photographs on display in the shop window. In an emotional (for him) letter of 20th December, 1942, when he was homesick and desperately sad about missing his sister's wedding, he wrote: "I must endure this exile". Charlie has missed out again, as he is the only person of significance not to see the photographs. Yet another sacrifice made, and another cruel reminder of how he is missing out on family events. I would like to think that someone did send him the photographs of the wedding.

Uncle Charlie studied "A Tale of Two Cities" for his Matric – (Matriculation) his former County School qualification in his final year.[5] He remembers studying the book for his exam and marking the relevant passages. This time he can read the book simply for the enjoyment of it, and he believes that this book is Charles Dickens's best.

Not able to write any details of the sustained German air attacks which are disrupting his concentration, and hinting he could write much more if allowed, Charlie signs off his letter in the usual way.

Sun. 21st Feb.

Went out in salmon tin with…? on recce. Several big hills in Medenine district. Were given 20 minutes' notice and then told off for being late! Returned to RHQ at 5-30. Slight air activity – much less than yesterday. My 11 set was repaired by George Grist. I waited for it. Valve change only after I had changed them all during day. New valve had no filament.

I am unable to make out the very faint seventh word in Charlie's first sentence. Perhaps it has faded with time. There is nothing very much to report today except for some slight air activity, and a mine which managed to knock out a Stuart tank. The regiment is still at Medenine.

Mon. 22nd Feb.

Moved off at 9-10a.m. Went to new Tac H.Q. position. Stayed all day but returned to main HQ position in evening. Stayed there all night. No enemy aircraft over. Whole area thick with Teller and S Mines[6] Two of our trucks went up on them. Nobody hurt. Tac. H.Q. was at the foot of a hill which reminded me of Werneth Low except that it had no grass on it. Heard BBC news. Clock back 1 hour tonight.

Two trucks were blown up today, and with great good fortune no-one was hurt. With help from the Royal Engineers, over one hundredweight of explosives were blown up and the mines made safe. The Royal Engineers were renowned throughout the Army for their bravery in tackling the dangerous and tricky task of disabling these explosive devices. There was a feeling of nostalgia for Uncle Charlie when the hill in front of him evoked a memory of Werneth Low, a hill above his home town – a hill he had probably walked on. The hill at Metameur perhaps had a similar shape to it, the difference being it was a long long way from his home town.

Tues. 23rd Feb.
Stayed in RHQ position all day. Had a good rest – both sets switched off. Wrote three letters. Phyllis, Dorothy Cooper and Jessie Morton. Finished "A Tale of Two Cities." What a great tale it is. Had a bath in the afternoon. Listened to news and brewed up in the evening.

Uncle Charlie had a much appreciated restful and peaceful day, with time to write three letters, (without interruption from the Luftwaffe this time) and he even managed a bath in the afternoon. I just can't remove a silly, incongruous picture from my mind of a large bath stuck somewhere between two sand dunes, in the middle of nowhere, with its old fashioned claw feet embedded in the sand. Common sense must prevail, so I am assuming the "bath" would be some kind of large improvised container, requisitioned for bathing purposes. Water must be so precious out there and yet so badly needed that the men would have been very grateful for any opportunity to get cleaned up. The inverted commas at either end of the book title have not been added by me. Charlie, always the perfectionist, had meticulously placed them there as if he was writing his Diary as an essay for someone else to read. Thank you Uncle Charlie!

Wed. 24th Feb.
R.H.Q. position this morning. Told to be ready to move at 1-0 o'clock. We moved off about two and after going about three miles up the road were shelled intermittently until dusk. Moved after dark to Bde. tac position. Loads of our aircraft went over – a fire burning in the east all night.

There is a discrepancy between the two accounts of the day's events. The timings are different, perhaps because Uncle Charlie was with R.H.Q. and the bulk of the Regiment moved off at a different time. Also Charlie reports some intermittent shelling, which held them up until after dark. There is no mention of shelling from the War Diaries.

Thur. 25th Feb.
In Tac. position until dusk when we moved 5 miles forward to another
Tac. Shelled intermittently all day. Nearest one 70 yds. away. Saw
a bloke on a truck going along the road hit in the hand by a piece of
shrapnel. Not badly hurt. Wrote home.

Today there has been intense enemy fire, the nearest shell landing only 70 yards away from Uncle Charlie. He witnessed a shrapnel injury to a fellow soldier who was travelling along the road nearby.

Fri. 26th Feb.
Stayed in same position all day. Shelling was worse – heavier and
nearer. Two landed 30 yards away – one on each side of the car. No
damage done but Jerry certainly had us "ducking". Were told to dig a
slit trench as well as a hole to sleep in. Then after we had dug it were
told we move at 9-0 o'clock tomorrow morning. "Never were so few"-

The shells are falling closer and closer to Uncle Charlie's vehicle; in fact too close for comfort – two landing hair-raisingly near – one on either side of the car, causing those inside to duck instinctively. It must have been very scary being a sitting target – like a plastic duck on a fairground shooting range: Charlie's heart hammering inside his chest, as he listened to the exploding shells getting nearer and nearer. Or, alternatively, he may have been bravely philosophical about the mayhem happening all around, thinking that if his name was on a particular shell, then so be it? Perhaps having survived all previous German assaults his fear threshold has become much higher; but this is pure speculation on my part. His writing only gives a small clue.

It is still neat, but the odd word is slightly less clear. I think I can forgive him this minute wobble in his usually meticulous writing. His final three words on this day: "Never were so few" is obviously a quote, possibly a slight variation of Churchill's speech during the battle of Britain: *"Never in the field of human conflict has so much been owed by so many to so few."* Unfortunately I cannot be sure whether it was an unlikely miss-quote, or if he was feeling particularly significant as: "one of the few."

> *Sat. 27th Feb.*
> *Did not move at 9-0a.m. after all but about 4-0p.m. Are now parked near an M.E.109 which was brought down this morning. I haven't mentioned that for the last three or four days we have been in the hills 15 miles S.E. of Mareth – in the Mareth line. So far have seen no concrete emplacements. Shelling eased off a lot.*

Uncle Charlie is up in the hills, parked near an enemy aircraft shot down that morning, fifteen miles South East of Mareth. Rather like El-Alamein the Mareth Line was vitally important to both sides of the conflict: the Allies needing to progress through it, and the Axis forces attempting to stop them. The Mareth Line stretched 22 miles inland from the sea to the Matmata hills, broadly following the Wadi Zigzaou, which was a natural feature, a seemingly insurmountable obstacle in its own right, with sky-scraper banks reaching 70 feet high in places. To the west of the Matmata hills there was only inhospitable desert. A smaller line of hills ran east-west along the northern edge of the Matmata range, causing more difficulties for those attempting to cross. To further thwart any would-be advance from the Allies, the area was bristling with man-made stumbling blocks built by the French prior to the war; it was full of anti-tank obstacles, concrete emplacements and fortifications. (Although Charlie has not seen any as yet)

At the extreme northern end of the Matmata hills there is just a narrow exit: the Tebaga Gap.

This area was reputed to be the most obstinately unbreachable military defence line in North Africa: the original French builders believed the hills to be impassable. It is to this heavily fortified place, hotly pursued by the Eighth Army, that the Germans have made a fighting retreat, crossing 1,400 miles across Egypt, Libya and now Tunisia. They had found the perfect defensive place to make a last stand against the Allies. For the Allies, after overcoming so many difficulties, they could be facing victory, if only they can conquer this final huge hurdle which could lead to the winning of the North Africa Campaign.

The scene is now set for some desperately hard-fought battles to come.

Sun. 28th Feb.
Static all day. Not much shelling. No air activity. Heard that RHQ got the only few shots fired on this area. Mr. Neary got shrapnel in his elbow. Harry went down to RHQ as he has to see the doc. every day. He has impetigo. In bed early as stand to's start in the morning at 6-0a.m. Several bats here in old Arab buildings, make a terrible noise at night.

Uncle Charlie is billeted with some unwelcome, very noisy nocturnal residents: bats – resulting in their playing havoc with a good night's sleep – when tomorrow morning he has to be up very early to start at six o'clock. Charlie's long-time companion Harry is seeing the doctor every day to help cure his impetigo (a highly contagious skin infection, consisting of small blisters that can burst and spread.) This could be the same Harry that Charlie has shared the last three years of a very eventful life with.

Mon. 1st Mar.

Static again. Fair amount of shelling. Up at 5-45 for stand to. Still dark. Heard in evening from 7th Armd. Div. that we are going out tomorrow and 58 Fld. is coming in. We are browned off with all this changing. Of course we knew as far back as England what it would be when we became an Army Fld. Reg. Wrote letter-card home. Maj. Walker killed.

Reg. War Diaries: *1100hrs. Small amount of enemy movement seen and engaged during day. British plane dropped bomb near R.H.Q. 1300hrs. Major E.B. Walker, R.A. was injured by and subsequently died from a round fired by his battery, whilst he was ranging. New D.F. tasks were registered by 212 and 476 Btys.*

1900hrs. Orders recd. for 111 Fld. Regt. to move on 2 Mar, two Btys. and RHQ to take over from 58 Fld. Regt. One Bty. (211) to go to 8 Armd. Bde. under Comd.

There are lots of changes taking place now, involving individual regiments and batteries. It is unsettling for the soldiers, even though, as Uncle Charlie writes, the men are aware that they will come under the command of different armoured divisions, for this is the role of the field regiment.[7] The officers in charge aim to deploy men and equipment in the most effective way possible, as they prepare for battle.

While out ranging the guns, Major Walker was killed by his own battery. I suppose in today's terminology a costly mistake of this nature would be called "killed by friendly fire" a term that sounds all wrong to me; but whatever its name, or however it is wrapped up or sanitized the unwanted outcome is still the same. There was another similar mistake, which fortunately did not end in tragedy, when a British plane dropped a bomb near R.H.Q.

Dear Mother and Dad,

Here I am again, reporting everything ship-shape and Bristol fashion. Today is the first day of a new month. The days, weeks and months keep slipping past and bringing us nearer the end of the war. They also bring me nearer home. I'm looking forward to the day which ends the war in the same way that I used to look forward to my birthday, Christmas or Summer Holidays when I was a kid. What a good day that will be, and what a tremendous relief for most of us.

Especially the "Desert Rats" in the Middle East. I'm one of the lucky ones, some chaps have been out here two and three years. Although, of course, I shall not be sorry to leave North Africa behind me. Perhaps this year will finish it all, I hope so, we are in the third month of it now.

Since I last wrote I've received an Airgraph from Mother dated Jan. 27th. Thanks mother. So they have finally caught Jack Taylor and are sending him abroad. If he comes to the Middle East pay office, he will still be on a good thing. He will in all probability end his journey in Jerusalem, lucky blighter. All the time I've been out here I've badly wanted to see Palestine which I believe is a green, well cultivated pleasant country. I never got the chance and I'm hardly likely to now. I don't think I shall ever go back to Egypt, let alone Palestine.

Two new operators have just joined the section. Mr. Hugo, our section officer, came up here yesterday and told me I might be interested to know that one comes from Denton. (the next town to Hyde) As soon as possible I must get back with the rest of the section and look him up.

Perhaps you are wondering why I say I must get back with the rest of the section. I don't think I've ever explained it before so I will now. Every unit has a main H.Q. and when in action what is known as a tactical or "Tac HQ". At main HQ is the Signal Office, stores, and in fact all the signal section except two wireless operators who are forward with Tac H.Q. I'm one of these two. The rest of Tac consists of the C.O. the Assistant Adjutant and a driver. We are issued with rations which we have to cook ourselves and don't see the rest of the boys for long stretches. It's not a bad life, but a little too exciting at times! There is this about it, we know what is going on, where Jerry is etc. and this makes life very interesting.

I think that the idea of Marjorie and Jim opening a shop is a sound one. They are both able to make what they will sell and I am of the opinion that they should succeed. They will both have to save up hard though, won't they? I suppose they are already doing this. By the way, how is my sum total getting along, I should very much like to know. Has the new allotment come through? You must forgive me if I keep harping on this blinking allotment, but there's ten and a tanner (10/6) a week of mine at stake and I'm naturally eager to know whether you are now drawing and banking it, or not. You see, you have received my letter-card of Jan 4th but as far as I know, not the one of about Dec 24th when I explained it all. But I must shut up or you'll be thinking I'm becoming miserly.

Have you heard or seen anything of Cliff recently? I haven't heard from him for ages. When I wrote to Dorothy I asked her to rouse him a little. Perhaps he's too busy thinking about his wedding to write to me. Poor blighter!

Well, the time has arrived for me to finish. When I end a letter to you, I always wonder how many more I shall have to write before I come home. I know what I'll do, I'll start numbering them. The next will be number one, I'll put it at the head of the letter. My guess is that round about no. 50 I shan't be far from home. We'll just wait and see.

For now,
Cheerio,
Charlie

The first paragraph of Uncle Charlie's letter describes his feelings as he looks forward to an end to the war. He feels a child-like anticipation to leaving the Middle East, a "desert rat" relieved to be leaving behind all that is military and returning home as a much-loved son, brother and cousin. He fervently hopes that 1943 will see an end to the war, and (thankfully), without foresight, he cannot know that the next ten weeks or so will bring a hard won victory for the Allies in North Africa – a victory he will not be given the chance to savour.

The cliché "It's a small world" seems to apply to all of us so many times in life, when, hundreds of miles away from home, we unexpectedly meet someone from the same town. For Uncle Charlie this will be the second time in less than a year that he has met someone from the same or neighbouring town. When he was on the troop ship he met a lad from Hyde, and now, in Tunisia, alongside soldiers from different parts of the country, Mr. Hugo informs him that a new operator in the signal section is from Denton, the next town to Hyde. Uncle Charlie looks forward to meeting him when he goes down to the regular signals section.

What follows is a very useful description of where Charlie is located in the Army scheme of things. He is travelling with the other wireless operator and the C.O., the Assistant Adjutant and a driver. This vehicle, during action, is known as Tac.H.Q. The rest of the Signal Section is based at H.Q. The problem could be that Charlie's forward vehicle may become a target. I think this could be why he thinks life can be a little too exciting at times. On the positive side the two wireless operators in Tac.H.Q. are not only the first to hear the latest news as it comes in, they also get to know where the Germans are.

In the next paragraph Uncle Charlie mentions that my mother and father are planning to open a shop. This is news to me as I have no recollection of them ever talking about this when they have been reminiscing about the past; so whether it was mooted, but never actually came to fruition I don't know. But as they were both working as confectioners, they would certainly be able to make what they were proposing to sell. Charlie wondered if they were both saving up, and this sent him off at a tangent again about his allotment of earnings from the Army. He is worried that his letter to my Grandma of the 24th December, detailing how his allotment is to be banked has not arrived, and she may be doing the wrong thing with his money! In one sense it makes me laugh when he says if he goes on about this too much they might think he is a miser. As if! But in another sense it indicates how much of a perfectionist he is about his affairs being carried out correctly. (After all: "there is ten and a tanner[8] a week of mine at stake.").

Keen to do the right thing for her son, and follow his wishes precisely, I believe Grandma's heart sank when she read her son's letter, particularly if his weekly allotment has not been coming through properly, or she has been dealing with his money in the wrong way.

In his final paragraph, Uncle Charlie decides to estimate how many letters he will write before returning home (typically using numbers as a reference point) he tells his family that starting from the next letter he is going to number each one at the top. He bets he will write fifty letters before the war is over. Attempting to be optimistic for himself and his family, as usual he is finding reasons to be positive.

Tues. 2nd Mar.
Stood to from 5-30. Moved at 7-0 to a Wadi near Medenine. Shelled in the morning. Supported Guards Bde. today and tonight. Talked to one of the new chaps who lives in Denton. Received N.C.H. (Oct. 16) gave it to him. German attack expected tonight or tomorrow. Might settle things in N. Africa.

Uncle Charlie has met the soldier from Denton and passed on the local paper (N.C.H.) to him. This is a little piece of home they can both share. It must feel quite strange to read about local events back home when they are living seemingly a million miles away in a completely different world.

But back to the reality of waiting for an imminent German attack. The 8th Army has paused at Medenine to regroup and prepare to face the enemy, whom the Allies expect will launch a pre-emptive attack sometime soon. Uncle Charlie optimistically believes this "might settle things in N. Africa" but he cannot know there is still a long, hard road to travel before their hard-earned victory is won. The Regiment's batteries and headquarters are being moved around, sometimes under heavy shelling, and 111 Field Regiment will be joining the 8th Armoured Brigade. This will be completed by 4th March. (See War Diaries account in Appendix A)

Wed. 3rd Mar.
Moved out of Wadi at 8-15. Went to North of Medenine to join 8th Armd. Bde. In reserve for a change! Jerry made three attacks today but they were all beaten off and no wonder. We've bags of stuff up here. He put up a respectable barrage at 10-0p.m. Quite noisy but I don't think much harm was done. No shelling near us.

I sense that Uncle Charlie, with almost nonchalant comments like "put up a respectable barrage" and "quite noisy, but I don't think much harm was done" when referring to the three German attacks, has become such an experienced soldier that he has become sufficiently detached to make a critical assessment of the enemy attacks. He is reassured by the "bags of stuff" the Allies have at their disposal; in other words a great deal of firepower helps to instill confidence in the "Cloud Punchers" – (an apt nickname for the Royal Artillery) It also helps knowing that in support of the 8th Armd. Bde. for now, 111 Fld. Rgt. is out of range!

Thur. 4th Mar.
Static all day. On half-hourly calls to Bde. and 11 set closed down, so we had an easy time. Two planes brought down about 5-0p.m. but from what I saw I think one was a Spitfire – pilot bailed out. Heard rumour that N.Z. Div. and us are going South into the Sahara and then round and North to help the Yanks. What a variety of units we support and interesting jobs we tackle. The Sahara Desert – ye Gods! Only a rumour yet though.

The prospect of going South across the Sahara seems to be an exciting one for Uncle Charlie, even though it may be just a rumour. He does revel in the prospect of experiencing different places. Thinking back to the occasions he looked forward to time off in Durban, Cairo and Tripoli, and his disappointment in not being given the chance to see Alexandria. He seems fairly contented with his lot at present, particularly with the variety of work he does, and the different roles within each unit.

Fri. 5th Mar.
Had a "Beefer" today. Stayed in same place and was on half-hourly call-ups to Bde. 11 Set closed down completely. Wrote two letter-cards, one home and one to Elsie. Erected tent at night but Ally had to take it down about 11-30 when I was in bed because Jerry's attack is expected tomorrow morning and we may have to move quickly.

Uncle Charlie had a quiet, easy day due to the 11 Set being closed down, meaning his only tasks were to make half-hourly call-ups to Brigade. This gave him the opportunity to write two letter cards home. I hope he enjoyed the quiet before the storm.

The War Diaries indicate that Charlie's regiment is permanently placed on the grid, for now at least, ready to face up to the expected enemy onslaught, thought to be imminent (see Appendix A) The tent had to come down, (even though Charlie had gone to bed in it) in readiness for action tomorrow morning.

Sat. 6th Mar.
Well, it's here. Heavy German attack started about 6-30a.m. We moved with Tac. Bde. to Operational Tac. Position about 7-0a.m. and got a severe shelling. No damage done to the White. Tank and infantry attacks all day and heavy shelling. Loads of Stuka's and M.E.'s. He did not break through. We knocked out 41 tanks and some guns. Battle considered to be going in our favour.

The anticipated pre-emptive enemy attack has arrived, announced with a fanfare of severe enemy shelling, supported from the air by action from Stuka's and M.E.'s. Cleverly, the Allies set a trap – an ambush – allowing the German tanks to come rolling in. Quietly, holding their nerve and with bated breath, the gunners[9] waited for the right moment to ensure success, before opening fire and letting loose their anti-tank weapons. Forty one enemy tanks were knocked out, and 476 Battery was successful in destroying guns and stopping an infantry attack. The Allies were well prepared and the German army was unable to break through their tough defences. When Charlie writes that there was no damage done to the White he is referring to the M3 Scout Car, often known as "the White" because it was manufactured by the White Motor Company of Cleveland, Ohio. It had various operational roles including patrol, scouting, command vehicle and ambulance. Uncle Charlie, still with the Commanding Officer, was travelling in this vehicle. Following their failed attack to break through the Allied defences the Afrika Korps and the Italian armies withdrew behind the Mareth Line and awaited the forthcoming British attack. All-in-all a pretty eventful day – not one designed to fall asleep out of boredom, that's for sure.

> *Sun. 7th Mar.*
> *We are still in battle position, but things have quietened down a lot. Jerry seems to have drawn in his horns. I think we have more men and stuff here than he bargained for. Plenty of air activity by both sides. At night we slept in an Arab house. Very warm and dry. First time I've slept in a building since Durban. Capt. Strutt and 476 Bty. did very well. Knocked out five 88mm guns which were shelling the Guards.*

After yesterday's challenging, pre-emptive strike by the German army, this day, thankfully, is much quieter. Uncle Charlie has written of the exploits of Captain Strutt and his men of 476 Battery, rising to the challenge of the German attack by knocking out five 88mm guns. From the Allies point of view yesterday was a very successful morale-boosting day, and on this night, the first one for seven months, Uncle Charlie slept in a house – a very warm and dry "Arab" one – a permanent, walled structure, which must have made a pleasant change from the usual insubstantial, cramped, portable sleeping arrangements of vehicles and tents.

Initially I wondered why the name "Strutt" sounded so familiar to me, and then I remembered that months previously I had found a letter penned by a certain Major M.F. Strutt written in November 1943, six months after Uncle Charlie was killed. Addressed to my grandparents, his letter explained to them how he had known their son. Apparently, Uncle Charlie had been one of his wireless operators; they had journeyed together all the way from El-Alamein to the Mareth Line. Captain Strutt (later promoted to Major) explained why it had taken him so long to write. He had been wounded; months had passed before he was fully fit again and able to return to duty. He felt the need to explain why he was so late in contacting my grandparents. He wrote that Charlie was dependable, always did his job, and had a ready smile, "even under the worst conditions". Major Strutt ended the letter by writing that if he himself had wanted any kind of epithet it would be the one he used to describe Charlie: "he did his duty."

It seems uncanny when Uncle Charlie writes of a certain Captain Strutt and then, nearly seventy years later, with the letters, the photographs and the diary, I discover a letter from that very same man who possibly knew Charlie Robinson as well as, if not better, than anyone. For five long months they travelled, worked and fought together. I believe Captain (later promoted to Major) Strutt was quite a man – mentioned in Charlie's diary twice, mentioned in the War Diaries three times for bravery in battle, wounded and evacuated. After returning to duty, finding that one of his wireless operators had been killed, and writing such a kind and thoughtful letter of condolence to Charlie's parents after so many months had passed, demonstrates the kind of man he was. The War Diaries have provided me with some background detail to Major Strutt's letter of condolence to my grandparents.[10]

Mon. 8th Mar.
Germans have withdrawn. We left the forward position and returned to main R.H.Q, 11 set closed down and 19 set went on to hourly calls. Closed down completely at 9-0p.m. Line through. Saw official description of battle. 33 enemy tanks were destroyed. We lost none at all! Good work. I suppose it's a matter of waiting until our attack starts now. Won't be long, I think.

The enemy's pre-emptive strike cost them dear with the loss of thirty three tanks – fighting vehicles they could ill afford to lose, and to make matters worse for the Germans, the Allies lost none. With spirits riding high, Charlie's regiment moved back to its former area without loss (apart from damaged tyres). Conversely, it was a poor day for morale within the German army: losing so many tanks and guns, knowing that the Allies, strong after their comprehensive victory, and with tails up, were preparing to do battle again.

> *Tues. 9th Mar.*
> *A very quiet day. Nothing to do and all day to do it in. McCully made two sausage duffs. Made Hay and McHugh ill! BBC news says that a total of 52 tanks of Jerry's were knocked out during the battle. Wrote letter card No. 2 home.*

Nothing to do today but eat McCully's sausage duff – so heavy it caused Hay and McHugh to be ill. McCully would have done much for the War effort by offering his lethal food to the German Army, and watch them fall by the wayside, one by one! Uncle Charlie is sticking to his letter numbering plan, and written letter card No. 2. home. There is more good news when the BBC announces a final total of 52 German tanks destroyed during the battle.

On this day Rommel left North Africa and travelled to the Ukraine to see Hitler. Rommel told his Fuhrer that he believed the German army should return to Europe, regroup, re-arm and bed down to prepare for battle there, as he believed the North Africa campaign was now lost. But Hitler would not countenance Rommel's proposal. The dictator saw himself as invincible, and one step in retreat would be a denial of his invincibility. As Hitler was unable to see the logic of Rommel's plan, he made the mistake of stubbornly fighting to the very end of the campaign in North Africa, losing two hundred and fifty thousand German and Italian soldiers when they became Allied prisoners of war after the surrender in Tunis. Due to his intransigence, Hitler had seriously depleted his own army. Rommel, on sick leave, was replaced by Von Arnim.

Wed. 10ᵗʰ Mar.
McCully made a sultana duff today – marvellous – had four pieces. Had a look inside a Sherman tank There isn't very much room inside, glad I don't ride in one. More talk of the Reg. going into the desert shortly. Seems as if it is actually going to come off. Listened to BBC news. Germans are advancing a little towards Kharkov. Hope Russians hold them.

McCully seems to have greatly improved his "duff" making skills, with a sultana duff that tasted so good it led to Charlie – the expert on sweets, puddings and desserts – eating four pieces! Rumours are still circulating regarding the Regiment moving into the desert, which may or may not happen.

Due to his role as wireless operator Charlie gets to hear all the latest news from the BBC. It occurs to me, as I type these three universally known capital letters that the Corporation, which has become such a part of daily life for millions of people today, connecting them to world-wide events, through television and radio, began in 1922 with John Reith's pioneering work on public service broadcasting. In the 1930s the Empire Service began, which was the forerunner to today's World Service. This has reached people who would otherwise be cut off from others: those who live in war-torn countries, isolated communities, and citizens who just need to hear a steady voice, providing a life-line to the outside world. What a marvellous invention – a world-wide service to mankind.

The radio was vital to the progress of the second World War; not only did it broadcast Winston Churchill's inspiring speeches, it also provided light entertainment which helped to raise the spirit of the British people, kept everyone up to date with news about the progress of the war, and allowed Uncle Charlie, like so many others far from home, to hear that steady, comforting, pitch-perfect voice, with its familiar unemotional tones, reading the latest news. Moreover, the BBC had standards to uphold. All evening newsreaders were formally attired in evening dress, despite the fact that nobody could see them! It set the standard for news: if the newsreader was dressed appropriately, their speech and unflappable demeanor would pass through the airwaves to be received by all who listened.[11]

The war was continuing on the Eastern front, with yo-yoing wins and defeats between the German and Russian armies. At the beginning of February the Russians recaptured Kharkov, but by the 19th February the Germans re-launched a counter-strike. The Russians bravely resisted, which led to house-to-house fighting before SS Panzer Division prevailed and recaptured the city on the 15th March. Unfortunately, Charlie's wish on this day for the Russians to hold off the Germans did not come about.

Thur. 11th Mar.
Same position. Still resting. Had my hair cut. Received three letters from home and one from Eric Holmes' wife. Came in two weeks, not bad. Listened to news in evening. Jerry attacked W. of Tatahouine – we knew nothing about it!

Fri. 12th Mar.
Same position. Wrote letter-card no. 3 home. Nothing much happened today. Very hot. Got rations for 10 days ready for move. Expect the last battle in N. Africa to start shortly. It will be great to see the last of Jerry in Africa. The question is where then? Italy, India, or home?

Still counting the letters, Charlie writes No. 3 home. He knows the end is in sight for the Allies in North Africa, but fortunately cannot foresee the days of mental trauma he will face in the next few weeks of heavy fighting. I notice he writes "Italy, India or home?" – home is the last and most important word of the day.

Sat. 13th Mar.
Same position. Having a holiday here. Our bombers are beginning to fly over again. – 18 today. 17 came back. Got airgraphs from Mrs. Holden and Ruth Pearson. There's really nothing doing these days. We are just lounging about reading and preparing meals!

The quiet before the storm. Enjoy the "holiday" while you can, Charlie. The bombers are taking off, and it is only a matter of time before 111 Field Regiment is in action again.

Sun. 14th Mar.
I spoke too soon. We moved off at 4-0p.m.back to Ben Gardane. Arrived at 11-0p.m. Lost 2 Armd. Had no bed or rations. Shared Elliot's bed. Loads of stuff moving up to Mareth Line. Looks like big battle shortly. Hope it's the final one.

Captain Strutt has been appointed to command 476 Battery – a just reward – following his decisive leadership in overseeing the destruction of five German 88mm guns on the 6th March. My Uncle is on the move again and somehow managed to lose 2nd Armoured, so what exactly happened I am not sure. After having nothing to eat, Charlie had to share a bed with Elliot, so a less than perfect day. What a difference a day makes: a "holiday" yesterday and no bed and no food today! Capt. (now Major Strutt) is in the news again, following his promotion. Charlie was not wrong when he wrote he had heard rumours about his regiment moving into the desert. They were not merely rumours, but a plan of action. The regiment, now part of the New Zealand Division, has moved south to Ben Gardane, a coastal town, 559km from the capital, Tunis, and not far from the border with Libya. The reason for this move is to begin an outflanking manoeuvre – to pass into the desert, entering the Tebago Gap from the Western end and to re-emerge on the coastal plain, thereby surprising the enemy by coming up behind the Mareth Line.

When the fortifications on the Mareth Line were built by the French, they believed that an enemy would have no viable alternative to attacking this narrow line head on, giving the defenders of the line a distinct advantage. An outflanking manoeuvre was thought to be impossible, given the sea and the Matmata hills on one side, and the impossibly rough desert terrain on the other, making the route impassable to mechanised transport. For these reasons, an enemy would be forced to attack a more easily defendable narrow line, and this is the area to which the Germans have retreated.

However, the Allies believed an out-flanking manoeuvre *was* possible for two reasons. Firstly the improvements made to military vehicles since the fortifications were built in the 1930s had led to purpose-built vehicles with four wheel drive and tracks, designed to cope much more efficiently with the kind of desert terrain they had to traverse. And not forgetting the men who drove and maintained these vehicles – soldiers of the 8th Army – had become expert in keeping vehicles moving across difficult desert terrain. Another vital consideration was that any force in the desert could be well supplied from Medenine by way of Wilder's Gap. (See map below.)

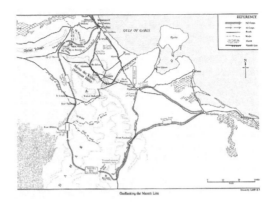

Outflanking the Mareth Line.
nzetc.victoria.ac.nz/tm/scholarly/WH2Bard-fig-WH2Bar-fo25.html
Thank you to Neill Atkinson of the National Library of New Zealand for
permission to reproduce the image.

Mon. 15th Mar.
"Z" Armd. came in at 11-0a.m. Had our breakfast and then slept
until 4-0p.m. Moved off West and South into the desert at 7-0p.m.
Passed through Foum Tatahouine of which I've heard a lot. Quite a
big place – bigger than Medenine or Ben Gardane.

"Z Armd." is the 2nd New Zealand Armoured Division; the one
Charlie's regiment has now become a part of.

Tues. 16th Mar.
Arrived at concentration area at 7-0a.m. Were towed in! Had breakfast
and then slept until dinner time. Worked on car during day. Made
scones for dinner. Wrote letter-card No. 4 home. A lot of transport
down here.

Time to pause, plan, repair vehicles and rest the men ready for
battle.

3454037 Sgm. C. Robinson,
Royal Corps of Signals,
Att. 111 Fld. Reg. R.A.,
8th Army,
M.E.F.
16-3-43

Dear Mother and Dad,

Please excuse the pencil, but I can't find the ink at the moment. I suppose someone has borrowed it and forgotten to bring it back.

I had an airgraph from Mr. and Mrs. Holden the other day. They tell me that Walter Harrison is a prisoner in Italy. I suppose he was taken prisoner out here somewhere. Do you know where exactly? We have been very close to his Division at times and I've been on the lookout for him. I'm glad to hear he's in Italy and not Germany – they get better treatment in Italy, or so I'm led to believe. Still, it's tough luck for Walter, he couldn't have been out very long before he was taken, could he?

Here's the ink turned up again like a bad penny! What we shall do when this bottle is finished I don't know, unless we reach Tunis before it is finished! There are five of us sharing it as it is.

I heard from Ruth Pearson yesterday. She didn't say definitely, but I gathered that she and Cliff will be getting married this summer. She said that she had heard from Stanley Lowe who was hoping to be home for the wedding. Well, this rumour about the Eighth Army going home after this campaign is over is still as prevalent as ever, but I have my doubts. There is a chance, of course, of our going home for a rest and re-fitting before our next little do. I sincerely hope so. It would be marvellous to have a week or two at home, wouldn't it? But I must not hope for too much.

How's the new electric fire going on? It's to be hoped you are not having any trouble with it. If Dad tries to repair it, he'll probably put *the whole of Hyde in darkness! You won't need to use any coal at all, this summer will you, and you'll have a good stock to start the winter with.*

Do you ever hear from the Raby's? I often wonder how they are getting along. Especially Rod and Paul. I never did write to Roderick, you know, and I've lost his address now. I should like to know what has been happening to him. Is Paul still in Canada? He's a lucky blighter if he is. It's getting near dinner-time now and we have a "Duff" to make so I must be rushing on. It takes about 45 minutes to boil a "Duff" so we have to get it on early. It's Tuesday today. Is it still potato pie day at home? I could sink two plates full right now. But enough of this gluttonous talk.

I think I shall write to Mr. and Mrs. Holden tomorrow. I was delighted to hear from them. Your next letter is due on the 20th (I write it on the 20th I mean) I'm trying to write every fourth day, so you should be getting plenty nowadays. That's all for now.

Cheerio,

Charlie.

The first two paragraphs of Uncle Charlie's letter – number four to his family- are written in pencil (at least Charlie takes the trouble to sharpen it, unlike the War Diaries which standard practice seems to dictate they must be written in the bluntest possible pencil!) Charlie apologises for using a pencil before the precious ink turns up. It is so unfair that five men have to share one bottle of ink for such an important task as keeping in touch with friends and family. After all a pencil is used to write everyday notes to the milkman; for important homeward-bound letters a pencil just doesn't cut it. Will the bottle run dry before they reach Tunis? Probably. Interestingly, when I compare the paragraphs written in pencil with those written in ink there appears to be no deterioration in either. To think, after almost seventy years pencil, ink and paper look as fresh as the day they were written. I think of Uncle Charlie, a young man of twenty five years, in his vehicle, or in his tent, surrounded by sand, big guns and all the weapons of war, writing this letter over two years before I was born; and here I am, now in my mid-sixties reading that very same communication from so long ago.

How strange. I have just had a flash-back to a childhood memory of my grandfather writing with a tiny stump of a pencil he had sharpened so many times, it was barely long enough to hold properly. He was not one to waste money on a new pencil when he could make the current one last – hopefully – for months! He also made his razor blades last longer by sharpening them against the rim of a glass. Those were the days when money was tight and nothing was wasted. A penny saved was a penny earned.

In his next paragraph Uncle Charlie expresses the generally well known fact that the present campaign is coming to an end, and of course rumours are flying round that the Eighth Army will be going home, at least for some leave if not permanently. He hardly dare believe he could actually be going home after so many long months away. Nevertheless, Charlie lives in hope – a small, but very powerful, four letter word. It has the strength to lift the spirit, only faces forward, and most importantly, provides the means to carry on.

Charlie's Mum and Dad have been splashing the cash on a new electric fire. Judging from Charlie's comment, I think he didn't have much confidence in granddad's ability to mend things, so hopefully it will not break down. The good thing to come with the electric fire is that it will solve the problem of any coal shortages this coming winter.

Uncle Charlie wonders if the Tuesday menu at home still includes potato pie, his favourite meal. Out in North Africa, he has to make do with a "duff" or pudding which takes forty five minutes to boil. The duff is probably another reason to wish he was back home, as there can be no comparison between a duff and his mother's potato pie.

Charlie is trying to stick to his promise of writing every fourth day. It must be difficult for him to think of something to say when there is so much he *could* write if it wasn't for the censor. But he knows how important it is to his family when they receive a letter from him: how it puts their minds at rest, if only in the short term.

> *Wed. 17th Mar.*
> *Same place. Still no wireless. Nothing at all to report. Rained today.*

Nothing written in the War Diaries either.

> *Thur. 18th Mar.*
> *Prepared to move at 5-0p.m. but didn't. Main R.H.Q. moved off. Rained again all day. Sutcliffe left us, thank goodness. Canteen opened – have now 470 fags! Made scones in the evening.*

Nothing written in the War Diaries again.

The above diary entry seems a little untidy today; the perfect spacing is absent, and a capital letter has been missed off. Also the number of cigarettes seems excessive. However, I have re-examined this day's diary entry very carefully with a magnifying glass and the figure is definitely 470. This imprecise writing is most unlike Charlie. Perhaps the incessant rain has made him a little careless. At least there is some good news, Sutcliffe (whoever he is) has left, which seems to have produced a sigh of relief. Charlie must still be with Tac.H.Q. as main H.Q. has moved off. I think this must be the quiet before the storm of battle, which is about to begin.

Fri. 19th Mar.
Were told to be ready to move by 1000hrs. Then 1300hrs then 1400.
Finally moved off at 5-0p.m. White broke down. I took all night to
reach new location! Got no sleep.

Uncle Charlie's vehicle, the White has broken down, leading
to a frantic search for the new location – and a sleepless night
– but they got there in the end. It cannot be a comfortable
feeling being out in the wilderness, separated from everyone
else. Meanwhile, the rest of NZ Corps travelled about thirty
miles, negotiating numerous wadis and sand dunes before
reaching the next staging area about thirty miles distant, just
after midnight.[12] The outflanking-manoeuvre, going deep into
the desert is well underway.

Sat. 20th Mar.
Changed White for a Marmon Herrington armoured car. There isn't
very much room but the plating is thicker. Were shelled about dinner
time but advanced quite a few miles. Closed down when in leaguer area.

Uncle Charlie has had to change from the unreliable White,
to a Marmon Herrington[13] Armoured Car. The downside to
this change means the new vehicle is not as roomy inside, but
the upside means they do have more protection inside a vehicle
with thicker plating, which would tick some boxes for Health
and Safety if there had been such a thing in 1943! They managed
to dodge enemy shells at dinner time and lived to fight another
day.

It was on the night of the 20th/21st March that a planned
combined attack on the Mareth Line was to begin. 30 Corps
was to start the main offensive directly on the Mareth Line,
while N.Z, Corps was to begin the outflanking attack on the
Gabes-Matmata road at the same time.

The 8th Armoured Brigade (containing Charlie's Regiment) were placed third in the order of march, out of a grouping of ten. Their objective was to capture the entrance to the Tebaga Gap. Meanwhile, 30 Corps was to break through the Mareth Line and advance along the main road to capture Gabes (see map 'Outflanking the Mareth Line' on page 167). This follows the plan made by the commanders on the 26th February, named "Operation Pugilist": "once operations have begun on the night 20-21st March, they will be conducted relentlessly until Sfax has been reached." Quote from Major General W.G. Stevens: "Bardia to Enfidaville." New Zealand Corps Operation Order No. 1.

The Allied objective was to take control of the coastal road, thereby blocking the enemy's escape route. Uncle Charlie would have to be on his toes as the above account states there were specific instructions for periods of wireless silence. Also employed were means of recognising Allied troops, plus target marking symbols for the enemy. Precision was vital to ensure accurate bombing by the desert air force.

The plan was for the 8th Armoured Brigade to break through the Eastern end of the enemy's defences; but it was not to be. Combining complex operations, given the mine fields, the harsh, rocky terrain and the barbed wire encountered by some units, resulted in slowing down progress and was proving impossible to co-ordinate, as the advance had become a stuttering, stop-start, piecemeal affair. Therefore, the planned offensive had to be postponed. Frustratingly, the rest of the day was spent on reconnaissance.

Notes

1 "Notes on Tactics and Techniques of Desert Warfare." by Major General George S. Patton, Jnr. 1942

2 See Appendix B – "Charles Robinson. Military Timeline".

3 "A Tale of Two Cities" by Charles Dickens is set in London and Paris during the French revolution. Written in 1859, the book compares the poverty in Paris with that of London, and highlights the cruelty of the aristocrats in France which led to the uprising of the impoverished population and ultimately to the revolution. It is also about love and bravery.

4 "Wireless Set 11 was a portable transceiver developed in 1938 as a general purpose low power set. Used as a vehicle station (Truck/AFV). Range up to 20 miles. Very successful design superseded by No. 19 and 22." Thanks once again to the comprehensive Website of Louis Meulstee's "Wireless for the Warrior."

5 The Matriculation was replaced some years later with the G.C.E. 'O' Level examination.

6 The Teller (German word for plate) mine was an anti-tank device, rounded and shaped like a plate. It reacted to pressure, usually of at least 200lbs. Only when the pressure was released, did it set off the explosive device within it. The 'S' version was designed specifically for use in the desert as its outer was composed of a ridged surface which prevented the covering of sand from being blown off and revealing its presence.

7 A field regiment, commanded by a Lieutenant Colonel, consisted of three batteries and a headquarters. Each battery, the basic fire unit, commanded by a Major, contained a troop of four guns; each troop was commanded by a captain.

8 Slang for sixpence.

9 A single gunner, working as a member of a team of six on each gun, had a specific task to perform. Each man had a number which corresponded to his task, e.g. layer, breach operative, etc. He knew his place in the gun firing order and acted accordingly.

10 On 6th March, 1943, Captain Strutt and the men of 476 Battery knocked out several enemy tanks. Following this action Captain Strutt was promoted to Major on 14th March and placed in command of 476 Battery. On 24th March he was wounded and evacuated, and on 13th April he was awarded the Military Cross for his actions the previous month.

11 The BBC was formed on the 22nd November 1922. On the 20th Anniversary of its formation – November, 1942 – Charlie's regiment was collecting salvage the Germans had left behind after the battle of El-Alamein, before making its way across North Africa. On the 22nd November, 2012, as I was listening to Radio 4, an announcement was made that the BBC had reached its 90th Anniversary.

12 New Zealand Electronic Text Centre: "Bardia to Enfidaville" by Major General W.G. Stevens.

13 At the outbreak of the Second World War, the weak South African motor industry needed to import parts from different manufacturers, and the Marmon Herrington Armoured car was no different. The vehicle was fitted with a four-wheel-drive train produced by the American company Marmon Herrington – hence the name. For British service in the Middle East, the Mark 11 was fitted with a Bren machine gun and a Boys anti-tank rifle.

CHAPTER ELEVEN

Hellish Shelling

Sun. 21st Mar.

Moved during morning but static after 12-0 noon. Fair amount of shelling. A lot of air activity during the night. Did not close down until 11-0p.m. Line was not through until then.

Apart from the shelling, and some progress from both batteries and regiments, the day was not too eventful.

Mon. 22nd Mar.

Moved at first light into a small Wadi. Were shelled and strafed heavily all day. One shell landed only three yards away! Ally Hay was wounded by shrapnel from it – 5 pieces in him, one in the small of his back. Hope he will be O.K. Poor old Al. Mr. Hugo sent up Cpl. Goodwin from the A.A. Sigs.

Major General Stevens[1] explains that the plan was to send the infantry in first which would open up a gap for the 8th Armoured to roll its big guns and tanks into. And although the initial infantry attack was successful, the 8th Armoured faltered, not following up quickly enough, thereby losing the advantage and allowing the enemy time to reform and regroup. Before evening the 21st Panzer Division was on the scene – moved up swiftly by the German commanders. This Division was a much tougher proposition than the Italian troops it had replaced, and therefore, there was very little progress made by the Allies as they were bombed, shelled, and machine-gunned from the air.

During times of War it is a given there will be casualties. All are regretted to a lesser or greater degree. Some are just names, others are good friends. Ally Hay, Uncle Charlie's fellow wireless operator has been wounded. Looking back in Charlie's diary I notice Ally was first mentioned on the 2nd January as he and Charlie erected a wireless aerial together; and again on the 12th February when they put up a "first rate bivvy." to keep out the rain after Charlie's blankets had been soaking wet for two days. I can only imagine how it feels to see a close friend and comrade in arms seriously wounded, only feet away from oneself; someone you have shared a life so closely with: eating, sleeping, sharing the days, weeks, months, the hardships, the quiet days, the days when you have both been scared witless; the days of shared laughter over some incident or joke. A close bond has been formed out of intense shared experiences. As "poor old Al." leaves the theatre of war for treatment to his wounds the replacement is on his way.

Tues. 23rd Mar.
Stayed in same Wadi. Shelled very heavily all day. It was hellish. A Colonel of the Tank Corps. and L/Cpl. were both killed. One shell landed only one yard away from the Marmon Herrington.

Reg. War Diaries: *Strafing by enemy continued. Capt. F.W. Gifford and several O.R's killed. Lt's. Charlesworth and Deer and about ten O.R's with wounds. Engaged enemy heavily, firing some 900 rds. during day. H.Q. established at 882041 for night, the Btys. being deployed to North and East of this.*

Major General W.G. Stevens' account of the day describes a frustrating, confusing one, with very few gains made by the

Allies. During the night the enemy had filtered back into the area, and enemy fire was enough to cause some Allied troops to retire. On this day the whereabouts of the 10th Panzer Division was uncertain. Unsure whether the Panzer Group had turned to face the Americans in the North, or were preparing to engage with the 8th Army, reconnaissance assistance was requested to discover the enemy's exact position. The answer came straight back that the Panzers were going to engage the Americans, but to be sure, they would monitor progress. 6th Field Company Engineers lifted a huge number of (between four and five hundred) mines; and another party of engineers began work on building an evacuation landing strip, which was finished the next day. Also, 500, mostly Italian, prisoners were captured.

Major General Stevens, in an understatement, concluded: "The day was an unsatisfactory one." Uncle Charlie describes his day as "hellish" and it is probably the most accurate word to describe a day about as far away from heaven as it is possible to get: stuck in a Wadi, with shells exploding all around all day long – the ear-splitting noise, the constant fear, the unrelieved stress; also knowing that others have been killed; without exaggerating, he is describing a kind of living hell. Remembering his diary is personal, the entries are usually quite factual, and he is not given to literary excesses and hyperbole, I can only conclude he truly has had a hellish day. His fear must have been at its height when a shell landed only one yard away from the vehicle; but Charlie's luck held today, as the shell didn't have his name on it. That particular personalised piece of ammunition would do its worst about seven weeks later.

Wed. 24th Mar.
We moved into a General Grant tank[2] as the A/C is again U.S.
Moved at first light. Very heavy shelling. Major Wale injured, Capt.

Hackett killed. The ridge which Jerry was holding is now in our hands, thanks to heavy concentration from Reg.

Reg. War Diaries: *Throughout day Rgt. engaged successfully enemy concentration as Rgmtal. Targets. Cmmd. 8th Armd. Bde. congratulated Rgmt. on its performance. Btys. were deployed in areas 8608 and H.Q. was established at 885060.*

1430hrs. Majors Strutt and Wale and Capt A… wounded, and evacuated. Capt. Hackett was killed. Several O.R.'s were also wounded. Rgt. was continually bombed and shelled during day.

Uncle Charlie is now travelling in a General Grant tank. Today seems to be a continuation of yesterday, with no let-up in the heavy shelling, resulting in Majors Strutt and Wale being wounded and evacuated and Captain Hackett losing his life. But overall there has been a victory for the regiment as, under continuous fire, they have made progress, taking ground previously occupied by the enemy. The commander of the 8th Armoured Brigade congratulated the men on their performance.

Thur. 25th Mar.
Same place. Shelling still as bad, beginning to tell a tale on me, I'm getting nervous. Moody came at 12-0 noon with relief. I'm going to battle H.Q. for a rest. Thank God. Up to tonight 212 Bty alone have lost 45 men.

After days of fierce fighting, although the routing of the enemy was not as comprehensive and the ground gained was less than the 8th Army would have liked, nevertheless there had been one major gain – the entrance to the Tebaga Gap had been secured, and: "a force of all arms threatened the enemy's flank and compelled him to react and redistribute his Divisions."[3]
It is a successful end to "Operation Pugilist" – the name of the

campaign for the fight to control the Mareth Line. Time to move on to the next stage.

But it has been a hard won victory with many losses. The fierce fighting resulted in forty five men losing their lives from 212 Battery alone. The constant bombardment has taken its toll in terms of loss of life and, for some, loss of nerve. Uncle Charlie is feeling the mental pressure when he writes: "It is beginning to tell a tale on me. I'm getting nervous." This is probably an understatement, as Charlie is not one to exaggerate. I'm not surprised, as I don't know how it is possible to hold your nerve when your life could be snuffed out at any second. Also, you are painfully aware that only three days ago your fellow wireless operator had been wounded and evacuated, and you pray he will survive. How do you manage to sit before a wireless set, as the never-ending bangs, crashes and thumps continue – trying to concentrate on the vitally important messages you are sending and receiving? Indeed, how can you think logically at all – amongst that amount of chaos? Additionally, in some dark place in your mind you are aware of forty five men losing their lives in one of the batteries attached to your regiment. Not surprisingly, the last few days of unremitting action have mentally taken their toll on Uncle Charlie. As a committed Christian, he writes a two-word heartfelt sentence: "Thank God" – for being given the opportunity to have a rest at H.Q.

Fri 26th Mar.
Didn't get up until 8-0. Had a great sleep. Fairly quiet here. Washed my hair & feet. Got five letters from home and one from Jessie Morton. I don't know when I'm going to write home again. We put up a heavy barrage between 4-30 & 6-0. Successful. Advance started. 350 Jerry prisoners.

After a good night's sleep, Charlie feels refreshed mentally and physically (he was able to wash his hair and feet). Also he enjoyed the added relaxation of a quiet day and the pleasure of reading five letters from home and one from his friend Jessie Morton. It has been a good day for the regiment too, having moved well forward, and achieving a "brew up" or a direct hit on an enemy objective. The Division has also captured 350 German prisoners.

> *Sat. 27th Mar.*
> *Advance continues. Now only eight miles from El Hamma. Major Barnes wanted a wireless op. to go out with him and of course, yours truly landed the job. The table came adrift and I had to hold it in! I don't know when I shall get back to main H.Q. now. Taylor is coming up to relieve me, sometime. Moved during night towards El Hamma.*

Uncle Charlie is on the move as Major Barnes's wireless operator, something Charlie is not too happy about; the table coming adrift did not improve his mood either! He hopes Taylor will not be long before coming to relieve him, and he can return to main H.Q. They are now only eight miles from El Hamma.

> *Sun. 28th Mar.*
> *Moved during night. Advanced another six miles. Were shelled again all day, but only lightly. Felt shaky in a "soft" vehicle. No sign of Taylor. Hope he comes soon. Am browned off with this C.O.2 job. It will be a holiday at Main. Jerry is reported to be evacuating Mareth Line. Will meet us shortly.*

General Freyberg[4] (C.O. New Zealand Corps) felt that rather than piling up in formation at El Hamma, it made more tactical sense to go directly to Gabes, avoiding the El Hamma bottleneck.

New Zealand Corps was to forge ahead at first light on this day and make for Oglat-Merteba – Gabes. A request for air cover for the NZ move was made. The 8th Armoured Brigade, containing 111 Field Regiment are now in the vanguard, forging ahead, ready to clash yet again with the German Army.

Uncle Charlie, still unhappy, is travelling with the second in command, in a "soft" vehicle, which I can only assume is without armour plating. Also, there is no sign of Charlie's relief showing up. The War Diaries report the meeting of some slight opposition before settling down for the night. I count myself lucky that right now I have the very best of all worlds: Uncle Charlie's diary, the War Diaries, and the official New Zealand Corps account of the action from Major General W.G. Stevens, which provides me with the theory and an overview of events.

I must pass on a fascinating story which has emerged from Major General Stevens' account of this day: 5 Brigade Group had rounded up some prisoners, and in recognition of a "worthy foe" Brigadier Kippenberger (2nd in command of New Zealand Division) invited the enemy commanding officer and his adjutant to take breakfast with him – the Adjutant acting as interpreter. Kippenberger then gave permission for the enemy C.O. to address his men, before they were rounded up and put into a prisoners' cage. The enemy C.O. and his adjutant were sent off in a 15cwt truck, and took with them, in the Brigade Major's words: "The sympathy of those who watched, for they showed good qualities to the very end." Gentlemanly conduct all round.

Mon. 29th Mar.
Moved off again at 5-30a.m. No opposition during morning.
Mareth Line broken, being mopped up by 50 Div. and 51st
Div. reported in Gabes. We passed Gabes in the South about

1-0p.m. Were shelled by Jerry's rearguard in the afternoon. Taylor has arrived. Took my kit off C.O.2 and put it on Signal Office. Pleased to go back for a time.

Uncle Charlie is pleased to be relieved by Taylor and back on the Signal Office truck. They reached their objective of Gabes at 1-0p.m., but were later shelled by the German rearguard.

The following map represents the 2nd New Zealand Division's route from Gabes to Enfidaville, charting Uncle Charlie's final journey. Thanks are due once again to Neill Atkinson of the National Library of New Zealand for permission to reproduce the image.

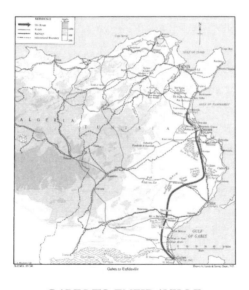

GABES TO ENFIDAVILLE.
http://nzetc.victoria.ac.nz/tm/scholarly/WH2.Bard-fig-WH2Bar-f057.html

Tues. 30th Mar.

Wrote letter No. 5 home. Left battle at 0600 hrs. with Sgt. Drew &
petrol truck. Met a battery truck on the way back and they handed over
to us a German prisoner. He rode on top of the cab next to me. He was
only about 18 and seemed quite harmless. I suppose he was dragged
into the war like myself. Had a lovely quiet day at Main. Jimmy Kay
was on duty on the Admin. Office set today. Stevie and I made some
bully and potato fritters, made far too much and had to sling some.
Junkers 88 raided at dusk.[5]

On his way back to Main Headquarters Uncle Charlie finds
himself sitting beside the enemy in the form of a young German
prisoner of the Afrika Korps. The British Tommy becomes
conscious of the fact that, sitting with the German on the front
of the battery truck, they have much in common: as soldiers,
as human beings with family and friends, thrust into combat
without much enthusiasm for fighting, doing their duty; the
only difference is that they are fighting on opposing sides. Both
soldiers are the owners of frail bodies that can be damaged or
snuffed out at any time. Today Uncle Charlie sees the human
face of the enemy.

On this day, Montgomery sent a message of congratulation to
the 2nd N.Z. Division:

> *on splendid results achieved by the left hook. These results have led*
> *to the complete disintegration of the enemy resistance and the whole*
> *Mareth position.*

Travelling deep into the desert and then swinging up to meet
the enemy in a surprise move has been a brilliant tactical
manoeuvre and a complete success.

3454037 Sgm. C. Robinson,
Royal Corps of Signals,
Att. 111 Fld. Reg., R.A.,
8th Army,
M.E.F.
30-3-43

Dear Mother and Dad,

There has been a big delay between letters four and five, I know, and regret, but I just have not been able to find time. If you've been listening carefully to the news, these days you will no doubt realise the reason. At the moment, though I have time, and will use it. I'm quite alright, although I've had several shocks and scares. Enemy shelling and strafing has been fairly heavy, and close. My co-operator on the Armoured Car, Al Hay, was wounded a few days ago. The shell landed only three yards away from the car. I was inside, and he was outside, shaving and caught a load of shrapnel. He has five pieces in him, but four will prove quite harmless, it is thought. The fifth, which entered just below his ribs, in his side, may be a nasty one. I sincerely hope he'll be alright. It was a lucky thing for me that I got in the car. I had been sitting on the bank, at the side of the car, about two yards in front of where the shell landed, until three or four minutes before it came. They had started dropping close and I decided that discretion is the better part of valour and got in. There will be more good luck stories later.

Four or five days ago I received a small bundle of mail. They were all letter-cards, mothers of the 11th Feb., dads of the 15th and 22nd of Feb and the 6th March, and Marjorie's of the 6th March. Thank you very much. I had a great time reading them. I'm glad you told me how much I'm worth, it isn't too bad is it? It should mount up quicker now that I'm sending 10/6 per week home. Sorry to hear about the alarm clock. I hope you've managed to get hold of one by now. As for me sending you one, or anything else for that matter, well it's rather a joke to me. I wish I was in a place where I could buy alarm clocks – I'd buy a dozen for you! In one of your letters, you tell me about Vera Holden stepping out of one of her shoes. It's certainly queer and rather amusing. When I used to travel to work on the 8-8, Marjorie Jones' shoe once came off and fell between the train and the platform, on to the lines. They had to draw the train forward before we could recover it! I've had many a laugh about that.

Now then, mother, you say you have been reading some of my letters at the Ladies Meeting. Well, I don't know what to think about that. I only hope that they didn't sound too bad. As for Mrs. Redfern saying that you had spent the afternoon in Africa, well, I can't remember ever describing Africa in so much detail. You surprise me when you say that Harold Shaw is out here. I shall certainly look out for him. And Eric is in the R.W.F., well, well, I didn't think either would be in the Army.

Now, Marjorie, a little paragraph for you (this is a Scotsman's letter). You are quite right. In 1939 I didn't think I should ever see South Africa, Egypt, Cyrenaica, Tripolitania and Tunisia, but I have. I wonder which other countries I shall see before the war is over? I wouldn't mind seeing Blighty right now! Yes, I'm having some narrow escapes, but I'm still here to tell the tale, and after all, a miss is as good as a mile. I'm very glad to hear that you're doing so well at work, and earning so much money. You'll be able to save up for after the war, won't you? Yes, I'm sure, Marjorie that you are happy, and I sincerely hope that the war will be over soon and you will have Jim back home. It doesn't matter so much for us single blokes, although the idea of returning to 159 doesn't sound bad to me. My regards to Jim. Tell him to keep a careful watch.

That's all for now, everybody. I'll be seeing you.

Cheerio.

Charlie

Knowing that their son was out in North Africa with the 8th Army, I am sure my grandparents at that time were avidly listening to as many news reports as they could; for they would have known that following that first crucial victory at El-Alamein, so many months before, and after fighting their way across many miles of tough desert terrain, their son was one of a crack team of soldiers who have just won their second most valuable prize of the campaign: the Mareth Line.

It is just as well that Uncle Charlie can laugh about his father's bizarre request for an alarm clock. Is he just in denial about his son's situation, or is it some form of naivety about the type of countries he is travelling through and the nonexistence of alarm clock shops? His father's request is about as sensible as asking General Montgomery to provide a signed photograph of Adolf Hitler!

On a serious note, Uncle Charlie describes to his parents the near-miss which could have led to an injury – or worse, if he had stayed outside the vehicle like his co-wireless operator had. Ally Hay, the man Charlie has shared so many miles and experiences with, had caught five pieces of shrapnel, the fifth piece, entering his body under a rib, potentially doing the most serious damage. The emotional impact of Ally's injuries was deeply felt by Charlie.

My Uncle's financial affairs are never far from his mind, and receiving a pleasant surprise from grandma's letter regarding the total amount of his savings, he is now looking forward to saving 10/6 per week It is a sad fact that he would never have the chance to enjoy a penny of this hardest of hard-earned money, so carefully set aside. I am sure that had he survived the war (not one to waste money) he would have put his savings to good use.

I am cheered that Charlie is moved to remember amusing experiences in his previous life. He relates the story of Marjorie Jones' lost shoe falling between the train and the platform, resulting in the train being drawn forward in order to retrieve it. I wonder if today's guards would have time to come to the aid of a maiden in distress. I hope they would. The picture in my mind of Grandma, reading Charlie's letters, standing in front of a row of seated, self-contained, devoutly temperate members of the Chapel Ladies Meeting: ladies-in-hats-not-too-brightly-coloured – nor too "racy" is quite a vivid one.[6]

Underneath every hat, the wearer would be listening politely. During the interval, from a large urn, tea was poured into cups and saucers and biscuits served. Perhaps it was during the lady-like sipping (no slurping) interval that drew an effusive response from Mrs. Redfern, who felt she had been transported to Africa for the afternoon. This statement made Charlie laugh, as it did me. Although his letters are interesting, amusing and informative, they are not exactly a detailed travelogue of his experiences in North Africa. I suppose Mrs. Redfern was just enthusiastically showing her support.

In the final paragraph devoted to his sister, Charlie lists the countries he has visited: South Africa, Egypt, and Cyrenaica, (located on the Eastern side of Libya, peopled and self- administered as an Italian colony), Tripolitania – (another Italian colony, occupying the north western side of Libya), and finally Tunisia. Despite his dearest wish he will not see number 159 again. His final words, referring to my father are: 'Tell him to keep a careful watch' for he knows how precious her new husband is to his sister.

Wed. 31ˢᵗ Mar.

Worked the 11set in the Admin. Office today. The control set at Tac. H.Q. is ten miles away. I heard it very faintly but they didn't hear me. We moved at 4-0 p.m. down to the beach. The whole regiment has pulled out of the line for a two day rest. They certainly need it. Got in position on the beach about 6-0 p.m. All sets closed down – lines out.

Had some chocolate from the Staffs canteen. It was pretty poor stuff but
I enjoyed it, I haven't had any for such a long time.

Uncle Charlie is relieved to have a day of rest in front of
him and writes "they certainly need it" when referring to the
work rate of his fellow soldiers. As a member of the Royal
Corps of Signals, Charlie, is just attached to the regiment, but
nevertheless he still experiences the same dangers as his fellow
soldiers.

Tac.H.Q. where Charlie was based previously, is now ten
miles out in front, and for a short period the whole regiment
can enjoy some relaxation without having to worry about
exploding shells. For the first time in a long time, Charlie, gets
the chance to taste some poor quality chocolate, and still enjoys
it! Sometimes it is the small things in life that make a difference
and can lift the spirits. Of course, back home, his family would
not have the chance to enjoy much chocolate either, whatever
the quality, due to food rationing.

Thur. 1st Apr.
Did not get up until 7-45. Cleared out the truck and straightened
things up a little. Had a swim in the Med. in the afternoon.
Glorious. First time since Boxing Day. What a long way we
have come since then! Col. Hill promoted Brigadier. New colonel
(Hobbs)[7] arrived.

On a rest day, Charlie reflects on the hundreds of miles he
has travelled since boxing day last year, when he last enjoyed a
'glorious' swim in the Med.

Fri. 2nd Apr.
Got up at 7-30. Went over to Admin. for breakfast. Swam in Med.
in afternoon. Short and sharp air-raid about dusk. Road bombed. Got

two letters from home and one from Elsie, bless her. Wish she would
write more often.

Reg. War Diaries: *Lt. Col. W.P. Hobbs, M.B.E., R.A. assuming*
cmd. of 111 Fld. Regt., R.A. Vice Lt. Col. J.G. Hill, M.B.E., M.C.,
R.A. on the latter's promotion to Brigadier, C.R.A. 50 Div.

Charlie enjoys a second day's 'holiday' and celebrates with
another swim. But what really makes his day is a long-awaited
letter from Elsie. She obviously means a great deal to him.

Sat. 3rd Apr.
Fairly cold today. Did not go for a swim. Wrote letter card No. 6 home
and one to Elsie. Had talk from new C.O.

I notice Charlie replied straight away to Elsie's letter which was
only received yesterday, so he must be keen. The War Diaries
record the arrival of some new vehicles.

Sun. 4th Apr.
General Montgomery came and inspected us. Gave us an informal
chat afterwards. He's an amusing speaker. Very sharp and eager
looking. Walked into Gabes with Jimmy Kay after Tiffin. Not a bad
little town. Loads of French flags flying. Air-raid at dusk. Were paid
400 francs, or £2. today.

Montgomery liked to keep a high profile, appearing in
person before his soldiers, presenting the human side of their
General. He did not want to be seen as some remote figure
in command. His presence would help to keep the morale
of his troops as high as possible, and during today's informal
talk, Uncle Charlie is impressed by his General's intelligent
optimism.

Mon. 5th Apr.

Moved off today at 3-0p.m. Took up position (Main) just across the road from where we were before. All quiet. Travelled with Jackie Stevenson. Jimmy Kay was on duty in Admin. Office. Picked up Italian copy of "Mein Kampf" – "La Mia Vita" by Adolf Hitler!

Uncle Charlie's choice of reading material seems strange: the Italian version of Adolf Hitler's "Mein Kampf" is an odd choice for an Englishman whose enemies are German and Italian. I doubt it could be classed as suitable bedtime reading, even if he could read Italian! However, he may have viewed the book as an unusual souvenir.

Written in 1925, Mein Kampf is part auto-biographical and part political theory. In the book, which is markedly anti-Semitic, Hitler warns against the rise of the Jewish race – a nascent belief then, which only comes to fruition during the war as the 'final solution' ; or the destruction of the Jews. Hitler's dream grew in the specially built concentration camps, housing barely alive human walking skeletons – unknown at this point in the war – but discovered by the Allies towards the end. Also, Hitler believed that it would be more humane to destroy the weak and the sick than letting them live. Hitler's political ideology alleged that by disposing of the Jews, the weak, the old and the sick, this action would result in the emergence of a strong German Master Race.

The regiment has moved into position, ready to meet the next encounter against those who, led by Adolf Hitler, were expected to believe in the ideology he promulgated.

Tues. 6th Apr.

On duty on set in Admin. Office. Our attack started at 0415 hrs. Big barrage. First objectives taken, 2000 to 3000 prisoners in. Never seen so many of our aircraft up before. Air support is magnificent.

Received two letter cards from home – mother and dad. Bombed at dusk. Nothing very close.

A total of 496 guns opened up simultaneously (the noise must have been deafening) but the enemy fired back, stubbornly refusing to surrender to the Allied barrage, which was compared to the first night's fierce attack at the start of El-Alamein Apparently, there was "magnificent" support from the R.A.F. which must have made a huge difference. Nevertheless, the task was not easy. The enemy counter-attacked strongly, and stalled the Allied advance, which was proving to be doubly difficult due to the number of mines laid by the enemy.

Wed. 7th Apr.
Moved off at 10-0 a.m. We travelled about 20 miles N.N.W. of Gabes. Finished in the dark. For the last hour there was a Junkers 88 bombing and strafing the column. Very unpleasant. Jimmy Kay jumped off the truck into a slit trench. Lost him. Started letter home.

The regiment made some progress today, but lost Jimmy Kay when he jumped off the truck. Matter of factly Charlie wrote: "Lost him. Started letter home."

Thur. 8th Apr.
Moved off at 7-0. Did about five miles and then stopped. Finished letter card No.7 home. Jimmy turned up early this morning. Saw loads of prisoners.

All three batteries were busy today and sustained casualties. Jimmy Kay turned up, but Charlie gave no explanation for his disappearance, and no clue as to where he spent the night. The advance continued very slowly over rough country. At times the bulldozers were called in to assist with flattening the surface.

Fri. 9ᵗʰ Apr.
Were moving nearly all day, did 35 to 40 miles. Raid by M.E.'s on
column about 11-0 a.m. Junkers 88s over at dusk and all night. Lot
of bombing, but nothing very near us. Country now cultivated. Very
pleasant. Are about 40 miles West of Sfax.

The regiment made good progress today. There was some
bombing activity but it did not get too close. Uncle Charlie
seems to be enjoying passing through a greener landscape.

Sat. 10ᵗʰ Apr.
Moved on again 40 miles today. Travelled through mile after mile
of olive groves. Saw thousands of poppies – big red ones. Lovely
countryside. Never expected it. Raid by Junkers 88 at dusk. Four
bombs fell 200 yards away near Arab village – poor innocents – hope
no one was hurt. Sfax fell this morning – Highland Division.

The regiment made good progress today, and, travelling
through the countryside, Charlie comments on the thousands
of poppies – "big red ones" lining the route as the soldiers pass
by. Since the end of the First World War, when the battle fields
of France and Belgium (where the bloodiest fighting took place)
were covered in poppies, their colour matching the blood shed
by thousands of soldiers, the poppy has become the symbol of
remembrance for those who have made the ultimate sacrifice.
It seems incongruous (apart from its blood-red colour) that this
innocent, fragile flower has become synonymous with death.
As I picture the tanks and armoured vehicles passing by the
nodding poppies, I imagine each one is paying a silent tribute to
a soldier as he passes. It feels like an omen – these poppies are
sending their tribute in advance of Charlie's own forthcoming
sacrifice. But, on this day, after so many months of enduring dry
desert conditions, with little greenery and no flowers, Charlie

would be unaware of the significance of the poppy – simply enjoying their colourful show.

In a strange coincidence, as I write these words on the evening of Sunday, 11th November, 2012, it is Remembrance Sunday, the 11th day of the 11th month, when poppies can be seen in abundance, laid on cenotaphs, and adorning the clothes of many citizens and ex-servicemen, as the nation honours those who have made the ultimate sacrifice beginning with the First World War, right up to the present day – the war in Afghanistan. I realise, without any prior planning, a strange coincidence is being revealed. I have recorded the Diary and letters in strict chronological order, writing each diary entry and letter in its time order. As I naturally reach this day's entry, I find myself reproducing Charlie's words on Remembrance Sunday as the Festival of Remembrance is being televised from the Royal Albert Hall. Copying his words at any other time of year would not have had the same impact. Yet tonight, as the red petals fall from the ceiling of the Royal Albert Hall during the two minute's silence, it feels like the nation is joining with me in honouring Uncle Charlie.

But it is not only the combatants of a conflict who lose their lives, sometimes the innocent can be caught up in the fighting. Uncle Charlie, revealing his kind-hearted spirit, realises that the enemy shells are landing close to an Arab village. He writes that he hopes these "poor innocents" are unhurt. I think in modern parlance, when civilians are accidentally killed the term used is "collateral damage". How much more heartfelt are Charlie's words: "poor innocents."?

Sun. 11th Apr.
Moved off at 1500 hrs. Travelled only 15 miles. Still mile after mile of olive groves. Our forces approaching Sousse – I wonder whether Jerry will try a "Dunkirk."

There was something of a stop-start situation today, as in the morning the Division was told there would be rest and reorganisation; the advance on Sousse would not take place until the next day. Then suddenly in the early evening the 8th Armoured was told to move towards Sousse. They had to detour the many road demolitions made by the retreating enemy, so progress was slow, and the engineers were very busy repairing the road surface.

Mon. 12th Apr.
Waited all day until 1700 hrs. before we moved. Then we went 38 kilometres along the main road. Finished up only 18 kilos. – 10½ miles – from Sousse which fell this morning. Jerry must be in a bad way now! Heard rumours that he is trying a Dunkirk. Wrote No. 8 home and to Mrs Smith.

The whole division was stretched out for 60 miles. Charlie's regiment must have been quite strung out too, as he left much later than the others. Also, while all three batteries were kept busy with the enemy, before bypassing Sousse, Uncle Charlie, seemed to have a quiet day, stopping ten miles short of the town.

As KDG were first to enter the town, they received a rapturous reception from the inhabitants, who presented the soldiers with flowers and bottles of wine. The locals told them that the enemy had left hurriedly, only minutes before. The German army might be retreating, but he certainly did not go quietly, engaging all three batteries from his rearguard. The engineers were kept very busy, repairing mined roads with huge craters in them. Also the enemy had laid charges on bridges, which needed to be made safe. All this work, combined with rough roads and a very rocky terrain forced the wheeled transport to use the newly repaired cratered and damaged roads, which further delayed the advance. Also, hindering progress, the terrain included huge cactus hedges with very narrow lanes between, which were difficult to negotiate; plus the aforementioned enemy rearguard shelling in which all three batteries had stopped to fight, meant that the advance was frustratingly much slower than planned. The enemy had succeeded in trashing the Allied plan, and was certainly not "in a bad way" as Charlie suggests, but on his way to bed down in Enfidaville, which will see the final desperate battles in the North Africa campaign.

> *Tues. 13th Apr.*
> *Moved off again at mid-day. Before doing so talked to an Arab in the village. who could speak French. Passed through Sousse. It was great. The people were beside themselves with joy. Girls were throwing flowers into the car. Everybody making the V sign. Giving away French flags. Made me feel I was fighting for something worth-while.*

In the morning, Charlie, being his usual friendly self, was able to have a conversation in French with a local man. This was followed in the afternoon by his regiment's triumphal march through Sousse. The enemy had hurriedly retreated from the town only minutes before the 8th Army's arrival, which makes their entry into town even more poignant and exciting for the local people. Charlie, for the first time in this campaign, felt that everything he had been through over the past seven months had been worthwhile: to witness their unadulterated joy as the people of Sousse are liberated from an occupying force gave him reason to be proud of all they had achieved. Tuesday, 13th April has been a good day for Charlie, his regiment, the 2nd New Zealand Division and the 8th Army.

But the good news does not end there, as the War Diaries record honours for Major M.F. Strutt, who has been awarded the Military Cross and Sgt. Roberts and Gunner Howarth who were both awarded the Military Medal for their "work" at Metameur on 6th March when, as members of 476 battery they: *"destroyed several enemy 88mm guns, and was instrumental in stopping an infantry attack."* It is a pity that merely eighteen days after these brave actions, on the 24th March, Major Strutt was wounded and evacuated.

Wed. 14th Apr.
Was sent for by Mr. Hugo to return to Battle H.Q. Knew it wouldn't be long. Am now on Adjutant's set. Moved up with George Grist – had the "Bridge Adventure." Saw Sgt. Read. I am very pleased to see that at last he has been promoted. Bit of shelling some distance away.

Under the command of Royal Artillery, 111 Field Regiment, 69 Medium, and 4, 5 and 6 Regiments are in position, ready once again to do battle. For the Allies the taking of Enfidaville is not going to be easy. I am not sure about the meaning of the "Bridge Adventure" unless Charlie is referring to the Bailey Bridge – a temporary bridge erected by the Royal Engineers.

Thur. 15th April.
Quiet day. Batteries did a little shooting. A single M.E. strafed in the morning, but did no damage. Lines out. Set closed. Had chicken for dinner.
Fri. 16th Apr.
Moved to a rest position for three or four days. Lines out again so set closed down. Wrote No. 9 home and one each to Eric Holmes and Margaret Ratcliffe. Received Xmas card from Elsie. Thought I should get one eventually. Had rabbit for dinner.

For two nights running the men have had a treat for dinner: chicken last night and rabbit tonight, which I assume would have been sourced locally. They will have savoured a welcome change from the usual bully beef, and both chicken and rabbit would be particularly welcome as a satisfying end to two restful days. The wireless sets have been closed down, the lines are out and action is on the horizon.

3454037 Sgm. C. Robinson,
Royal Corps of Signals,
Att. 111 Fld. Reg., R.A.,
M.E.F.,
16-4-43

9

Dear Mother and Dad,

Thanks for the mail I received two days ago. I got Dad's No. 3 of April 3rd and Mothers of March 31st. They really are coming through well at present. Yes, sometimes I'm "not in a position" to receive mail and it has to wait until I am. I was in a position to get the last delivery, and I certainly got them, six of them! That's the way I like to be handed mail. I had your two, one from Elsie, one from Jessie Morton, one from Eric Holmes, and, a pleasant surprise, this one, one from the C.H.A. at Ashton. It appears that they had just celebrated one of the club's birthdays and it was decided to write to all the members in the services. A girl who Cliff and I were friendly with at C.H.A. "Do's" wrote to me. I studied the sender's address for five minutes and I just couldn't imagine, until I opened it, who had sent it!

I've made inquiries amongst the blokes and have discovered that none of the altered allotments made at the same time as mine have got through. If nothing is heard shortly, we shall put in another form exactly the same as the other one. That should remind the pay office blokes.

I can well imagine you having a good laugh, mother, as you were climbing the steps at the Theatre. You seem to be able to laugh under practically any circumstances and you can't beat it. A laugh a day keeps the doctor away.

Two or three days ago I passed through a liberated French town. I don't think I've spent a grander and happier half-hour since I joined the Army. The people – men, women and children – were out in force, lining the streets. They smiled, they laughed, they jumped, yes, and they trembled with joy. The girls threw flowers into our truck and French flags. The mothers, whenever we stopped, opened the door and placed their babies into our arms. The fathers shook hands with us and wished us "Bon Voyage." The boys climbed on to the vehicle and rode through the town with us. It was like a carnival day, everybody was laughing and shouting as if they had just come out of prison, and so they had. I certainly didn't feel like a conquering hero, but I did feel a thrill of pride that I was one of many who had made this joy possible. We were greeted everywhere with cries of "Vive L' Angle Terre." I've never seen so many people looking absolutely carefree all at the same time. It was a great reward for months spent in the desert. It also gave us proof of what we are fighting for and strengthened our determination to liberate millions more. May the day soon come when the whole of occupied Europe will feel as happy and free as did the people of… I shall never forget passing through this town. We are drawing towards the end of this campaign now, and everyone is wondering "What is in store for the Eighth Army?" It can be anything and anywhere. Rumours are flying round, some people have definite information or "Pukka Griff" in our slang. However we must wait and see. For now, Cheerio, Charlie.

I think Charlie has excelled himself in the fourth paragraph of this – the final letter – in what I consider to be his best piece of writing to date. On reading this paragraph, I wonder if there could be a more descriptive, more vividly detailed piece of writing anywhere. His experience of passing triumphantly through Sousse (he could not name it in his letter for censorship reasons) made such an impact on his emotions that it led to a freely expressed, unrestrained, creative piece of writing. His words are normally amusing and informative, and he pens a very good letter; but this paragraph is a gemstone amongst the gold.

In writing these words to his family, Charlie brings to life the unforgettable scene played out before his eyes. The reader – rather like Alice in Wonderland – finds herself falling through the words on the page, landing with a bump in another world. Feeling like Alice, I can vividly 'hear' the shouts and cheers of the people of Sousse as the convoy passes through town. I can 'see' the colourful flowers landing softly (seen, but unheard) on the dull, hard shells of the vehicles of war. I can 'hear' the excited shouts of the local boys as they scramble to climb on the vehicles – thrilled to be riding in triumph with 'real' soldiers on 'real' tanks, trucks and armoured cars. These are soldiers' fighting vehicles, shared for a few moments with excited boys, who normally have to make do with pushing small cars along the ground. For soldiers, men, women and children alike, this day will never be forgotten. Now the invader has been seen off by the 8th Army, the people of Sousse are free. Is it any wonder that their gratitude and happiness overflows? Uncle Charlie modestly claims he doesn't feel like a conquering hero, but he does allow himself a feeling of pride – pride in a job well done, and as he absorbs the cries of joy, surrounded by so much happiness, he feels it is a just reward for all that sacrifice and hard work.

The fourth paragraph of Charlie's letter engendered quite an emotional effect on me. I felt touched that my Uncle – only weeks before his death – was deservedly given the opportunity, on entering Sousse, to feel a sense of satisfaction and pride in the culmination of almost two thousand hard, travelled miles. As he absorbed the spectacle of unbounded joy and gratitude of the local people, he knew it was a vindication of all he had been fighting for. But what really touched my emotions, as a mother and grandmother, was when Charlie related what happened whenever there was a pause in the procession: the door would open and a mother with babe in arms would enter the vehicle, and, showing complete trust, place her most precious possession in the arms of an unknown man – a soldier and a killer of men, trusting that his strong arms would be gentle enough to hold her baby, as he would his own child. I thought of the word "trust" realising there are so many levels to this small, five letter word. Surely, handing your precious child into the arms of an unknown foreign soldier is the ultimate expression of the word. Those mothers are offering something more valuable than any hoard of gold or silver. Trust has blossomed out of gratitude for the sacrifices the Allies have made in fighting for the cause of freedom and justice.

Uncle Charlie received a letter from the C.H.A. – an organisation he was involved in, which had decided to write to all their members in the armed forces. Unfortunately, I have not been able to discover the meaning of the acronym.

This is the second of the two letters of condolence that have survived down the years. Dated, 4th Oct. 1943, the final sentence of the letter from the Hon Sec of the C.H.A. reads: "His many friends, both in and out of club circles, will mourn his departure, and find his place difficult to fill, for the world cannot afford to part with men like your son." Uncle Charlie's letter from the C.H.A. is one of six he received at the same time. Reading the six letters will have cheered him up no end. As usual, Charlie keeps a keen eye on his finances, and it seems there has been some delay in receiving his pay or 'allotment' so, perhaps with the instigation of Charlie, getting together with the other men, they have decided to submit another pay request, just to make sure.

In the third paragraph of his letter Uncle Charlie comments on some amusing incident which his mother has related to him in her letter. This had happened when she was climbing the steps of the Theatre. I notice that Charlie uses a capital letter 'T' when referring to this and I think it was probably the local theatre, the Theatre Royal in Hyde. On a visit to Hyde a few months ago, I took a photograph of this, now dilapidated, but once beautiful old theatre, showing its sadly neglected façade.[8] It is many years since I was last inside this beautiful old building, and to my disappointment, I cannot remember what must have been a very ornate interior. I wish the Theatre Royal Onward Trust good luck in their work. Uncle Charlie comments on Grandma's ability to laugh in all situations, showing a positive outlook on all events. This strength of character will stand her in good stead in the following months, as she tries to cope with the tragic loss of her eldest son. Following the worst of all news, she will need to draw on every ounce of strength she has within her to carry on. Knowing her quiet, but strong, demeanour, I know she would keep going, with the help of her Faith, her Hymns, her Family and her Friends.

Originally I was unsure how many letters Uncle Charlie had actually written, and whether or not the twenty three I have were all, or only a part of, a much larger number. But from early on in the letters Charlie intimated he liked to write a regular weekly letter. Out in the Middle East he tried to write every fourth day to make sure his family knew he was alright. Allowing for busy periods, schemes, fighting and times when it would have been impossible to write, I estimate that he would have written at the very least one hundred letters home during the three years he was in the Army. A further clue is that Charlie made a note in his diary every time he wrote a letter: from the 1st January, 1943, until his last diary entry of 6th May, 1943, he has written, in these final three and a half months, a total of twenty three letters, some of which I have acquired, most I do not have. The number may be incomplete, but I feel privileged to own such a fine selection of my Uncle's letters. Beginning with the very first letter to his parents in which he describes in detail his first few days in the army, and ending with his final letter in which he describes so eloquently the 8th Army's triumphal march through Sousse.

There is a gap between letters from June 1940 to April 1941, when Charlie joined 111 Field Regiment, Royal Artillery. After passing basic infantry training in Carlisle, he was stationed in the United Kingdom as a member of the regiment of the Lancashire Fusiliers, part of the 125th Brigade, where he continued with signalers' training. The soldiers of this Brigade did not serve abroad, but were sent on to other units, ultimately to be posted overseas, as was the case with Charlie. This possibly explains why his letters during that time were not saved, as his stay in this country was probably uneventful. Taking these points into consideration I can only conclude that they were sorted by someone – someone who kept a range of letters in memory of their loved one.

But who went to the trouble of sorting his many letters into a manageable selection: relevant, important, historical, interesting and funny? Could it have been my grandmother? Could she bear to grade *any* of her son's precious letters into order of importance? No, definitely not. Could my grandfather have steeled himself to rank any of Charlie's precious letters? No, I don't think so. They would all have been equally priceless. My Uncle Norman? – I doubt it very much. Thinking of the people Uncle Charlie left behind I can only come to one conclusion: In my opinion it could only have been one person: my mother – who read Charlie's letters again, many years later, when she was sorting my grandmother's possessions after she had passed away. I think Mum kept them in memory of her brother, a written testimony to the sacrifices made by Charlie and his family. It is the only explanation that seems possible to me. Additionally, in my Uncle's diary, in the empty space on the day of his death, 12th May, 1943, I found some words written by my mother, forty years later in which she wrote about the impact of Charlie's death, and how she still mourned his loss even after the passage of so many years. Assisted by the passage of time, I think Mum found the strength to carefully, and with much thought, sort through his many letters to select the most meaningful ones. Although Charlie wrote four more letters, she chose the one above as a fitting tribute to end the series of twenty three. Alas, I wish my Mum was well enough to ask if she did indeed perform that labour of love in memory of her brother.

> *Sat. 17th Apr.*
> *Another very quiet day. Nothing to do and all day to do it in. Big do starts on Monday night.*

> *Sun. 18th Apr.*
> *Quiet day. Spent most of day with Signal Office blokes. Am operating C.O.2's set on coming operation. Had chat with New Zealanders in evening.*

These two days will be the proverbial quiet before the storm of the next battle.

Notes

1 Major General W.G. Stevens. "Bardia to Enfidaville" New Zealand Electronic Text Centre.
2 There were two types of these American made tanks: the General Grant with a British turret style and the General Lee with an American turret style.
3 Taken from: "Bardia to Enfidaville" by Major General W.G. Stevens. NZETC. Victoria .AC
4 General Freyberg was as tough a man as it is possible to find. Compared to the Salamander, a mythical creature who could walk

through fire unharmed, he won the Victoria Cross at the Battle of the Somme during the First World War, sustaining 27 shrapnel wounds in the process. He swam the English Channel; he was a boxer and a sculler. Rick Atkinson, author of "Army at Dawn." wrote the following tribute to him: "No greater heart beat in British battle dress." p.427.

5 Involved in the air attack on Poland in 1939, the Junkers 88 first entered service. Although this high speed bomber was vulnerable to the faster spitfires and hurricanes, it could carry a record payload of 4,400lbs.worth of bombs which could wreak much destruction on the ground. The Junkers 88 was also quite tough – able to withstand a good deal of damage and still keep flying. It continued in service until the end of the war in 1945.

6 I remember, as a child, being taken by my grandma to these Meetings with 'proper' tea-time etiquette observed. Hard wooden forms for seating, with movable back-rests which could face either way, fascinated me; but what I really liked was when someone would find me a sweet, and they usually did!

7 Post Script: On consecutive days both Uncle Charlie and the Regimental War Diaries noted the arrival of a new Commander of 111 Field Regiment, Lieutenant Colonel W.P. Hobbs. Two days later 2nd Lt. Cassell joined the Regiment. Within a matter of weeks, the wireless operator, the Regimental Signals Officer and the Commander will all suffer the same fate.

8 The Theatre Royal, Hyde, now a listed building, also has Trust Status., and is run by a group of dedicated volunteers: ("Theatre Royal Onward") who have taken on the task of fundraising, aiming to restore this once beautiful theatre to its former glory. Their website is: http://www.hydetheatreroyal.co.uk

CHAPTER TWELVE

The Horrible Hill Of Takrouna

Mon. 19th Apr
Wrote letter-cards to Elsie and Jessie Morton. Moved off in C.O.2's
M.H (Marmon-Herrington) at 7-0p.m. Stayed night, what little
there was of it, at Battle H.Q. Barrage started at 11-0p.m. Am bitten
to death by gnats. There are mosquitoes, too.

Charlie found some quiet time this morning to write two letters
before – bang-on-time – at precisely eleven o'clock that night,
the exploding guns heralded the barrage commencing the
next confrontation with the enemy, this time on the Takrouna
Feature. The barrage was set to provide cover for the attacking
infantry who had fifteen minutes to close up to the barrage
start line. Thereafter the barrage would lift one hundred yards
at two minute intervals, finally pausing for eighty minutes,
allowing the infantry to consolidate. At this stage, General
Stevens remarks on a pervading sense of optimism from the
whole Brigade following their many triumphs over the enemy.
There was a sense of invincibility amongst the troops: that this
next skirmish near Enfidaville would be "a piece of cake." But
to militate against this understandable over-confidence, there
were, he claimed, several errors made by reconnaissance patrols,
as well as poor quality maps of the area. The patrols reported
that the enemy had been routed from the Enfidaville area,

when in fact the patrols were looking in the wrong place. This was a serious miscalculation of enemy positions. The eyes of the planners should have been focused to the left of Enfidaville, on the Takrouna Feature, which was right on the enemy main line, and therefore would be vigorously defended. This led to some unexpectedly fierce fighting from both sides: each side fighting for supremacy to secure the feature. This "piece of cake" would prove to be virtually indigestible – almost, but not quite, choking the 2nd New Zealand Brigade.

Uncle Charlie writes of being pestered by mosquitoes (fortunately non-malarial) Many of us have experienced the high-pitched whine of this tiny pest as it goes whizzing past our ears, on the lookout for some bare skin to sink its mouthparts into. Their bite can cause such misery: itching skin as well as the constant irritation of trying to bat them away. Major J.G. Stevenson,[1] writing his account of the contribution of the 2nd New Zealand Division, to the Second World War, writes of the severity of the mosquito attack, causing soldiers to be hospitalised with swollen faces and eyes so severely affected that they were unable to see. Also, a side-effect of the bites, Major Stevens believed, was one of extreme tiredness experienced by those men who were severely bitten. Did they have mosquito nets I wonder? As if these soldiers have not had enough to contend with, without the long, irritable, sleepless nights adding to their woes.

Tues. 20th Apr.
Swanned around during the morning with Major Barnes. Static in afternoon. A certain amount of shelling, not very close. Wrote No. 10 home.

Uncle Charlie seems to have had a fairly easy day, with only some distant shelling to be concerned about. He is very lucky to hear distant shelling, and not to find himself in the middle of some of the fiercest fighting in the whole of the North Africa Campaign.

Whilst up on the front line the War Diaries report mixed results: some engagement with the enemy, without sustaining serious casualties, and some ground gained. From the 19th to the 21st April, the advantage swung backwards and forwards – in favour of the Axis forces, then the Allies – reverting to the Axis and back again, as the enemy vigorously defended its ground, before finally losing the Takrouna Feature to the Allies.

> *Wed. 21st Apr.*
> *Marmon-Herrington was lent to R Bty. as O.P. car, complete with set and operator – me! Were very heavily shelled in afternoon. Was murderous – thought my last minute was coming at any time. Shrapnel burst water & petrol cans, blew my aerial off. Very unpleasant.*

> Reg. War Diaries: *A day of great Arty. activity on both sides. The Regt. fired numerous concentrations on enemy Inf. and guns; some of these were in support of an attack by Staff. Yeo. on the Takrouna Feature. None of the enemy concentrations fell on the Regt. and only a few stray rounds landed near the guns. No casualties were caused thereby. However, 212 Bty. had one premature which killed one man and injured one or two others.*
> *1800hrs. Takrouna feature finally cleared, some 300 P.W.'s being taken. O.P.'s were withdrawn at last light.*

Today, Uncle Charlie finds himself up on the front line in the Observation Post car. Charlie's regiment was in support of the Staffordshire Yeomanry, fighting for control of the Takrouna Feature.[2]

★★★

The enemy had the advantage of looking down on the Allies from on top of the hill and could throw shells down on them at will. This hill, formed by nature and defended by big guns, proved impossible to climb. For two days, the Allies had been facing a tenacious enemy and a hill that was even more determined to prevent access to the top. To make matters worse, the enemy had planted mine fields at various points at the bottom of the hill. Then, plumbing the depths of disastrous events, the Allies began to experience problems with the guns. The gunners tried and tried to land shells on the enemy at the top of the hill, but either the shells landed short, and thumped harmlessly into the side of the hill, or flew right over the top, landing behind the enemy. Could things get any worse? Something had to be done. So the Allies brought to the front a seventeen-pounder gun which, having greater accuracy began to cause damage to the enemy. Meanwhile, a Maori Sergeant from one of the Maori regiments of the 2nd New Zealand Division,on his own initiative, with a group of men, managed to get round the other side of the hill, while, at the same time, more soldiers entered the village from the opposite side, driving the enemy towards the Maori and his men. Led by their sergeant's uncompromising leadership skills, this brave group of soldiers brought about the capture of over three hundred prisoners (mostly Italian) and the desperate battle was finally won.

Uncle Charlie, sitting in his Marmon Herrington, in the middle of the action, was rocked by enemy fire. I can just picture the scene (like a Hollywood movie) shrapnel pinging off petrol and water cans and blowing Charlie's aerial off. His heart must have been hammering in his chest for most of the afternoon. Luckily none of the shrapnel was meant for him today. That particular piece of destruction with the name "Charles Robinson" stamped on it would do its worst in roughly three weeks' time.

The War Diaries report that despite all the "great artillery activity on both sides" the Regiment's casualties were surprisingly light. Only one man was killed and others injured when a gun went off prematurely.

But other units were not so lucky. At the culmination of two days of fierce fighting, the 2nd New Zealand Division finally took the Horrible Hill of Takrouna; but they paid a heavy price for the victory, with a total of 536 men either killed or missing. The Allies' over-confidence and miss-information had caused them to be ill-prepared for the tough battle of Takrouna,[3] taking over two days to prevail. Rick Atkinson[4] in his account of the battle stated that the fighting became so fierce that men lost control, resorting to hand to hand fighting (hurling stones when they ran out of ammunition) and the Gurkhas, part of the 4th Indian Division, were driven to use their ceremonial knives on the enemy, resulting in many deaths.

A further explanation for the supreme struggle for supremacy was, Rick Atkinson believed, due to a change of terrain from the flat desert landscape in which the 8th Army excelled, to the tree-laden, cactus-covered, fissured ground of

Takrouna. Photo: Ref. DA-10929 – Summit of Takrouna 1943.
URL: http://www.nzhistory.net.nz/media/photo/summit-takrouna. With
grateful thanks to the Alexander Turnbull Library of New Zealand for kind
permission to reproduce the above photograph.

Tunisia. Even with the superior fire power which Montgomery enjoyed, shells were now rendered harmless, missing their mark and landing uselessly in the undergrowth, falling prey to a cultivated and hilly landscape.

After a day of so many near-misses, Uncle Charlie can breathe again. He was lucky it was only cans and his wireless aerial that were destroyed.

Before reaching the hill on the 12th May, 2013, I could see its bulk rising menacingly above the plain, and shuddered at the thought of soldiers attacking this fiercely defended monster seventy years ago. Twisting, turning and climbing, we drove to the top, finally reaching the summit where we were treated to a wonderful panoramic view of chequerboard fields filled with olive trees; below us, to the right, a large blue lake shimmered in the sun. (Probably almost identical to the view Uncle Charlie would have seen had he managed to reach the top.) We enjoyed a coffee with the direct descendants of the Berber family who originally settled there.

> *Thur. 22nd Apr.*
> *At O.P. again, but Major Winterbottam told me I was returning to Battle H.Q. Good. Were shelled heavily in the morning. A Maori was killed near us. Were at the side of a farmhouse. It was hit direct three times. Returned to Battle at 4-0 p.m. Very glad. Bty. kept the car.*

Uncle Charlie is still in the firing line. This time he is near a farmhouse which is drawing enemy fire, and is hit three times, killing a Maori nearby. Uncle Charlie is glad to be going back to Battle [H.Q.] later that afternoon. The War Diaries report a great deal of firing from the enemy resulting in the death of a Lieutenant, and damage to vehicles. It appears the regiments needed to change position, but were only able to move one troop from 212 Battery.

Fri. 23rd Apr. Good Friday
St. George's Day
Spent the day at Battle H.Q. Quite a lot of shelling. Terrible thing
especially on Good Friday. Did a short duty on Tac set until 11-30.
Slept with Mat and Bert in their hole. Quiet night. New Zealanders
advanced two or 3 miles without opposition.

Uncle Charlie has experienced a more relaxed day, despite the continued shelling. For everyone at home today is Good Friday – a bank holiday, a day for religious observance, and an opportunity for Charlie's family to rest and to enjoy some relaxation. Although the family will be enjoying a break from routine, for the 8th Army, Friday the 23rd April is a non-holiday, and it will be "business as usual". Soldiers have to take impromptu "bank holidays" whenever they can. I am sure Uncle Charlie's thoughts will frequently turn to his loved ones today.

Sat. 24th Apr.
Wrote No. 11 home. Did another two hours on Tac. set. Shelled again.
He seems to be going for the track. We are very close to the track. New
Zealanders pulled out of line. 56th Div. came in. They have been told
not to associate with the 8th Army as they are an undisciplined lot!
They have come up from Syria!

Today Uncle Charlie found time, despite the shelling, to write letter number eleven. The 56th (London) Division, having travelled three hundred miles from Libya in record time, have come in to relieve the 2nd New Zealand Division, temporarily taken out of line to rest. I wonder if this is some sort of rumour, or have the newly arrived inexperienced soldiers really been told not to associate with the battle-hardened veterans of the 8th Army?

Sun. 25th Apr. Easter Sunday.
Went down to the sea for a swim after Tiffin. Very enjoyable. When
coming back saw that Enfidaville was being shelled. Waited outside
and when it quietened down we made a dash for it. Got through O.K.

The fighting continues around Enfidaville, forcing Charlie to wait until the coast is clear before rejoining his regiment after his relaxing swim in the Mediterranean. Previous reports about Enfidaville being clear of the enemy are not true, as combat continues with German units still fighting a rear-guard action.

Mon. 26th Apr. Easter Monday.
Heavy shelling again. Have to keep down in holes at present. Very
nerve-racking. Puts me off my grub. Shall be glad when this campaign
is over. Getting too hot for my liking.

Another non-holiday for the 8th Army, as the fighting continues. Charlie, having to take cover from the almost constant shelling, seems to be affected in both body and mind – being under constant stress – not able to relax and not eating properly. He will be ready for tomorrow's break from hostilities.

Tues. 27th Apr.
Left for 24 hours rest at sea-side at 2-0 p.m. Got there at 3-0 p.m.
Had a swim and a walk round village before tea. Had hair-cut in
Arab shop! Had to sit cross-legged on stone slab! However, he didn't
make too bad a job.

The regiment begins a new system of resting one of the three batteries in turn, which seems, to me a very good idea, as it still allows two thirds of the fire power to do their job, whilst giving some respite to the men in the remaining battery. I hope this day away from the fighting soothes some of Charlie's nerves and he can rest and relax. He did enjoy a swim, a walk round the village and an unconventional, (but quite good) haircut by a local barber.

Wed. 28th Apr.
Got up at 9-0 a.m. It's great not to have to worry about shells. Swam again before Tiffin. Left at 1-0 p.m. When we got back to camp they were still being shelled. Felt worse than ever after a rest.

It seems Uncle Charlie needs more than one day of relaxation to fully recover from his "nerves" for although he enjoyed the rest, without having to worry about the destructive power of an exploding shell, returning to the battle proved to be quite an ordeal for him. "Operation Cholera" in which 56 London Division and 4 Indian Division were tasked to capture a line running from the coast to Djebel et Tebaga has been postponed for twenty four hours.

Thur. 29ʰ Apr.
Shelled again. One landed on track just over our heads. Kept my head down! Wrote No. 12 home. Received long-awaited parcel from home also 2 Reporters. Account of Marjorie's wedding in one.

Ratcheting up the tension again, Uncle Charlie had to duck to avoid a shell as it whistled over his head; but he makes no comment about his state of mind today. Happily his spirits were lifted by the arrival of "a long-awaited parcel" from home. He has received two local papers, one of which contains a report of his sister's wedding on 22nd December 1942 – during the period when he was so desperately homesick and frequently thinking of her.[5]

It is seventy years since Charlie's sister exchanged vows with my father. If Charlie sent a prayer from the sands of North

Africa across the many, many miles to England, with a loving wish for his sister to enjoy a long and happy marriage, then that prayer was certainly answered, because both my parents, now ninety and ninety one, celebrated their admirably long and happy marriage with the family. They are still together, both with health problems and living in a nursing home, but crucially: still together.

As planned, the newly arrived inexperienced 56 Division, along with 4 Indian Division began "Operation Cholera" but, as is often the case with the best laid plans of mice and men, it turned out to be something of a disaster after 56 Division came under fierce enemy return fire, and were forced to seek support from Charlie's regiment to assist with their retreat from the onslaught. The planned outcome was that the 8th Army would fight its way through Enfidaville, travelling north to meet up with the U.S. Corp. having taken Bizerte, while the 1st Army would attack the capital, Tunis. But the plan went awry in Enfidaville, following the fierce enemy counter attack. The 56 London Division and 4th Indian Division had been asked to perform an impossibly difficult task. It seemed unrealistic to expect two divisions – one of which (the 56th) was too inexperienced to take on such a demanding role, particularly when there was insufficient infantry to support them. Enfidaville was nestled between the hills and the sea, making an outflanking manoeuvre by an attacking army impossible. There was no alternative to a full frontal attack, a serious disadvantage in the type of terrain which had become easily and vigorously defended by the German army. The Allied plans were doomed to failure and "Operation Cholera" was postponed indefinitely. Major Stevens[6] maintains that the attempted capture of Enfidaville was an uncharacteristic error of judgment and planning by Montgomery, and was his first failure.

Fri. 30th Apr.
Heavy shelling. Vic Burley and Hyams killed and Tommy Gibbons
wounded this morning. I had my narrowest escape to date. Ten of us in
a dug out with roof on. Shell landed on corner! Whole dug-out moved
but didn't collapse – thank God. Decided to move. Went back to Main
H.Q. About time too.

Another day another round of shells: the fighting continues.
It must be very frustrating for these men wondering when on
earth their hard-won victory in North Africa would actually
come to fruition, as it surely must. Today two more men were
killed and one other wounded, and Charlie had his "narrowest
escape to date" when a shell landed on the corner of his dug
out, thankfully only shaking the structure without collapsing
it.

But the grim reaper is hovering, slowly but inexorably honing
in on the small soldier with glasses: his days are numbered.
Charlie, thanking God for his reprieve, moves again, this time
to Main H.Q. Is it any wonder that soldiers suffer from combat
stress? Now it is the turn for 211 Battery to go out of line for
three days of rest.

Sat. 1st May
At Main H.Q. all day. Were told to go down to the beach to meet
Major Barnes but stopped at the last minute. It seems that the whole
regiment is coming out for a rest. Nice work, they need it.

Again, Uncle Charlie refers to "they" when writing of the
regiment's hard earned break from fighting. He acknowledges
his fellow soldiers' need for rest, but unselfishly doesn't
mention his own..

Reading Major General Stevens account of the time, he

relates there were some tricky decisions to be made for the 8ᵗʰ Army. If they were to push northwards through the fiercely defended bottleneck of Enfidaville towards Tunis, ultimately to meet up with the 1ˢᵗ Army, (who were making steady progress from the North,) they would have to fight their way through, and the loss of life would be such that, as General Horrocks Commander of 10 Corps gloomily pointed out to Montgomery: "we will break through but I doubt whether at the end there will be much left of the 8ᵗʰ Army." General Freyberg, commander of the 2ⁿᵈ N.Z. Division, also had misgivings about the proposed push north, as he was under some pressure from the New Zealand Government to reduce what seemed to be a disproportionately large loss of life for such a small country. A further consideration, possibly in Montgomery's mind, was the fact that his soldiers had fought so hard and travelled so far, they had earned the right to be present at the finale. But the price to be paid for such a push would result in too great a loss of life. A third consideration was that the 1ˢᵗ Army and the U.S.A. Corps were well on their way to Tunis and Bizerte, possibly arriving there first, precipitating the complete collapse of the Axis forces, so any prior loss of life in the South of Tunisia would be completely unwarranted.

Sun. 2nd May
Moved with Battle H.Q. to new position in rear. Actually a rest position. Left for sea-side at 5 o'clock. Arrived at six. Had sing-song after dinner.

Today the men can enjoy a well-earned rest at the "sea-side." Also, the decision had been made to abandon the planned push North to Tunis. The 8ᵗʰ Army would stay where they were in a holding position. Most of the 8ᵗʰ Army would not be present at the triumphal march through Tunis, although

Montgomery did transfer the 7th Armoured Division, the 4th Indian Division and 201 Guards Brigade up North to assist with the coup de grace. General W.G. Stevens felt that Montgomery's choice of units to go up North was, for him, a morally correct one: they were the origins of the 8th Army, formed as the Western Desert Force in 1940. He probably felt that they were a fitting (and capable) force to be in at the very end of a long campaign.

Mon. 3rd May
In the sea three times today. One of the battery chaps got into difficulties and had to be rescued. He recovered after artificial respiration had been applied.

Reading Charlie's account of today's relaxing swim, it seems that shells, bombs and bullets are not the only threat to a soldier's life. One of those endangered by nothing more sinister than the warm, clear blue waters of the Mediterranean, was a soldier who got into difficulties and had to be successfully resuscitated. It makes me think that a precious life can be snuffed out at any time and for a variety of sometimes innocuous-seeming reasons – even on a peacefully quiet day of rest.

Tues. 4th May.
Left for H.Q. at 7-30. Arrived at 8-30. Nothing outstanding happened today, but it's a pleasure to have things running smoothly on. Wrote No. 13 home.

For the first time in a long time I sense that Charlie, taking the opportunity to write home, is completely relaxed today. He is savouring a simple, peaceful, non-eventful day. I like to think of myself as a pragmatist, that the number thirteen is just another number. But I have to admit to a little uneasy feeling, thinking that the letter he numbered thirteen, could be the last one to land on the doormat of 159 Great Norbury Street.

Wed. 5th May
Played football this morning. After about 10 minutes I had no wind left. Ye Gods! To think I used to play for 1½ hrs. I must be out of training. Got letters from mother and Phyllis Booth.

Charlie laments his lack of fitness today, but thankfully there were no shells to worry about. This day is just a lull in proceedings, as the Germans have not finished fighting yet.

Thur. 6th May
We were told to go again to the sea at 2-30 by Jimmy Kay. At 5-15 we were sent for and told to return. When we got back Major Barnes said he hadn't given permission! Misunderstanding. Straightened out later. A band came down and played to us for half an hour. Harry evacuated.

Charlie's final diary entry is a fairly innocuous one, with no exploding shells, no enemy bombardment, no exchange of unpleasantries with the Germans or the Italians, no near-misses, near-death experiences, or close shaves – just a misunderstanding with Major Barnes. But Charlie's final two words, written in a tiny space, in tiny letters (I had to use a magnifying glass) leave me with some questions: Was this the Harry Withington who trained with Charlie in Carlisle over three years ago? Was this the Harry who was attached to 111 Field Regiment with Charlie and mentioned occasionally in his diary? If it was the same Harry, why was he evacuated? Was he injured, ill, or wounded? Ultimately what happened to the man who had travelled so far and shared over three years' worth of highs and lows with my Uncle – probably forming a close bond with him? Their many shared, unforgettable experiences would number more than most people experience in a lifetime. I suppose I will never know the answers to these questions. Perhaps Harry survived the war and continued with the rest of his life. But there is one thing I am certain of: he would not forget the friend who didn't make it – Charles Robinson.

Notes

1 "Bardia to Enfidaville." by Major General W.G. Stevens. 2nd N.Z. Division. New Zealand Electronic Text Centre,

2 This hill was seriously nasty. It was high, it was almost vertical and it was covered in loose scree. But the hill's coup de grace was an impossibly large overhang right at the summit, guaranteeing its complete victory over any would-be climber who had managed to get thus far (see photograph of Takrounataken in 1943 on page 210).

3 Major General Stevens account of the action.

4 From: "An Army At Dawn." By Rick Atkinson.

5 A few weeks ago my parents celebrated their platinum wedding anniversary on the 22nd December, 2012.

6 Major General W.G. Stevens "Bardia to Enfidaville" – Conclusion

CHAPTER THIRTEEN

The Final Days

Uncle Charlie's final diary entry was written six days before he died on the 12ᵗʰ May. The five blank days are puzzling. From the day of his first entry on 1ˢᵗ January, 1943, until the 7ᵗʰ May, there were no blank days; despite being busy or tired at the end of a long day, he always found the time and the inclination to write up his experiences. Even on days when nothing much happened – when he would write: "nothing to do and all day to do it in." – rather than leave a blank. I know he was not wounded. I know that at this stage they were not fighting, but training and resting, and I doubt he was ill as he would have taken his diary with him (wherever soldiers went they took their kit with them). I feel he had some reason for not writing up these days, but I have to reluctantly accept that his last few days of life will go unrecorded and I will never know what kind of days they were. The Regimental War Diaries continue:

8th May
Tunis and Bizerte taken by 1st Army & U.S.A. Corps.

9th May
ENFIDAVILLE – 1530 hrs. Regt. moved back to old positions and continued firing concentrations.

10th May

ENFIDAVILLE – Daily average of 4,000 fired. Expenditure accelerated in afternoon owing to 10 Corps message that Bosch would surrender when his Amm. was finished.

11th May

Continuous firing, chiefly H.B. and multiple mortars.

Despite, (or perhaps as a result of) the fall of Tunis, the enemy, holed up in Enfidaville is throwing everything it has at the Allies in a last gasp attempt to use up all its ammunition and cause as much damage as possible to the 8th Army before the inevitable surrender of the Axis forces in North Africa. While the Americans, British and Commonwealth units in Tunis are enjoying a victorious entry into the capital city, those left behind in Enfidaville are pinned down under aggressive and indiscriminate enemy fire. Kippenberger (now in temporary command of 2nd New Zealand Division) noted that the enemy were: "pitching shells at random in a most disconcerting fashion" and a total of thirty one hostile batteries were engaged in a four hour period. The situation is not unlike the last round of a boxing match when, in a final all-out effort the combatants are throwing punches as hard and fast as they can in a last ditch attempt to achieve victory. Unfortunately, in this case the aggressor must know he has already lost the fight, and despite the Allies sending out invitations to, and terms of, surrender, the enemy will not give in gracefully. How disappointing for the soldiers in Enfidaville that they had not been able to share in the triumph of their colleagues in Tunis, and to add insult to injury, they are still fighting!

Wed. 12th May.
1030 hrs. 155mm mortar from rocket Bty hit office truck. Lt. Col. W.P. Hobbs, M.B.E., R.A., and 2nd Lt. D.W.G. Cassell, R.A.

(R.S.O.)[1] killed. Many Regt. records destroyed. Total 4 vehicles brewed up.

1930hrs. Regt. withdrew to S. of Enfidaville the campaign being virtually over.

From the wording of the above report it seems a 155mm mortar from the regiment's own rocket battery hit the office truck, killing the Commanding Officer and the Regimental Signals Officer and destroying many regimental records. A total of four vehicles were "brewed up." I read those sentences so many times, attempting to decipher the wording of what must have been, after so much mayhem, some of the most difficult words any officer would ever have to write. I tried to imagine the chaos, the deafening noise of explosions as vehicles were blown up. I am not surprised that the writer struggled to record events legibly and in detail. This incident serves to highlight the gratuitous loss of life in the dying hours of the campaign: at this stage the enemy knew it had lost the war in North Africa. The above account left me puzzled and with some unanswered questions: As my Uncle's official date of death was the 12th May, why wasn't he mentioned in the above report as an O/R death? Where was he and how did he die? How could a mortar from the regiment's own rocket battery, manage to cause so much death and destruction?

The War Diaries' report of this day's events threw up more questions than answers. However, thanks are due to W.E. Murphy and Major General W.G. Stevens[2] whose accounts have provided more details of the events on that morning of 12th May, 1943.

The Germans have added a powerful rocket to their arsenal, named Nebelwerfer, which literally means "fog thrower". As its name suggests – the rocket should simply be used to produce a smoke screen. But the German Army began to pack this large, thin skinned rocket with high explosives, designed to deliver a massively powerful blow.

On the morning of the 12th May a Nebelwerfer (one of many fired by the enemy that morning) burst by the artillery board of the rocket battery, containing the live shells and mortars of 111 Field Regiment, setting off missiles which went shooting out on their various destructive paths, blowing up a total of four vehicles, resulting in several deaths, one of which was the regiment's Commanding Officer, Lieutenant Colonel W.P. Hobbs, and somewhere in all this mayhem (perhaps with his Commanding Officer in the office truck, or in one of the other vehicles) was my Uncle.[3]

It is a sad irony for me that after surviving the intense fighting during March and April when he was lucky enough to survive so many near misses, that at the final last gasp of the campaign, my uncle should succumb to a rogue shell. It may seem surprising after so many years have passed that it still matters to me how my Uncle died. It does. I understood from my mother that the vehicle he was travelling in received a direct hit, which, when compared with the above accounts of that morning's events, seem to indicate he would have been killed outright. I hope so. I would not like to think of him lying injured, in severe pain, perhaps having lost his spectacles, confused and possibly without anyone nearby capable of helping him. I believe he died instantly, without pain, knowing nothing. If there is such a thing as a heaven, and no doubt he had faith that such a lovely place existed, I hope he achieved the paradise he so richly deserved.[4]

Charles Robinson's life may be over, but the beating heart of the regiment continues.

The War Diaries record that by 7-30 that evening they had withdrawn to the south of Enfidaville:

"the campaign being virtually over."

At 2-45p.m.on 13th May, 1943 General Alexander signalled to Mr. Churchill:

> *"Sir, it is my duty to report that the Tunisian campaign has ceased. We are masters of the North African shores."*

On this day surrender was complete: there were no pockets of enemy resistance anywhere in North Africa.[5] The number of German and Italian prisoners numbered 250,000! But the 13th May brought with it a feeling of anti-climax for the 2nd New Zealand Division, as Major General Stevens wrote:

> *"There was no excitement, no cheering, and it can only be said that the campaign came to an end very quietly."*

The men were probably feeling cheated – cheated out of taking part in a victory parade of which, without doubt, they had earned the right to be a part. They had also been cheated of the lives of their commanding officer, the Regimental Signals Officer and a certain O/R named Charles Robinson, of the Royal Corps of Signals, as the fighting continued long after it should have ceased. Even after the BBC had announced the Allied victory in North Africa, these lads were still fighting! For them, on this day, there was no cause for celebration. But finally, two years on, they *would* have the chance to celebrate their contribution to a complete and overwhelming victory at the end of the war in Europe.[6]

During the next few weeks the regiment rested, took part in training exercises and maintained, cleaned and replaced vehicles, guns and machinery in readiness for the next campaign, the invasion of Sicily.[7]

Charlie's death may, mercifully for him, have been quick and painless, but for those left behind the pain of his loss would be unbearable. Whilst mindful that there was always a chance he would lose his life in the conflict, the family lived in hope that someday Charlie would return home for good, and the family's enforced separation and worry would all be over. The more frequently he wrote, the more often they could breathe a sigh of relief and say: "We know you are alright Charlie." I am reminded of his letter written on Christmas Eve 1942 in which, writing to his parents he describes one of his near-misses having to dive under a truck with bullets lashing the sand, as a Stuka dived down and strafed the ground. He emerged unscathed, but promised to write home more frequently to allay their fears. He kept his promise.

Charlie's death occurred on the morning of Wednesday, 12th May, 1943, the day after Grandma's potato pie day at home. Which household tasks was Grandma carrying out on that fateful Wednesday? Perhaps she was on her way to the shops that morning, or (accompanied by her hymn singing) doing some baking at home, or changing the bedding. Working on those mundane tasks, Grandma was unaware that she was about to receive the worst news of her life: her son had lost his life in the conflict, and a telegram (in essence just a piece of paper) was on its way to deliver more pain than any destructive piece of shrapnel could inflict.

My grandfather would be working in the carding room at Slack Mills, my mum would be working in her aircraft factory, my Uncle Norman, having joined the Army would probably be still undergoing his initial training, my father would be away at sea, and the rest of Charlie's family and friends would be going about their usual daily business.

The 12th May would become an anniversary monster,

skulking and spoiling the happy, carefree days of Christmas, Easter, summer holidays, birthdays and days out: family celebrations from this day forward would be muted brought about by a pervading sense of loss in the absence of a much-loved family member. Future family get-togethers would never be the same. This young man died in the very prime of his life, at the age of twenty five. He died believing that he was fighting for freedom, not just in defence of the citizens of the U.K. but to help free most of Europe occupied by the Nazi regime. If there was any consolation for the family it would be that he died fighting for a just cause. They carried on: they had to. Unlike today, bereavement counselling was unheard of. Charlie was one of so many to make the ultimate sacrifice: each family receiving a telegram containing the dreaded words: "killed in action" – a world of grief contained within that short, three word sentence. But someone (perhaps Charlie's newly appointed Commanding Officer) kindly wrote to them personally, and thankfully, enclosed Charlie's precious diary.

In seeking to understand, the family would want answers: How did he die? Did he suffer? What was he doing at the time? And something very important in those days: Did he do his duty? Charlie's bravery did not take the form of single-handedly knocking out a German machine gun nest or hand-to-hand fighting with bayonets; he was not awarded any medals for bravery or for outstanding conduct in the line of duty, he was not the last man standing throwing every last piece of ammunition at the enemy before succumbing to a German bullet. No, he died doing his duty. When shells were exploding round him, and he was very afraid, he suffered the trauma of so many near-misses, he saw friends hurt; he saw friends killed and again he was very afraid. There were times when he thought that the last few minutes of his own life were being played out. His bravery took the form of facing up to a soldier's harsh life, never giving in to bitterness, never complaining or grumbling, never descending into malicious name-calling or even unkind words about anyone. He showed empathy for local people as he passed their villages, realising they were innocents caught up in a war that was none of their making. He made attempts to communicate with people of all nationalities and languages (in schoolboy French if necessary) as he passed by their dwellings. Over the past seven months he had witnessed the horrific sights and sounds of war. Unwilling to fall out with anyone, this friendly, peaceful man did his duty under the most trying conditions and retained his basic humanity in the midst of so much aggression, death and destruction. Like all those men who faced up to War, in all its best and worst aspects: he was a hero.

Notes

1 Regimental Signals Officer
2 NZETC 2nd New Zealand Divisional Artillery. Operations Around Djebibina. By W.E. Murphy. NZETC "Bardia to Enfidaville." "Conclusion." By Major General W.E. Stevens.
3 The above question was answered in May 2013, when I visited my Uncle's final resting place in Enfidaville War Cemetery, Tunisia. He was laid to rest next to 2nd Lt. Cassell, R.S.O. who was next to Lt. Col. W.P. Hobbs, the Commanding Officer. All three men had died together. No other grave nearby had the same date of death inscribed on it.
4 Post Script: When I wrote the above I was unaware of the words inscribed on the base of Charlie's headstone, until I visited his final resting place on the 70th Anniversary of his death I was moved to see the words: "Of such is the Kingdom of Heaven."
5 In the six months between the 8th November, 1942 until the

surrender on the 13th May,1943, 6,233 British and Commonwealth soldiers lost their lives, 21,528 were wounded and 10,599 missing. The American losses were 2,715 killed, 8,978 wounded and 6,528 missing.

6 The 2nd New Zealand Division took part in the invasion of Sicily, from July to August 1943.The Division also saw action on the Adriatic Coast, the Gustav Line at Monte Casino and the Gothic Line in Italy in 1944. The Division took part in the Allied Spring Offensive in 1945 which led to the German surrender. They were in at the end of the 2nd World War and received their well-deserved moment of glory.

7 111th Field Regiment, still part of the 8th Army group, but now under the command of the British X111 Corps saw action in Sicily. During 1943-4 the Regiment, attached to the 8th Indian Division, took part in the Italian Campaign. Finally, in 1944/5 the Regiment saw service in Yugoslavia as part of 2 Special Services Brigade. Having manfully done its job, the Regiment was disbanded in 1947.

CHAPTER FOURTEEN

Conclusion

The Letters

The twenty three letters Charlie wrote to his family, so carefully sorted and preserved by my mother were written between February 1940 and April 1943. Each letter may be viewed as a small, but significant, historical document detailing social, military, monetary and civilian life during the Second World War. The family's daily lives were akin to the majority of families throughout the length and breadth of Britain: making sacrifices, pulling together; united in supporting the war effort; standing shoulder to shoulder in the belief that their combined solidarity and determination could beat off the threat of Nazi Germany. Charlie's letters provide a lens through which we can view civilian life during the Second World War. The family's daily lives were akin to the majority of families throughout the length and breadth of Britain: making sacrifices, pulling together; united in supporting the war effort; standing shoulder to shoulder in the belief that their combined solidarity and determination could beat off the threat of Nazi Germany. Charlie's letters provide a lens through which we can view civilian life during the Second World War.

Charlie's first descriptive letter written two days after he arrived in Carlisle to begin his infantry training, is full of detail about receiving his uniform, describing Hadrian's Camp, the huts the men slept in, the food and the men or "chaps" he found himself sharing his new life with. Within his first letter is a small, but fascinating, snapshot of military history, as he describes his impressions as a new recruit on being called up during the early months of the war. To continue in a military vein; in a later letter, it is thanks to Charlie that I learnt of his role on the front line with the commanding officer in Tac.H.Q. He made a point of explaining as much as he could to his family without incurring the wrathful black line of the censor. This information was very helpful to me too!

The first and last of Uncle Charlie's letters are so different, yet have many similarities, and not simply from a military perspective. Both are full of hope: the first as a naive young man of twenty two years ready to start a new life in the service of his country, and his last, three years on, as an experienced battle-weary twenty five year old, also full of hope that the people of Sousse, so ably liberated, will be just the first of many to experience the freedom of release.

Charlie's letters reveal something of the personality of the uncle I never met. From the many pre-war photographs I have, there are several images of a smiling, relaxed young man, captured in a fleeting second of time, usually with a group of friends, on choir trips and all within the U.K. Found within Charlie's letters is evidence that he enjoyed the adventure of travelling. But what really whetted his appetite for adventure was, when sailing the thousands of miles from the Clyde to Durban on his "cruise" – as he commented in his letter of July 1942: "I like the prospect of seeing a strange town in a strange country." He was always keen to experience a new place – even if it meant walking round on his own. Although walking round Cairo was something of a culture shock, he still savoured the experience and was able to write an interesting and amusing letter to his parents. He was very disappointed not to be offered the chance to visit Alexandria due to his regiment moving on. He was even looking forward to the experience of travelling deep into the Sahara desert as part of the Division's outflanking manoeuvre during the battle for the Mareth Line.

I believe Charlie also had a sense of natural beauty, particularly enjoying his time in Caithness, amongst some beautiful scenery where, on his days off, he loved to walk in the hills, enjoying the spectacle of the rising and setting sun. As Charlie travelled across North Africa he was never too preoccupied with the business of soldiering to revel in the change of scenery: from the dry, arid, dusty desert terrain of Egypt and Libya to the green, cultivated fields full of olive trees, (and poppies) stretching mile after mile as the 8th Army passed through Tunisia. He must have seen a number of shocking, gruesome images during his many days of fighting; but I imagine there were times in the quiet of the night when he looked up in awe to see millions of stars shining above him in the clear desert air. I believe he was that sort of person.

His letters reveal my uncle had a well-developed sense of humour. There was usually a small part of every letter in which he described some amusing incident. He could appreciate the funny side of life in the Army, even during the serious business of fighting a war. The shoeblack's frantic efforts to clean the soldier's other boot; the soldiers' scramble to leave, then return to the open-air cinema following an air-raid warning, Mrs. Redfern's gushing over-reaction to one of his letters, are just three examples of the many amusing incidents he related to his parents; perhaps in some measure to alleviate their anxiety about his precarious life; and much more positive than grumbling about the tough, unpleasant conditions he had to contend with.

When Uncle Norman bought a violin it provoked a titter from Charlie, as he imagined some odd sounds emanating from Norman's practice sessions at home. But on a serious note, for each member of the Robinson family music played an important part in their precious few leisure hours. Granddad sang the bass in Slack Mills Male Voice Choir. Charlie sang in the chapel choir, Uncle Norman played the chapel organ and the piano, mum sang in the choir and grandma, not to be outdone, sang her hymns with great gusto. There is nothing like music to soothe, inspire, lift the spirits and comfort the troubled soul; I hope that their collective love of music helped the Robinson family, in some small measure, to cope with their loss.

If there was one particular subject with which Charlie was preoccupied, it was the subject of money, mentioned so many times in his letters. But the letter which stands out above all the others is the one he sent to his parents on the 24th December, 1942 in which he wrote two very large and confusing paragraphs (taking up two thirds of the letter) explaining how grandma was to deal with his money. I notice that someone has marked a cross in pencil at the beginning and end of the two paragraphs. I am not surprised because no-one could read them just once and take in all Charlie's instructions. In the early letters he often asked for money, stamps or razor blades; on one occasion explaining he was down to his last 4½d. and would his parents: "please help me out with the usual" – not wanting to borrow because he would have to pay it back! By the time he reached North Africa there was probably little to spend his money on, and perhaps he had also become a better money manager, as his requests for financial "assistance" appeared to dry up.

Periodically Charlie would ask how his finances were faring in the Post Office back home. He seemed to take pleasure from his growing savings, and by 1st March, 1943, grandma was banking 10/6d a week for her son, diligently placing the money in his Post Office savings account back home. The amount, equivalent to just over 50p in today's money, seems miniscule However, he generously asked Grandma to give his sister £1 for a wedding present: amounting to almost two weeks' allotment. The amount seems so tiny when compared to the inflated spending power of today, and how little £1 can buy; but in the

1940s literally every penny had to be counted and "luxury" items like cars and foreign holidays were out of the question. There was only enough money to afford a small mortgage, coal and electricity for heating, some clothes (many items were knitted and sewn in the home) and plain home cooked food. If there was any money left at the end of the week, it might just pay for a visit to the cinema.

The subject and importance of money was never far from Charlie's mind. It was not simply that he was a "miser" as he wrote in one letter, but I think he liked the precision and order of both number and language, evidenced by the care he took to write legibly (even in his personal diary) with correct spelling and punctuation. In all his words I have found only four misspelt, (thanks to Spellchecker) and one or two I was unable to make out. He even used inverted commas in his diary when writing the titles of books he had read. I can see how his love of figures and order led him to declare (in his letter of 1st March 1943) that he proposed a bet with his father, predicting he would write a total of fifty letters before the end of the war. Thereafter he started to number each letter on the top left hand side of the first page, opposite the address. I am sad to say he only reached number thirteen.

For soldiers, travelling in a hot country, meals (out of necessity) consisted of tinned or dried food – probably very boring most of the time. The men tried to liven things up a little by making home-made "duffs" with various fillings, and making porridge out of Arnott's rock-hard biscuits. Charlie missed home cooking, of course, but if there was one meal he missed most of all it was Grandma's potato pie, mentioned more than once in his letters. On one occasion he imagined enjoying a "beefer" at home where he could savour a hot soak in a bath filled with lots of hot water, followed by a large helping of his mother's potato pie.

Uncle Charlie was a friendly, outgoing man, evidenced by the many friends he corresponded with as well as the number of people of different nationalities he attempted to converse with as the 8th Army passed through their towns and cities. But there was one friend in particular he seemed extremely fond of – Elsie, mentioned twelve times in his diary. She never wrote as frequently as he wished and he always replied to her letters as quickly as he could. He cherished the thought that she would meet his mother and father and fervently hoped they would like her. This hoped-for event didn't seem to happen, despite Charlie's encouragement. But it suggests she meant a great deal to him, and I wonder if they would have married if my Uncle had survived the war.

To fully understand something I think one has to live through it. Over the years I had learnt a little of the Blitz, bomb shelters, food rationing, and the sacrifices made by the population as a whole. Thanks to his letters Uncle Charlie has helped me to gain an insight into what it *feels* like to be at war with another country not too far away. Charlie's letters shine a light into the dark recesses of a different world, so many decades ago, when families made sacrifices and endured so many deprivations. Added to that was a real fear of invasion in the early days of the war, losing one's home to a bomb, working harder to meet production demands, generally having to make do and mend, and all this amid fears for the family's welfare. Charlie's letters are more than pure fact; they speak a truth about the every-day life of his family, and in doing so offer me a family bond, stretching back seventy years. I know how precious those letters were from service-men to their families, for they were the only form of communication.

Whenever I unfold a page of one of Charlie's letters I feel a little thrill to think that I am actually reading words written by his hand seven decades ago with a pen dipped into a small, shared, pot of precious ink. Charlie's meticulously neat writing with a primitive nibbed pen that required frequent dipping into liquid ink – too much would make unsightly blots, and too little would be too faint to read – required skilled handling in its use. I am proud to claim there is not one ugly blot in or around any of his words.

Charlie's letters have allowed me to share something of the daily lives of his family and friends as they went about the business of coping with the Second World War. I feel a sense of admiration for the fortitude of men and women, who, under the most trying of circumstances pulled together in the face of adversity; they refused to be beaten or cowed. Most of all, I thank Uncle Charlie for writing these treasured letters and I thank my mum for saving and so carefully preserving them.

The Regimental War Diaries Of 111 Field Regiment, R.A.

If I was aware of the bare bones of the war from a civilian standpoint, which Uncle Charlie's letters fleshed out for me, then my knowledge of the North Africa campaign and his regiment's part in it was non-existent. After accidentally discovering the War Diaries I have been absorbed in charting the progress of Charlie's regiment through North Africa, as they record the daily events, methods and means of warfare. The War Diaries have been so valuable in the writing of this book it would be remiss of me not to mention their significance – providing a perfect companion to Charlie's Diary in the way they complement, enhance and inform his experiences.

My first attempts to read the War Diaries filled me with dismay as I balked at the unfamiliar hand writing with its (to me) alien language liberally sprinkled with abbreviations and acronyms. But I persevered and slowly but surely I became accustomed to the formal style of writing and the esoteric language of War. It was the War Diaries – crucially filling a ten month gap in my uncle's letters – that informed me of Charlie's artillery training in Northumbria before embarking for Durban on the troop ship "Awatea". Weeks later I learnt the Regiment was bound for Egypt on board the troop ship "Kosciuszko". But it was when the regiment reached the Middle East that the War Diaries came into their own. Firstly, when the regiment reached Almaza, near Cairo, they assumed the prestigious duties of Depot Regiment at the Middle Eastern School of Artillery. The War Diaries have provided me with detailed accounts of 111th Field Regiment and the part it played in winning the desert war: marching and fighting across almost two thousand miles of unforgiving terrain. The Diaries informed me that Charlie's regiment was part of the 50th Northumberland Division during the battle of El Alamein, allowing me to pinpoint his pre-battle position on that long front line.

From the War Diaries I have learnt some surprising and impressive facets of Army life. For instance, I discovered a considerate side to the Army: praise for effort, achievement and recognition to individuals and regiments when it was due. After the battle of El-Alamein, 111 Field Regiment were acknowledged by the C.O. for working conscientiously on the thankless task of being part of the salvage drive: collecting guns and ammunition left behind by the retreating enemy, when I am sure they would have much preferred the more prestigious job of chasing the enemy out of Egypt. Then there was the occasion when 476 Battery was praised for its "good work" in knocking out several enemy guns during the German Army's failed pre-emptive strike on the 6th March. Also Montgomery himself made a point of praising the work of the regiment during their successful outflanking manoeuvre which contributed to the Allied victory at Mareth. After Uncle Charlie had spent a few horrendous days being heavily shelled and working under an unbearable strain, a wireless operator was sent to relieve him, giving Charlie a chance to rest at H.Q. To me this demonstrates some compassion for the men, their efforts and their bravery, and I believe that despite the large number of deaths, lives were not devalued: every soldier mattered, which convinced me that the Army had a soul. I think back to Major Strutt's compassionate letter of condolence to Charlie's parents written six months after he died when the Major returned to the fray after recovering from his wounds. Montgomery himself liked to keep a high profile by face-to-face communication with the men as often as possible, and due to his demonstration of the common touch, the soldiers of the 8th Army not only identified with their General, they would have gladly followed him wherever he led, such was their loyalty and respect for 'Monty.'

I was also struck by the efficiency of the 8th Army. I have heard the saying: "Military Precision" but not really appreciated the phrase until it became clear as I read about the regular, organized training sessions, designed to improve effectiveness in combat. The exercises were spread throughout the eight months of the Campaign; but – not resting on any laurels – the Royal Artillery gun training sessions began merely weeks after their victory at El-Alamein.

Regiments were moved around different Brigades and Divisions to make the most efficient use of men and equipment. Nearing the end of the North Africa Campaign when enemy shelling was fierce, one of the three regimental batteries was rested each day, and after days of fighting with very little respite the whole regiment was pulled out of line for a rest. This demonstrates not only consideration and compassion for those men in the stressful and life threatening positions on the front line, but also shows efficiency in having men rested, thereby improving effectiveness and morale. It is the War Diaries that recorded the repulse of the enemy's pre-emptive strike on the

6th March, and the resulting awards of one Military Cross and two Military Medals.

The 8th Army was master of the desert terrain it moved through. Each man understood the conditions he was facing and, despite the clogging sand, dust and dirt, ensured vehicles were well maintained (and more importantly) kept moving. Another factor worthy of note was the efficiency of the supply line in coping with the Army's insatiable demand for food, water, fuel, equipment, replacement vehicles and parts. During the outflanking manoeuvre the long supply line was efficiently managed from Medenine through Wilder's Gap and beyond as it drew an ever lengthening line in the sand. In early December the regiment travelled an incredible 300 miles in two weeks, stopping along the way to prepare for more battles with the enemy.

On the 14th March 111 Field Regiment passed to the command of the reputable 2nd N.Z. Division where it remained until the end of the North Africa Campaign.

Charlie's Diary, letters and the War Diaries represent a perfect Triumvirate, each one with its own part to play; slotting together, they complete the story of the North Africa Campaign. The War Diaries record an eventful history in the curves, loops, dots and dashes of a pencil, and, just like Charlie's letters and diary, after seventy years have not been dulled by the passage of time: they seem to be as fresh as the day they were written. The Diaries have been an invaluable aid to me, recording the daily conflict in precise detail, providing the bigger picture and increasing my knowledge and understanding of military history. I really appreciated the strong sense of history the War Diaries engendered in me, and again, as with Charlie's letters and diary, I felt privileged to be reading the digitized copies of the original documents so many years after they were written. Without the Regimental War Diaries Charles Robinson's story would have been incomplete.

I am proud to say that my signalman uncle was attached to a regiment that fought at El-Alamein, was part of a successful outflanking manoeuvre leading to victory in the battle for the Mareth Line, the taking of the Takrouna Feature and finally their enforced holding position at Enfidaville, when it became a war of attrition – a stalemate of guns and ammunition and the place where he lost his life. The Regimental War Diaries detail the regiment's contribution to the winning of the North Africa Campaign, and the vitally important task of receiving and relaying messages from the commanding officer to the three regimental batteries: a task performed by one small man with glasses, Charles Robinson. For this, his contribution to the success of the Campaign, I feel very proud and privileged to be his niece. He was part of a revered group of thousands of men who fought and travelled so many hard miles, and endured such harsh conditions; but I will let Winston Churchill sum up the contribution of these men to the victory of the North Africa Campaign:

> Let me assure you, soldiers and airmen, that your fellow-countrymen regard your joint work with admiration and gratitude, and that after the war when a man is asked what he did it will be quite sufficient for him to say 'I marched and fought with the Desert Army' And when history is written and all the facts are known, our feats will gleam and glow and will be a source of song and story long after we who are gathered here have passed away.[1]

The Diary

I can't help wishing that Uncle Charlie's Diary had been larger as it may have encouraged him to write more each day. As it is, even with his neat and tiny writing, one day's entry only transfers to about four lines of typing on the page. I feel sure that given his writing skills and with additional space he would have grasped the opportunity to express more of his thoughts, feelings and observations. Many of Charlie's daily accounts mirror the War Diaries by describing factual events. However, there were times when Charlie's feelings took precedence over more practical concerns: for example when he described the mental stresses he was suffering when under fire. Also Charlie notes numerous personal accounts of his experiences with people, places, and daily events that the War Diaries (with an official regimental daily record to write) cannot describe. But these two very different versions of daily events complement each other very well.

It feels like I have travelled the same two thousand miles with my Uncle Charlie (not quite the same as spending the afternoon in Africa, as Mrs. Redfern claimed!) but beside him in spirit, feeling an empathy with his long journey nevertheless. He passed through Egypt, Libya and Tunisia: through places with strange sounding names like Tatahouine (when his regiment dropped deep into the desert on their outflanking manoeuvre) Takrouna, Metameur, El-Samen, Gazala – just a small sample of the fifty nine named places: hamlets, towns, cities, collection of dwellings, or simply grid reference points on a military map – that the war diaries record having passed by or passed through since the regiment left El-Alamein. Charlie obviously enjoyed arriving in different places, looking round colourful towns and cities whenever he was given the chance to take some leave. On one occasion he walked into a nearby village and sat cross-legged on a stone slab to experience a local haircut, meeting and talking with the locals with whom he would converse, preferably in English, or, if not, then French would have to suffice (better than not communicating at all). Being his usual friendly self, and keen to make contact with others, he made strenuous attempts to converse with the Italian family he met in Libya. Demonstrating his friendly, outgoing nature to all, Charlie also talked with New Zealanders, Maoris, South Africans, Libyans, Egyptians, and Tunisians.

My Uncle did express some grumbles in his account of experiences from 1st January until 6th May 1943: wet blankets in heavy rain which took three days to dry out fully; caught in a rain storm when he had to get up very early to wake Mr. Hugo, wryly saying "just my luck"; setting out in a sandstorm to go out on a gun calibration exercise (luckily it was cancelled). On the 14th February, back at Tac.H.Q. he was on set for a very long eighteen hours. Mosquitos were a serious problem when the 8th Army reached Tunisia, and on top of all that there was sand – sand everywhere – it must have found its way into everything. I am sure Charlie could have expressed many more complaints than the above irritants had he a mind to.

Understandably, there were tensions too: on the 9th January Charlie had a "silly row" with Mat Read about milk – I suppose it could have been about anything – given the close proximity to each other – relationships would inevitably become strained at times. But the argument was soon resolved. Then there was the occasion when both wireless set and truck broke down, the result being they lost touch with the regiment – having to stop for the night – before finding their way back. This incident occurred just when the C.O. required Charlie and his wireless set to be fully operational. When Charlie explained the situation, Mr. Hugo thought he was pulling his leg. Again, the misunderstanding was sorted out.

There was evidence within the diary that Charlie was becoming inured to a soldier's life. By January of 1943 he had come through the fierce fighting of El-Alamein the previous October/November, and was well on his way to chasing the German and Italian armies out of North Africa. With comments like: "Action again I suppose" following the Regiment's half hour notice to go; then on the 15th January, on the eve of another battle, he was not too tense to enjoy a good night's sleep, which I think demonstrates some resignation to his daily challenges.

In his diary, as in his letters, the subject of money was never far from Charlie's mind. He always noted when there was some anomaly such as a delay in receiving his allotment. On the 4th April he noted that he had been paid in French francs. Then there was his neat back of diary account where he totaled his weekly pay from 1st January to the 7th May. To me, those entries on the back page – simply a list of dates and figures – are as touchingly significant as anything else he has written; the figures he so neatly entered, seem to shout out the price of his sacrifice: from the 1st January to the 7th May he earned a mere £13.18.00.

Charlie was well trained by Royal Signals to do the vitally important job of sending and receiving messages via a wireless set. His task was to relay instructions using a combination of Morse code and a form of three letter code signals and abbreviations to the Regiment's three batteries. In 1943 the Army used the phonetic alphabet, similar to the one in use today by the emergency services. Royal Artillery always had the highest priority of fire order as it was vitally important to relay messages – without delay – to the readied and waiting guns. It was very stressful during the heat of battle – right up on the front line – amongst the noisy chaos of bangs and booms all around, under severe and unremitting enemy fire; yet still demanding complete concentration for long hours "on set". During very intense fighting in March, Charlie suffered from the stress of battle, writing of his mental anguish as the "nerve-racking" shelling lasted an interminable three and a half days, compelling Charlie to record his suffering. He wrote that enemy fire was "hellish" and "it is beginning to tell a tale on me, I'm getting nervous." For Charlie, often reluctant to express his feelings, he is sending a clear message that he is suffering from combat stress. Fortunately his commanding officer arranged for a replacement wireless operator to relieve Charlie, who thankfully returned to the relative safety of Head Quarters, away from the front line, where the majority of his fellow wireless operators were based. Eventually he seemed to recover from the living nightmare of those few days in March and he did return to Tac.H.Q.

During Charlie's six month journey from El-Alamein to Enfidaville he writes of the two joyous occasions when he managed to procure some bags of water – enough to have a bath! Oh Joy! Two baths in six months! How he reveled in those makeshift baths. And then there was more enjoyment to be had: swimming in the Mediterranean. His first swim of 1943 on the 1st April reminded him of his previous swim, way back on the 26th December – when he wrote of the novelty of swimming in the sea on Boxing Day! Charlie was lucky enough to have enjoyed eight swims during his time in North Africa. He always made the most of "bathing parties" as the War Diaries termed them, and on his last day of swimming on the 3rd May, he entered the water three times. The long journey from El-Alamein to Enfidaville, thankfully, was not all bad. As well as the glorious swims and baths, he also enjoyed the changing terrain, from the desert landscapes of Egypt and Libya to the cultivated, green land of Tunisia, where he savoured the spectacle of passing mile after mile of cool green olive groves.

Charlie also experienced some memorable highlights of his "enforced exile." He had the privilege of seeing Montgomery four times, and each time he was impressed by the man and the occasion. He also enjoyed the spectacle of seeing Winston Churchill drive past his waiting regiment, as they lined the road out of Tripoli. But the final most memorable and meaningful event was the victory parade through Sousse, making such an impression on my Uncle, and giving him the conviction that the very long journey he and his companions had undertaken – enduring so much – had been utterly worthwhile.

Charlie had some lucky days, too, with lots of near-misses. Like the day a piece of shrapnel smashed into the back of Charlie's truck, passed through it and exited the front – incredibly without damaging any flesh – but wrecking the wireless set on its way through. Then there was the time when, without mishap, the regiment picked its way through an area "thick with mines". There was the occasion when two shells landed, one on either side of the vehicle. His final piece of luck happened when a shell landed on a corner of the dug-out he was in, shook it, but did not collapse the structure. One lucky day for Charlie was not so lucky for Ally Hay who was seriously wounded only feet away from where Charlie had been sitting after he had gone inside the truck.

From his first diary entry on 1st January to his last one on the 6th May, Charlie survived air-raids by Stuka's, M.E.9's, shells, mortars, mines, bombs and bullets, several of which were near misses, each one seemingly closer than the last, until sadly, the Grim Reaper honed in and Uncle Charlie's luck ran out on the 12th May. Out of 126 days of diary entries, almost a third – thirty seven – were spent fighting – more than one of those days he described as "hellish".

Some clichés come to mind as I near the end of my *"long journey"* in my *"quest"* to learn about Uncle Charlie, his *"trials and tribulations"* in North Africa and details of his *"ultimate sacrifice"* not forgetting: *"only the good die young"* before reaching the *"final chapter"* of my *"labour of love"*. To use another cliché this has been the story of a man who: *"never had a bad word to say about anyone"*- (with the exception of his scathing criticism of the Japanese – following their unprovoked attack on Pearl Harbour, found in his letter of the 10th December, 1941.) Clichés are convenient, ready-made expressions and are so prevalent that their true meaning becomes blunted by frequent use. A "Labour of love" can become something enjoyable – achieved after only one hour's work. A "long journey" can become a week's "quest" on the internet. "Only the good die young" doesn't seem to be heard so much today; but Mum uses the phrase in her heart-felt words at the end of Charlie's diary, when, perhaps that expression was more prevalent then. Finally the "ultimate sacrifice" rolls off the tongue so easily, and, due to the conflict in Afghanistan we are still hearing that expression today, when most of us feel sad that another young man has lost his life, and are aware that his family and friends will be grieving. Everyone understands the meaning of the ultimate sacrifice, and it remains just as poignant as ever.

For me, the years I have spent writing this book have truly been a labour of love, as Uncle Charlie's story is a story about my family, a part of me and therefore part of my D.N.A. Having watched T.V. programmes when famous faces are researching their family tree, they become emotional about a troubled ancestor, perhaps going back generations – never known, but *touched* by the unbreakable bond of D.N.A. I understand their emotion, having experienced it for myself. My attachment to my uncle increased by the day as his story unfolded, as I discovered new gems of information. My former ignorance on the history of the North Africa Campaign dissolved then reformed into a new and respectful understanding.

My Mum always spoke of Charlie's "goodness" – feelings which are understandable following the loss of her beloved elder brother. When someone passes away, it is unseemly to criticise their memory, and when a family member makes the ultimate sacrifice, the sheer power of their sacrifice will over-ride everything except heart-felt eulogies. So what have I observed for myself about the character of Charlie? In his photographs I see a confident, relaxed individual –

comfortable in his own skin, with an outgoing personality that belies his small stature. Judging by the number of letters he sent and received from friends and family, he was well liked (and loved) by many people. Reading his letters I know he had a sense of humour. I also know that he felt empathy for others, particularly the many local people he met by chance on his "walkabouts" or when passing through their villages and towns: people who were different in colour, creed, and language. He was meticulous, (perhaps perfectionist) in his writing and in his preoccupation with money and the recording of figures. He loved chocolate (and other sweet things),

Before I started to write this book I only "knew" my Uncle Charlie from a large black and white photograph on a sideboard. Despite its unremarkable familiarity, the image has stayed with me for over sixty years, fading with time, and almost – but not quite – forgotten: waiting patiently for resurrection when I read his diary for the first time. Mum's cousin Hilda, uncannily, wrote of *her* memory of that very same iconic photograph and vase of flowers in her letter to me.

I understood that he had been killed in a truck travelling through the desert in the Second World War. Now, via his letters, diary, accounts from my mother, father and cousin I feel I know him almost as well as if I had actually spent time in his company, because in a sense I *have* spent time: reading and thinking about his words, so neatly written on the page, words brought to life again after so many years of lying in a box amongst old photographs. I may not have literally walked in his desert boots, but I feel I have walked beside him, absorbing something of his daily life in North Africa and reliving his memorable experiences, thanks to his diary and letters. The photographs, showing a smiling, relaxed, confident person, with an out-going personality shouts of a bigger man, adding extra height to his small frame. When I eventually received Charlie's service records, I was surprised to see his height on enlistment was only 5 feet four and a half inches. I imagined him to be taller. But he *was* a big man – big hearted with a generosity of spirit, friendly and outgoing towards everyone, regardless of colour or creed. He was helpful too, his meticulous nature coming to the fore when he identified and wrote the names of friends on the back of many photographs – thank you. Before being called up he lived life to the full, mixing with many people in the clubs and activities in which he participated.

Now I know so much more about him. He was a perfectionist, a Christian, a Methodist, a choir member, an enthusiastic traveller, a great communicator, and his complaints about his "exile" were few. He loved swimming in the turquoise waters of the Mediterranean sea, (who wouldn't!) He had a well-developed sense of humour, appreciating the funny side of life. He was outgoing, open to new experiences, thoughtful as well as capable of empathy. He was loving and in turn was much loved. I know that any faults he had were pushed aside by the sheer weight of the sacrifice he made.

He gave his life so that others could be free. In a sad irony, after surviving so many battles and near-misses during March and April, he was one of the last soldiers to lose his life in the dying hours of the North Africa Campaign. I am proud and thankful for what he did for me and for a few million others. He surrendered his future – perhaps fifty more years of living – eventful years in which he may have married, experienced the joys and challenges of becoming an uncle and a father. His early death had stolen away his future.

The final few words, written in Charlie's diary were not his, but, in fact, written by his sister in heartfelt, touching, words, expressing her loss, forty years after his death, in tellingly large capital letters written in the blank spaces of his diary on the 11th – 23rd May 1943:

Tues. 11th May
NEVER A DAY GOES BY BUT I THINK OF HIM WITH REGRET.

Wed. 12th May.
CHARLIE KILLED TODAY. HIS TRUCK BLOWN UP IN ACTION. GERMANS HAD SURRENDERED, BUT CHARLIE'S REG. PLUS GERMANS DIDN'T KNOW.

13th – 23rd May
THEY WERE IN THE HILLS IN A SMALL POCKET. I'M WRITING THIS WHICH I FOUND 40 YEARS AFTER, ON EMPTYING MOTHER'S HOUSE. IT BROUGHT IT ALL BACK. THE TERRIBLE SADNESS OF LOSING SUCH A WONDERFUL BROTHER. EVERYONE LIKED HIM. I FEEL SO UNHAPPY TO HAVE GONE THROUGH LIFE WITHOUT HIM. HE WAS ALWAYS FAIR, HAPPY AND UNDERSTANDING, HARDWORKING AND ENJOYING HIS LEISURE HOURS WITH SO MANY PEOPLE WHO ALL WANTED TO BE HIS FRIEND. AS HIS SISTER, I FEEL PRIVILEGED TO HAVE GROWN UP WITH HIM. HE WAS ALWAYS MY CHAMPION. HE UNDERSTOOD MY SLOWER WAYS, WHICH MUST HAVE MADE HIM IMPATIENT, BUT HE ALWAYS SHOWED ME PATIENCE AND KINDNESS, PRAISED ME WHEN PRAISE WAS NEEDED. TRIED TO GET MY FATHER TO LET ME GO TO TO DANCES, WHICH I WANTED. SO BRIGHT, SO QUICK SO – CHARLIE. I NEVER

RECALL EVER HAVING A ROW WITH HIM. HE WAS
TOO PERFECT FOR ALL OF US, BUT HOW WE ALL
LOVED HIM. IT'S TRUE ONLY THE GOOD DIE
YOUNG. 25 YEARS OF AGE

It has been a privilege to write the story of Charles Robinson: Charlie, the uncle I never met; the soldier in the black and white photograph, standing beside the snowdrops, fresh, innocent and unknowing.

> *They went with songs to the battle, they were young*
> *Straight of limb, true of eyes, steady and aglow,*
> *They were staunch to the end against odds uncounted,*
> *They fell with their faces to the foe.*
>
> *They shall grow not old as we that are left grow old*
> *Age shall not weary them, nor the years condemn*
> *At the going down of the sun, and in the morning,*
> *We will remember them.*
>
> *Laurence Binyon. "For the Fallen."*

Notes

1 Speech made at Tripoli on 3rd February, 1943 to General Montgomery and men of the Joint Headquarters of the 8th Army. It was on the following day Churchill drove past Charlie's regiment as they lined the road out of Tripoli.

War Diaries Of 111 Field Regiment, Royal Artillery.

1943 1st January – 13th May.

1st January: 476 Bty. exercised with 1RB. 212 Bt. and 211 Bty. with 5RTR

2nd January: …30 Corps visited Rgt.in morning… 8th Army arrived 1000 hrs. & watched Rgt. Practice with live shells on ranges. B.R.A. expressed himself satisfied.

3rd January: "Rgt. went to ranges to calibrate guns. However, a sandstorm blew up and it was impossible to carry out …? detail. Rgt. returned from ranges and battled against the storm in the lines.

4th January: Sandstorm continues all day.

5th January: Regimental Exercise. This was to test out methods of producing:

a) Rgt. concentrations under conditions of no grid and no maps

b) As above, but with Rgt. on arbitrary grid fixed by Rgt. Survey Section.

c) Quick Barrage in support of Tanks. This exercise produced many lessons, but showed that what had been projected was possible within reasonable times. 1930 hrs Conference held in evening to discuss lessons from Exercise.

6th January: The Regiment's guns were calibrated by the comparative method. A Troop of 4th Field Surrey Regiment assisted.

7th January: C.O lecture to officers was followed by an exercise on Regimental concentrations. In the afternoon course shooting under b…took place. Reinforcements 5 officers and 56 O.R's arrived.

8th January: (Illegible report.)

9th January: C.O. & Adj. left for Army Cmmds. Conference.

10th January: C.O. attended Army Cmmdr. Conference. Rgt. Moved 70 miles West and came under Cmmd. 22 Armd. Bde. Corps Arty. Orders received.

11th January: Rgt. moved S.W. of Sirte.

12th January: O.O. No. 8 issued. Bde. O.O. rec'd. C.O. gave confidential talk to officers, giving Army Cdrs. Message.

13th January: Preparations were made for the westwards advance.

14th January: Regt. under command 22 Armd. Bde. 211 and 212 Bttys. in support 5 R.T.R. and 476 in support. Regiment moved to 60 miles west of battle position.

15th January: Advanced 5 miles to a spot 7 miles East of SONDA

16th January: Retreating enemy pursued with 12 Lancers on patrol. No actions during the day. Route Zonda-Zem-Zem to S. of CHEDDAHIA. Very bad going through Zem-Zem…?Single line ahead. 0700hrs. Advance continued N. past Ghaddania to Babdel Gader

17th January: Advance continued N. past Ghaddanir to B Abdel Gader.

18th January: Advance cont. N. and N.W. area. Good going to S.W. of Zliten

19th January: Enemy in force at Homs and Tarhuna. Bde. halted while suitable road between these places was being recc'd. 7th Armd. Div. towards Tarhuna.

20th January: Col. & Adj. recc'd …? for guns to go on to Homs. 212 Btty. moved forward to Homs. Remainder of Rgt. spent day on refitting, refuelling and maintenance. 7th Armd. toward Tarhuna.

21st January: Remainder of Rgt. less 212 Bty. Moved via Zliten to 3 miles W. of Homs

22nd January: 111 Tac. H.Q. moved forward with Army Cdr. 5 RTR with 476 Field Bty. in support to escort Army Cdr. into Tripoli. Very bad going owing to blown bridges and deep Wadis delayed column. Halted for night at Castel Verde.

23rd January: 11th Hussars entered Tripoli 0540hrs. 5 RTR at 0640hrs. 111 Field Regiment moved to an artillery concentration area S.W. of Tripoli.

24th – 30th January: Days spent in washing, cleaning and maintaining equipment.

30th January: O.O. No. 8 issued for move into 30 Corps GMC area.

31st January: Detachment from Rgt. attended victory parade and march past in Tripoli.

February.

1st February: Tripoli – 1000hrs. Regiment reverted to 30 Corps and moved to Corps Artillery concentration area 9km S.W. Tripoli.

2nd February: No report

3rd February: TRIPOLI 1200hrs. – Guns and men lined Tripoli-Garian Rd. for Corps. Cmmdrs. Inspection. Under 12 hrs. notice to join 7 Armd. Div. 1500hrs. Regt. to join 7 Amd. Div. forthwith. C.O. and Adj. went fwd. to 131 Bde. H.Q. 6 reinforcements arrived.

4th February: TRIPOLI – 1100hrs. Tripoli-Garian Rd. lined by Rgt. to cheer Rt. Hon. Winston Churchill, P.M., C.I.G.S. Gen. Sir Alan Brooke, C. in C. Middle East, Sir H. Alexander and General Montgomery as they passed. The turnout of the Regt. after crossing the Libyan desert was very favourably commented on.

1300hrs. 21 reinforcements arrived. Rgt. under Cmd. 131 Bde. and moved to 50 miles W. of Tripoli.

5th February: The pursuit of Rommel's remnants taken up again.

1500hrs 212 Bty. moved fwd. to 2 miles S.W. of Pisida and remainder of regiment …? 5m E. of Pisida for night. The main road was strafed and dive-bombed twice during the day. 2 O.R's injured and two guns slightly damaged.

6th February: Lt. Col. Hill assumed command of 111 Field Rgt. Group consisting of 111 Field, 69…? 150 Light AA Bty, 231 Lt AA Bty…? No. 1 Composite Bty., 4 Surrey Rgt. for current operation of securing a firm base at Pisida. Group O.O. No. 1 issued During the day O.P's pushed forward W. of Pisida to border, and came back at night

7th February: Regimental area shelled by 175mm. gun.

8th February: 211 Bty, 476 Bty moved forward securing a firm base at Pisida. Holding strong positions on Tunisia frontier and road. Pisida frontier under obs and shellfire. One O.R. killed by shellfire.

9th February: Sniping section from 211 Bty. went up and attacked O.P's and M,G. posts. O.P's pushed up to frontier.

10th February: 1600hrs. 212 Bty. remained at Pisida and regiment moved back to Zuara. O.O. No. 4 issued.

11th February: EL-ASSA 0700hrs. Regiment turned West again and went to positions at El-Assa forming a firm base there with one fifth and one sixth Queens. Rgt. in support of 131 Bde. reverting to command C.R.A. 7 Armd. Div.

12th February: Regiment held up while causeway was being built over Tunisian border.

13th February: 212 Bty. moved to El-Assa

14th February: 476 Bty. moved with one fifth Queen's across border N.W. of BIR-SAMEN. During the day remainder of regiment followed and leaguered for the night in TUNISIA.

15th February: A day of movement pursuing the retreating enemy. The Bde. Adv. in desert formation with one fifth Queens and 476 Bty. in support leading with OP's pushed well forward. BENGARDANE was taken and the regiment leaguered there for the night.

16th February: Rgt. remained at Ben Gardane all day. Considerable air activity by enemy. 211 Bty. position bombed. 5 casualties,

3 evacuated. Lt. MacLeod Carey hit a mine in jeep and was evacuated with…? Lt. Barton came to RHQ as…? Officer.

17th February: Rgt. Moved to Nefatia under 131 Bde and formed there a firm base. No opposition on advance.

18th February: NEFATIA.

19th February: Regiment advanced by night to a position East of Medenine. Regiment in action 0400hrs.

20th February: Rgt. supported advance of 22 Armd. Bde. to outflank Medenine. 3 O.P.'s out. O.P''s withdrew when Rgt. was out of range. Rgt. then supported 131 Bde. in forming firm base. 212 Bty. sent out a …? section forward in evening. Capt. Nott wounded by shell fire and evacuated. Considerable enemy air activity all day.

21st February: Rgt. remained in position all day except 211 Bty. which advanced at first light in support 1/7th Queens to the west of Medenine. 211 lost one Stuart tank on mine field. Track blown out.

22nd February: METAMEUR – Rgt. Advanced to Metameur with 211 Bty. and 476 Bty. covering de-bussing of 1/7 Queens in the morning. These Btys. then moved up with 212 Bty. to a Rgmt. area at Metameur. The area was covered with mines which were removed during the day with R.E's assistance. 1.15 cwt. was blown up.

23rd February: 0800hrs. I.O.S. and D.F. tasks were registered by firing live shells.

24th February: 0700 First light vis. Poor…?. Visibility improved later in morning. 1500 Received orders to move and was moving at 1600 hrs. 1640 Arrvd. new location E6785

25th February: D.F. Tasks registered… Moved 1500hrs. to E639889. "A" troop was heavily shelled after occupation of its position. No casualties. Troop moved to new location during night. One … undertaken.

26th February: D.F. tasks registered. Regimental area was intermittently shelled all day. Considerable enemy air activity. 1300hrs Div. target engaged. 1500hrs Div. target engaged.

27th February: 131 Bde. was relieved by 154 Bde. – consequently had to alter the way it was facing, but did not change location. D.F. tasks on new 131 Bde. front and registered in evening from…? Positions.

28th February: D.F. and S.O.S. tasks for 131 Bde. Issued during day in the form of a trace and task table.E639889 Rgt. H.Q. was shelled in afternoon. Lt. F. Neary L.O. at R.H.Q. was wounded and evacuated. Rgt. Op…? was produced and attached as app. Orders for all round defensive position issued.

March

1st March: 1100hrs. Small amount of enemy movement seen and engaged during day. British plane dropped bomb near R.H.Q. 1300hrs. Major E.B. Walker, R.A. was injured by and subsequently died from a round fired by his battery, whilst he was ranging. New D.F. tasks were registered by 212 and 476 Btys. 1900hrs. Orders recd. for 111 Fld. Regt. to move on 2 Mar, two Btys. and RHQ to take over from 58 Fld. Regt. One Bty. (211) to go to 8 Armd. Bde. Under Comd.

2nd March: 1000hrs. 211 Bty. moved out. Whilst moving out they came under considerable enemy shell fire, without sustaining damage. 1100hrs. RHQ and 212 and 476 Btys. closed down at old location. RHQ in new location. 1230hrs. E727771 were shelled on coming in. 1503hrs. Both Btys. in action in new location. Orders received for 111 Fld. Regt. To join 8 Armd. Bde. Complete by 4th March

3rd March: 0300hrs. 30 Corps Arty. ordered to engage Corps Tgt.) suspected enemy movement in sq. 5892. 111 Fld. Rgmt was out of range. 0800hrs. 30 Corps. Arty. engaged HB tgts. 111 Fld. Rgmt. was out of range. 1000hrs. 111 Fld. Rgmt. Moved to sup. 8 Armd. Bde. 1230hrs. RHQ and 476 Bty. established and in action at new location. 211 Bty. joined Rgt. again. 1745hrs. A German attack developed in area 260. Enemy tanks showed themselves in area E46. 2200hrs. 212 Bty. Established at new location.

4th March: Nothing to report.

5th March: 111 Fld. Rgt. Placed on permanent grid.

6th March: 0700hrs. German tank attack developed from West of Medenine. 0945hrs. 8 Armd. Bde. with 111 Fld. Rgmt. in sp. moved towards Metameur to engage enemy tanks.1100hrs. Tac. H.Q. established at 700816. Btys. in action area 7081. E706824 1400hrs. 7082. Main H.Q. 111 Fld. Rgmt. established at 706824. All Btys. engaged enemy to West of Metameur, but 476 Bty. in particular carried out successful shoots, destroying 88mm guns and being instrumental in stopping an infantry attack. 111 Fld. Rgmt. moved into close leaguer with 8 Armd Bde.

7th March: 0600hrs. 111 Fld. Rgmt. moved out of leaguer into Bty. positions in same area as 6th March. H.Q. returned to 755895.1030hrs. 212 Bty. moved fwd. to pos. west of Metameur at 68075 followed by other Btys. 1800hrs. Enemy activity on Rgt. front on greatly reduced scale. Rgt. prepared to put down concentrations during night, but these were not required.

8th March: 0900hrs. Regt. complete moved back to former area E7588 to E7689. 1705hrs. Regt. Strafed by enemy fighters, but no damage caused except to tyres.

9th March: Capt. M.F. Strutt appointed to command 476 Fld. Bty... Major E.B Walker. Lt. W.R. Middleton appointed Adj. and promoted.

10th March: Rgt. Received extra 3 tonnes and 15 cwts. to make up to scale for future operations.

11th March: 35 reinforcements recd. Mainly D.U.B. and Sigs.

12th March: Regt. Recd. 8 Armd. Bge. Movement Order 8 and Admin. Order No. 16.

13th March: Capt. J.B.H. Daniel promoted A/Major from 1st March and took over duties of second in Command

14th March: Capt. M.E. Strutt promoted A/Major via Major R.M... who was evacuated. 111 Fld. Regt. moved to ... area at 1300 hrs.

and arrived at 2330hrs.1800hrs. 8 Armd. Bde. and 111 Fld. Rgmt. passed to commd. of N.Z. Div. from 7 Armd. Div.

15th March: 1900hrs 111 Fld. Rgt. Left Staging Area . Each Btty. moving with its affiliated Armd. Rgmt. as per 8 Armd. Bge. Movement Order 9.

16th March: 1800hrs. 111 Fld. Rgmt. Arrived in assembly area with 8 Armd. Bde. 111 Fld. Rgmt. lay up in this area for several days during which time its MT situation and organization for the battle was considered and adjusted.

17th March: No Report.

18th March: No Report

19th March: 1800hrs. 111 Fld. Rgmt. moved under command 8 Armd. Bde. as per their Op. Order No. 19 to lying-up area. 2400hrs.111 Fld. Rgmt. leaguered for night at...E1033

20th March: 0800hrs. 111 Fld. Rgmt. continued march northward. Contact with ...units of enemy at approx. E1253. After being shelled, enemy withdrew. 111 Fld. Rgmt. deployed in Rgtal area and prepared to support Buffs by D.F. This was not, however, required.

21st March: 0800hrs. The Btys. moved off with their Armd. Regts. Followed by H.Q. 111 Fld. Rgmt. Btys. deployed in area D8898 and engaged enemy heavily with shell fire. 1800hrs. H.Q. established at 898980 for night.

22nd March: 0700hrs. 111 Fld. Regt. moved forward but Rgmtal. target engaged whilst on move. Guns were widely dispersed in area 8701 to 8804. During day all parts of Regt. was subjected to bombing, shelling and M-gunning from air.1300hrs. H.Q. Established at approx. 870010.

23rd March: Strafing by enemy continued. Capt. F.W. Gifford and several O.R's killed. Lt's. Charlesworth and Deer and about ten O.R's with wounds. Engaged enemy heavily, firing some 900 rds. during day. H.Q. established at 882041 for night, the Btys. being deployed to North and East of this.

24th March: Throughout day Rgt. engaged successfully enemy concentration as Rgmtal. Targets. Cmmd. 8th Armd. Bde. congratulated Rgmt. on its performance. Btys. were deployed in areas 8608 and H.Q. was established at 885060.1430hrs. Majors Strutt and Wale and Capt A… wounded, and evacuated. Capt. Hackett was killed. Several O.R.'s were also wounded. Rgt. was continually bombed and shelled during day.

25th March: Activity on both sides was on a reduced scale, but further concentrations were put down. At 1700hrs Regt. concentrated in area 8507. 8508 in preparation for attack on following day. Lt. Watkinson injured and evacuated.

26th March: 1600hrs – No firing during early part of day. At 1600hrs Rgmt. fired concentrations as part of an Arty. programme of N.Z. Corps and 1st Armd. Division in sp. of an attack by N.Z. Corps and 1st Armd. Div. in direction of El Hamma. Armd. O.P's went fwd. with 8 Armd. Bge. 2130hrs The Regt. Achieved a "brew up" on one of its concentrations. A report received – that objective was reached.

27th March: 0700hrs. 8 Amd. Bde. moved fwd. with Rgmtal. O.P.'s in sp. 1055hrs. Regt. Moved fwd. into area 8811 and at 1400hrs. H.Q. was established at 880102. 2300hrs. Rgt. advanced in Armd. Rgmtal. Gps. and at 0630 went into open leaguer at 975178

28th March: 0900hrs. Rgt. and 8 Armd. Bge. was directed on Gabes, but met slight opposition. Several Rgtal. targets were engaged and the Rgt. was shelled intermittently. 1900hrs. Rgt. moved into close leaguer in area 1019.

29th March: 0900hrs. Rgt. Ordered to move with 8 Armd. Bde. To cut roads out of Gabes. However, Gabes was reported occupied and Rgt. moved north into action at 205346. H.Q. established. for the night at 203060.

30th March: 0820hrs. Rgt. moved on and came into near Oudref. 1400hrs. R.H.Q. established at 176446. Rgt. engaged light enemy forces holding the Gabes gap during the afternoon.

31st March: 1300hrs. A quiet morning. At 1300hrs. Regt. was taken out of line for a period of rest. Rgt. went into open leaguer in area 308366

April

1st April: 308366 Day spent in maintenance and rest.

2nd April: Lt. Col. W.P. Hobbs, M.B.E., R.A. assuming cmd. of 111 Fld. Regt., R.A. Vice Lt. Col. J.G. Hill, M.B.E., M.C., R.A. on the latter's promotion to Brigadier, C.R.A. 50 Div.

3rd April: 2nd Lt. E.D. Roberts, R.A. posted to Regt. A number of new vehicles arrived.

4th April: 10-30 hrs. Gen. B.L. Montgomery inspected the regiment and spoke to the men . A new draft arrived and more new vehicles. Also Lt. A.G.A. Owen arrived from hospital. Cassell, Lt. Idle and 2/Lt. Lacy were posted. Major W.H. Cheesman arrived to assume cmd. 211 Fld. Bty.

5th April: Z2037. 1400hrs. Regt. moved off to rejoin 8 Armd. Bde in area 2037.

6th April: 0600hrs. Regt. moved to west of Oudref and formed up for advance.

1530hrs. Regt. came into action in area 130545 and engaged enemy guns and infantry. The enemy resistance was stubborn and no further advance was possible. At nightfall Regt..leaguered with Armd. Regts.

7th April: 0800hrs. The enemy having withdrawn, the Regt. advanced with objective Chebket En Nouiges (Z19), Tanks and enemy guns were met in area 1879 and the Regt. went into action in area Z0777

1730hrs. A tank battle started in area Z08, which ended in the enemy's withdrawal.

8th April: 0545hrs. Regt. continued its advance U1405 area Z0777 0815hrs. 211 Bty. came into action in area 1405 followed by 212 and 476 Btys.1745hrs. Tanks and M.E.T. were engaged. 211 Bty.

moved fwd. with 8 Armd. Bde. in direction of Retba (U32) Lt. Blyde injured and evacuated 4 men in 211 Bty. killed and several wounded by A.P. shot.

9th April: 0530hrs. Remainder of Regt. moved towards Retba and advance continued beyond there. Regt. eventually came into action in area U220550. There were numerous enemy tanks to the North and West and two brew-ups were achieved. 1800hrs. Bde. engaged these tanks and the enemy withdrew. The Regt. went into leaguer in area U300540.

10th April: 0900hrs. Regt. moved towards U770790. 1355hrs. 211 Bty. came into action at U760790 followed two hours later by the other batteries.1700hrs. Spasmodic firing at assorted targets took place. 212 Bty. moved fwd. to sp. Staffs. Yeomanry but did not come into action.

11th April: 1740hrs. Regt. moved fwd. on El Djem. 1930hrs. Regt. moved towards Sousse in rear of Notts. Yeomanry. 2200hrs. Regt. halted at P6317.

12th April: 0800hrs. Regt. advanced to Msaken, and then North, bypassing Sousse.1040hrs. 476 Bty. came into action in area P5349. 211 and 212 Btys. went through. 476 came into action in area P5254. There was intermittent shelling by both sides. 1700hrs. Regt. moved into action in area P5060 and remained there during night.

13th April: (Continuation Sheet 4.) 0715hrs. 211 Bty. moved fwd. with 3 R.T.R. Opposition was not in area 3578. 1130hrs. Regt. moved into area P3673, being deployed by 1345hrs. Enemy guns and M.E.T. were engaged as Reg'tal and Bty. targets during afternoon. Towards evening our Inf. patrol line was well formed and the guns were out of range (Continuation Sheet 5 missing.)

Continuation Sheet 6. The position was, however, subject to spasmodic and inaccurate enemy gun fire. Major M.F. Strutt, Sgt. Roberts and Gnr. Howarth were awarded the M.C., M.M., and M.M. respectively for their work at Metameur on 6th March.

14th April: 1100hrs. One Tp. From each Bty. Moved fwd. to square P3578 and carried out successful shoots in sp. of Staffs..Yeo. and Inf. who tried to take Enfidaville. They were heavily shelled by the enemy and 21 casualties were sustained mainly by 212 Bty. During this and the previous few days there was a noticeable absence of enemy air activity. At last light O.P.'s and fwd. troops all returned to area P3673.

15th April: Regt. remained in area P3673 and was not in action.

16th April: 0915hrs. Regt. moved to rest area P3571. Some additional vehicles were received and preparations were made for the forthcoming attack by 10 Corps.

17th April: No entry in War Diaries today.

18th April: No entry in War Diaries today.

19th April: 1800hrs. Reg. H.Q. established in battle position at P288740. 2300hrs. Btys. deployed in area P2978. Barrage in sp. 5 N.Z. Bde. Started at 2300hrs.

20th April: 0146hrs. Barrage completed. Report received that objectives partially taken and Enfidaville clear. 0900hrs. Btys. commenced to leapfrog up to square 3284. H.Q. bringing up the rear at 1200hrs. During the afternoon the Regt. area was shelled and bombed without there being any casualties. One O.P. tank was hit by shellfire and two other O.P. trucks went up on mines; a few minor casualties. The Regt. fired concentrations on enemy M.E.T. and Inf.

21st April: A day of great Arty. activity on both sides. The Regt. fired numerous concentrations on enemy Inf. and guns; some of these were in support of an attack by Staff. Yeo. on the Takrouna Feature. None of the enemy concentrations fell on the Regt. and only a few stray rounds landed near the guns. No casualties were caused thereby. However, 212 Bty. had one premature which killed one man and injured one or two others. 1800hrs. Takrouna feature finally cleared, some 300 P.W.'s being taken. O.P.'s were withdrawn at last light.

22nd April: Much artillery activity on both sides. Numerous concentrations were fired by the Regt. Several enemy concentrations launched in the Regimental area, one on 211 Bty at 1130 caused the death of Lt. C.R. Harris, R.A. and two in 212 Bty. between 1640 and 1710hrs. caused two minor casualties, "brewed up" two tractors and damaged other vehicles. As a result 212 Bty. moved one Tp. forward. It was however found impossible to move the Regt. as a whole because most other available positions were already occupied.

23rd April: 0845hrs. O.P.'s reported that enemy guns had withdrawn. Activity was therefore on a greatly reduced scale.1445hrs. A small scale enemy advance was dispersed by gun fire. 2200hrs. N.Z. adv. forward to the next ridge without meeting opposition in force.

24th April: 1005hrs. Enemy infiltration was stopped by heavy Arty. concentrations. Many regimental targets were engaged during the day.

25th April: 0938hrs. Regiment fired 15 r.p.g. on enemy mortars which were concentrating in Tarhouna. N.Z. Div. moved forward to Tarhouna feature with 3 RTR in sp.

26th April: Many "stonks" on hostile batteries. Lt. W. Simmons killed by direct hit.

27th April: Spasmodic shelling and mortar fire throughout the day. 400 r.p.g. were dumped in troop positions. The system of having one Bty. silent resting was instituted.

28th April: Regt. in support of 152 Bde. 51 H.D. (Highland Division) for the day. General attack ("Cholera") in whole front postponed for 24 hours. Arty. duels throughout day.

29th April: 0930hrs. 56 Div. took over front from N.Z. Div. 1000hrs. Regt. fired on 6 D.F. tasks. Counter-attack by enemy caused 56 Div. to withdraw and Regt. called in to spt. this Div.

1655hrs. 4 Indian Div. ordered to stand to. "Cholera" postponed indefinitely. ENFIDAVILLE – During morning 56 Div. thickened up and reorganised. L.O. sent to 111 Fld. & 4 Indian Div.

30th April: Lt. R.V. Seddon, R.A. and Lt. J.W. Nicholls evacuated through illness.1500hrs.Regt. Fired 112 r.p.g. on counter-battery programme. 1945hrs. 211 Bty. R.A. went out for three days' rest.

May

1st May: ENFIDAVILLE 1210hrs. Quick barrage fired over enemy M.G.'s and Mortars.1500hrs.Task table of concentrations commenced which continued during afternoon to 1725hrs. Many "stonks" fired during day resulting in expenditure of 200 r.p.g. 476 Bty. and 212. Bty.and Battle H.Q. withdrawn from the line to rest.

2nd May: Main R.H.Q. joined Regt. in rest area.

3rd May: Lt. G.G. Owens, R.A. evacuated (sick).

4th May: 1030 hrs. 211 Fld. Bty. R.A. returned from Hergla and joined Rgt. in rest area.

5th May: Training commenced with special attention to signallers and layers.

6th – 7th May: Training continued in rest area.

8th May: Tunis and Bizerte taken by 1st Army & U.S.A. Corps.

9th May: ENFIDAVILLE – 1530 hrs. Regt. moved back to old positions and continued firing concentrations.

10th May: ENFIDAVILLE – Daily average of 4,000 fired. Expenditure accelerated in afternoon owing to 10 Corps message that Bosch would surrender when his Amm. was finished.

11th May: Continuous firing, chiefly H.B. and multiple mortars.

12th May: 1030 hrs. 155mm mortar from rocket Bty hit office truck. Lt. Col. W.P. Hobbs, M.B.E., R.A., and 2nd Lt. D.W.G. Cassell, R.A. (R.S.O.) killed. Many Regt. records destroyed. Total 4 vehicles brewed up.1930hrs. Regt. withdrew to S. of Enfidaville the campaign being virtually over.

13th May: Resting. Major C.H.A. Barnes, R.A. (2nd I.C.) assumes Command and rank of Lt. Col.[1].

Notes

1 At 2-45p.m. on this day, General Alexander signalled to Mr Churchill: "Sir, it is my duty to report that the Tunisian campaign has ceased. We are masters of the North African shores."

Charles Robinson – Military Timeline

1940

15th February – Joined 310th Infantry Training Company, Lancashire Fusiliers.

12th August – Training completed. Posted to Lancashire Fusiliers

11th September – Posted to 125th Infantry Brigade, Headquarters (Preston)

1941

31st January – Transferred to 42nd Divisional Signals.

28th March – 42nd Divisional Signals – Signalman.

24th April – Attached to 111 Field Regiment, Royal Artillery.

8th August – Passed "OWL" (Operator of Wireless & Line Grade 3) Signalman.

1942

11th – 17th June – Redesdale Military Firing Range, Northumbria. (Rgt. Att. 50th Div)

17th June – Left Glasgow for Durban on HMT "Awatea"

20th July – "Awatea" docked Durban, South Africa.

16th August – HMT "Kosciuszko" left Durban for Egypt.

7th September – "Kosciuszko" docked Port Tewfik, Suez Canal, Egypt.

7th September – "Under canvas" at Kabrit Camp

20th September – Regiment arrived Almaza Camp, near Cairo

23th October – 4th November Battle of El-Alamein. (50th Division)

1st November – Daba Alex, El-Mreir

4th November – Rgt. in support S.E. Yorks holding Ruweisat Ridge

16th November – Rgt. came under command 30 Corps as Corps artillery.

28th November – Rgt. Left Fuka.

3rd December – Entered Libya.

1943

14th January – Rgt. came under command 22nd Armoured Brigade.

3rd February – Rgt. under command 7th Armoured Division

14th February – Entered Tunisia

4th March – Joined 8th Armoured Brigade.

14th March – Rgt. and 8th Armoured Brigade came under the command of 2nd N.Z. Division.

12th – 28th Rgt. passed deep into the desert, outflanking the Mareth Line.

April – Sousse, Takrouna, Tarhouna, Enfidaville.

May - Enfidaville.

A Soldier's Prayer

Stay with me, God.
The night is dark,
The night is cold:
My little spark
Of courage dies.
The night is long;
Be with me God,
And make me strong.

The above verse, written by an unknown British soldier, is the first part of a much longer poem that had been blown into a slit trench in Tunisia, sometime after a fierce battle at El-Agheila, in Libya, early in the Second World War.

The verse was found in a work of fiction by Dean Koontz called "The Husband" on page 431. My husband was reading this book whilst we were on holiday in Tunisia, and read the above poem contained within it, two days before we were due to visit Enfidaville War Cemetery. It was quite an uncanny experience for us in its timeliness and relevance.

The complete poem can be found on the website: www.Holistic-online.com A Soldier's Prayer.

APPENDIX D

Letter To Uncle Charlie

Dear Uncle Charlie,

Hello. My name is Karen. I am your niece, and the first member of the family to visit your final resting place, seventy years to the day since you were laid to rest with your combat companions. My husband Terry is with me. I am the daughter of your sister, Marjorie. You will be pleased to learn that at the age of ninety one your sister is still living – physically well – but her memory is not as good as it used to be. Just a few days ago I went to see her in the nursing home and told her of my planned visit to Enfidaville. As always, when she speaks your name she becomes tearful, and despite her problems with memory, has never forgotten the loss of her beloved brother. She sends her love to you. Incredibly, Jim, her husband of over seventy years is still her constant companion in the care home. Over seven decades ago when you sent a prayer from North Africa to England, your intercession was received, and answered, as your sister and her then new husband are still together, enjoying a long, fulfilling relationship that has moved beyond the test of time. Your father died first at the age of sixty eight after losing his fight with cancer. Your mother lived till she was ninety one. Your younger brother Norman came through the war, but sadly died in an accident at the age of fifty one. Despite losing her husband and two sons, Grandma stayed strong, her faith and her hymns providing comfort. She must have been a good mother to you as she was a good grandma to me and loved me unconditionally. Your father, also was a very loving granddad. I like to compare Grandma to a marshmallow – with a difference – soft and round and squidgy, but with a hard nut in the middle (a tough nut to crack.) because she stayed strong, coping with three major losses in her life. I have received several letters from your cousin Hilda, who is now in her eighties, recalling the good times you had when you were young and happily energetic, boarding the tram for a day out in Vernon Park, Stockport. Your family, of which I am proud to be a part, were close-knit, enjoying each other's company during Christmases, high days and holidays.

The diary you so helpfully filled in every day from the 1st January, 1943 detailing all your military experiences, those challenging days, as well as the vast number of places and people of different nationalities you communicated with, was sent back home to your family (a poor consolation for them at the time, but ultimately became very precious) Thirty years ago, your sister inherited the diary from your mother and touchingly, wrote on the blank day of your death and the days after, about the continuing sadness she felt. Even as the years stretched out behind her, she still thought of you every day.

She also sorted through your many letters, preserving twenty three of the most informative, memorable, historical and amusing examples. I have now inherited these precious items, and in writing my book, reading about your many and varied experiences so many years after they happened, I feel I know you very well.

I know there were many times you wrote with anticipation when you were on your way to somewhere different, somewhere you could walk round, savouring the sights and sounds of a new and unusual town or city, and you appreciated the out-of-the-ordinary flavour that foreign travel brought – even though sometimes you had to fight your way out with big guns! I know you had a sense of humour, you enjoyed sweet things (particularly chocolate). You were not really a miser, even though you obsessed about your "allotment" and wrote a long list of

figures at the end of your diary. Mentioned twelve times in your diary,
Elsie was the person you most longed to receive a letter from. Despite
all the hardships you endured and the threats to your life, I know you
appreciated the special times. You saw Montgomery four times, you saw
Churchill, Alexander and Brooke on the road to Tripoli, and last but
not least you and your fellow soldiers were the object of unadulterated
joy from the people of Sousse as the 8th Army triumphantly marched
through their liberated town – so ably freed from Nazi occupation.
You also enjoyed a total of two impromptu baths when you were lucky
enough to procure some bags of water. I have also read about your total
of eight glorious swims in the Mediterranean.

Of all the words in your letters and diary, there are only a few
disparaging ones – all found in one letter dated two days after the
unprovoked Japanese attack on Pearl Harbour, which obviously
created in you such a deep outrage towards the Japanese people.
Despite the vulgarities of war: the killing, the wounding, the fear, the
deprivation and the battle-hardening conditions, you had the strength
to remain the person you had always been – naturally friendly and
open-hearted. Your spirit and humanity did not succumb to the
brutality of battle. Your tough life had not hardened your heart.

After reading your letters, diary and different accounts of the
history of the war, I know what you did for me, the citizens of this
country, and most of the people of Europe; you gave your life so millions
of human beings could be free. You made the ultimate sacrifice and I
am proud and grateful to you for that. From the niece you never met I
thank you Uncle Charlie.

Karen

APPENDIX E

Acknowledgements

Firstly I would like to thank Tim Berners Lee, who, as inventor of the World Wide Web, has enabled me to access a tiny fraction of the vast sea of instantly accessible information contained within it. In similar vein, Wikipedia has provided excellent, basic information, images and photographs – a valuable starting point for someone like me who is starting out with very little prior knowledge of the Second World War.

Martin Skipworth, researcher at the Royal Signals Museum, has helpfully passed on information regarding my uncle's role as a signaller. Also thanks are due to Paul Evans of the Royal Artillery Museum, London, for conducting research into slang terms used by soldiers for the vehicles they travelled in.

Thank you to the Army Personnel Centre in Glasgow for sending Charles Robinson's Service Records to me.

I would like to express my gratitude to the staff of the Dock Museum in Barrow for finding and reproducing photographs of the Barrow built ship, the "Awatea" which transported my Uncle from the Clyde to Durban.

Many thanks are due to Jacob Corbin of Tameside Archives for digging around, finding and sending me a copy of a particular letter published in the local newspaper in December 1942.

Thank you to Neill Atkinson, historian of the National Library of New Zealand for permission to reproduce images held in the library.

A special thank you to the following:

Louis Meulstee and his comprehensive website: "Wireless for the Warrior" and for his advice, interest and kindness in ensuring I was sent the correct, digitised, quality photographs of wireless sets 9, 11 and 19.

To Lee Richards of Arcre Document Copying Service, for first class service and for drawing my attention to the Regimental War Diaries in the first place, as I didn't know such documents existed. The original documents were released by the National Archives, (P.R.O.) who have kindly given me permission to reproduce them in this book. The War Diaries have proved to be the perfect companion to my uncle's diary, and have been an invaluable source of historical, military information. (See Appendix A)

I wish to express my thanks to the New Zealand Electronic Text Centre for providing the official history of the 2nd World War, with particular reference to the 2nd New Zealand Division's significant part in the North Africa Campaign, of which my Uncle's regiment came under the command, from mid-March until the end of the campaign.

I wish to make a special mention of Hilda, Mum's cousin who thoughtfully wrote to me with lots of valuable additional family information in her many letters. Finally, I send love and thanks to my immediate family: my husband, who patiently explained about aspects of vehicles and guns. To my son Ian who advised some constructive editing, my younger son Phillip, who made many positive comments. Finally, to the two people who have made this book possible, I send my love and gratitude to Mum for preserving Uncle Charlie's letters and diary and to Uncle Charlie himself for making the decision over seventy years ago to begin such a precious diary.

Karen J. Yates.

APPENDIX F

References

Books

Addison, Paul & Crang, Jeremy A. "Listening to Britain. Home Intelligence Reports on Britain's Finest Hour. May-Sept. 1940."

Atkinson, Rick, "An Army At Dawn."

Koontz, Dean. "The Husband" Extract from the poem "A Soldier's Prayer" p. 431. The complete poem can be found on line at: www.Holistic-online.com

Matanle, Ivor. "50th Anniversary of World War 2" Colour Library Books.

Neillands, Robin. "The Desert Rats. 7th Armoured Division 1940-1945."

Thompson, Julian "Desert Victories – Forgotten Voices".

Paper

British Journal of Industrial Medicine – Feb. 1951. 877. "Cardiovascular Disease in Cotton Workers" By Richard Schilling & Nancy Goodman, from the Nuffield Dept. of Occupational Health, Manchester University. Published by: group.bmj.com (oem.bmj.com)

National Archives

Regimental war diaries of 111 field regiment, royal artillery

W.O. 169/4602 111 Fld. Rgt. June – Dec. 1942.

W.O. 169/9512 111 Fld. Rgt. Jan. – Jun. 1943)

Internet

Alexander, Harold: https://en.wikipedia.org/wiki/Harold_Alexander-1st-Earl-Alexander-of-Tunis

Alexander Turnbull Library of New Zealand: www.natlib.govt.nz/researchers

Army Museums: www.armymuseums.org.uk

Arnott's Hardtack Biscuits (history of). www.cookiesloungebar.com.au/history/

Artillery Gun Firing Order: http://nigelef.tripod.com

"A Soldier's Prayer." www.Holistic_online.com

"Awatea." H.M.T. "An Army at Dawn" by Rick Atkinson. (p.174)

Also: http://www.navy.nz and www.dockmuseum.org.uk

Battles 1942: www.btinternet.com/ianapaterson/battles1942htm www.criticalpast.com/libyahtm

Battles 1943 www.btinternet.com/ianapaterson/battles1943htm

Battle of Kharkov: www.wikipedia.org.ThirdbattleofKharkov

Battle of Velikiye Luki: www.historynet.com/velikiyeluki

British Army Officers: 1939-45 www.unithistories.com

British Army: Royal Signals History: http://www.army.mod.uk/signals/heritage1309.aspx

British Artillery Organisations: http://nigelef.tripod.com/RAorg.htm

British Artillery in World War 2: http://www.ra39-45.pwp.blueyonder. co.uk

111 Field Regiment: http://nigelef.tripod/regt.summ.htm

BBC (History Of): www.bbc.co.ukhistoryofthebbc/innovation

B.B.C History: World Wars: www.bbc.co.uk/history/interactivemap/ northafrica

BBC 2 – People's War – Stories: www.bbc.co.uk/history/WW2peopleswar

Brooke, Alan, Viscount: https://en.wikipedia.org/wiki/Alan_ Brooke1stViscountAlanbrooke

Censorship & Propaganda: http://www.johndclare.net/wwii12. htm

Churchill, Winston: http://www.winstonchurchill.org

"Coal Distribution": http://www.hansard.millbanksystems. com.Lord'sSitting. 29th January, 1941. Vol. 118.

"Comforts for the Troops." By Ian Durant: http://www. sentimentaljourney.co.uk/tl/comfort.htm

Cue Sports (Billiards): http://www.wikipedia.org/wiki/cuesports

Cwm Rhonda. Hymn No. 839 "A Collection of Hymns – For the use of the people called Methodists" By John Wesley www.ccel.org/w/wesley/hymn/jwg0839html

Desert Rats: www.desertrats.org.uk http://en.wikipedia/wiki/ desertrat

Distance Calculator: http://www.distance-calculator.co.uk

42nd Divisional Signals: http://nigelef.tripod.com/RAorg.htm

Document Copying Service: http://www.arcre.com

Durbin, Deanna: http://www.wikipedia.org/wiki/deannadurbin

El-Alamein: www.spartacus.schoolnet.co.uk/secondww

www.historylearningsite.co.uk/El-Alamein.htm

www.secondworldwarhistory.com

www.El-Alameinorbat.com (Order of Battle)

www.wikipedianorthafricacampaign

Engagements 1943: www.btinternet.com/ianapaterson/battles1943htm

Film: "Cottage to Let" http://www.wikipedia.org/wiki/Cottage to let

General Grant Tank: http://wikipedia.org/wiki/M3Leehistory

Graces Guide to Industry: (Rexine) www.gracesguide.co.uk

Guide Bridge Railway Station: http://www.wikipedia.org/wiki/guidebridgerailwaystation

Hadrian's Camp, Carlisle: www.carlislehistory.co.uk

Hay, Ian (John Hay Beith) http://en.wikipedia.org/wiki/John_Hay_Beith

Heliograph: http://wikipedia.org/wiki/file/heliograph

History of British Army Wireless Sets: "Wireless for the Warrior." http://wftw.nl/

Humber Armoured Car: www.en.wikipedia.org/wiki/Humber_car

Impetigo: www.nhs.uk/conditions/impetigo

Junkers 88: http://en.wikipedia.org/wiki/Junkers_Ju88

Kabrit R.A.F. Station, Egypt: http://www.wikipedia.org/wiki/kabrit

Lancashire Fusiliers: www.lancs-fusiliers.co.uk

Libya 1942/3 http://en.wikipedia.org/wiki/Libya

"London Gazette" http://www.londongazette.co.uk

M3 Stuart Tank: (Honey) https://en.wikipedia.org/wiki/M3_Stuart.

M3 (White) Scout Car: www.wikipedia.org/wiki/M3Scoutcar

M4 Sherman Tank http://en.wikipedia.org/wiki/M4_Sherman

Marmon Herrington Armoured Car:

http://en.wikipedia.org/wiki/MarmonHerringtonArmouredcar

McAdam, John Loudon: www.About.com.inventors

ME109 (Messerschmitt BF109) http://wikipedia.org/wiki/messerschmitt_Bf_109

Mein Kampf: http://www.wikipedia.org'wiki/meinkamph

Money Values 1943/2013: www.thisismoney.co.uk/money/hist oricinflationcalculator

Montgomery, Bernard Law: http://en.wikipedia.org/wiki/Bernard/montgomery

National Archives: www.nationalarchives.gov.uk

National Army Museum: www.national-army-museum.ac.uk

Nebelwerfer: http://en.wikipedia.org/wiki/Nebelwerfer

New Zealand Electronic Text Centre: "The Official History of New Zealand in the Second World War 1939-1945. www.nzetc.victoria.ac.nz

New Zealand HistoryOnline: http://nzetc.victoria.ac.nz. "Bardia to Enfidaville". by Major General Stevens

2nd New Zealand Divisional Artillery. "Operations Around Djebibina." By W.E. Murphy: http://nzetc.victoria.ac.nz/tm/schorlarly/tei-WH2Arti-c15-11.html

North Africa Campaign: www.britishmilitaryhistory.co.uk. www.nzhistoryonlinethenorthafricacampaign

"Notes on Tactics & Techniques of Desert Warfare": by Major General George S. Patton Jnr.1942.www.patonhq.comtextfileshtm

Pearl Harbour: www.widipedia.org/wike/attackonPearl-Harbor

Pendlebury Hall: http://www.britishlistedbuildings.co.uk/en21 0861_pendeburyhall

Pounds, Shillings and Pence currency: www.woodlands-junior.kent.sch.uk

Rommel, Erwin: http://en.wikipedia.org/wiki/erwin-rommel. http://www.spartacus.schoolnet.co.uk/GERrommel. htm#source. www.topedge.com/panels/ww2na/tacticshtml

Royal Artillery: www.firepower.org.uk

Royal Signals Museum: www.royalsignalsmuseum.co.uk/ website/index.php/archives

Stuka: http://en.wikipedia.org/wiki/Junkers-Ju87 http://plane crazy.purplecloud.net/aircraft/stukahtm

Takrouna Feature: http://www.nzhistory.net.nz/media/photo/ summit-takrouna

Tameside Archives: www.tameside.gov.uk/archives

Teller Mines: http://www.wikipedia.org/wiki/Tellermine_35

Theatre Royal, Hyde: www.hydetheatreroyal.co.uk

Timeline: www.worldwar-2.net

Trove Digitised Newspapers: http://trove.nla.gov.au

Tunisia 1943. www.britishmilitaryhistory.co.uktunisia

www.wikipediatunisiacampaign

www.wikipedia.org/wiki/marethline

Walpole, Hugh: http://www.wikipedia.org/wiki/Hugh_Walpole

Warship Week: http://www.wikipedia.org/wiki/warship_week http://www.hydonian.blogspot.co.uk/HMSWrestler

APPENDIX G

Illustrations

p.8. Two photographs of C.R. (Charles Robinson) as baby and toddler.

p.9. C.R. in the Scout movement.

pp.10-12. 4 photographs taken from 1936 to 1938 depicting C.R.'s pre-war travels.

p.12. Copy of photo-card featuring the full cast of a three act play. (C.R. in centre of photo.)

p.15. Copy of original envelope addressed to C.R.'s parents.

p.26. "Signalling Class, Carlisle, 1940."

p.34. On leave with family and friends.

p.57. The troop ship "Awatea".

p.122. Wireless Set 19. "Wireless For The Warrior" www.wftw.nl Thanks to Louis Meulstee.

p.142. Wireless Set 11 Thanks once again to the comprehensive website of Louis Meulstee's "Wireless for the Warrior."

p.167. Outflanking The Mareth Line: Map:nzetc.victoria.ac.nz/tm/scholarly/WH2Bard-fig-WH2Bar-fo25.html Permission granted from neill.atkinson@mch.govt.vuw.ac.nz http://natlib.govt.nz

p.183. Gabes To Enfidaville: http://nzetc.victoria.ac.nz/tm/scholarly/WH2.Bard-fig-WH2Bar-f057.html

p.210. Takrouna. Photo: Ref. DA-10929 – Summit of Takrouna 1943. Taken from New Zealand History Online:www.nzhistory.net>Medialibrary>information@natlib.govt.nz Alexander Turnbull Library of New Zealand.

APPENDIX H

Glossary

ACCUMULATOR An electrical storage device: a type of battery.

ADJ or ADJUTANT A Commanding Officer's administrative assistant.

Adv. Advance/advanced

A.F.V. Armoured Fighting Vehicle

A.G.R.A. Army Group Royal Artillery

A.P. Advanced Patrol.

A.P. Armour Piercing

A.P.O. Army Post Office

ARMISTICE A truce in war to discuss terms for peace.

ARTILLERY or ARTY. Heavy guns, canons, large calibre weapons, and the soldiers who use them.

Att. III Fld. Reg. R.A. Attached to 111 Field Regiment, Royal Artillery

AWATEA Troop Ship that transported Charles Robinson from the Clyde to Durban in June/July 1942.

AXIS World War 2 fascist powers. The military and political alliance of Germany, Italy, and later Japan that fought the Allies in World War Two

BARRAGE Precise meaning for an artillery regiment. A moving or stationary belt of fire, in lines or lanes, providing a protective screen, behind which attackers advanced or defenders were positioned. A moving barrage could be creeping, rolling or block, and set to advance at a specific rate.

BATTALION A military unit typically consisting of a headquarters and three or more companies, batteries, or other subunits of similar size.

BATTERY A group of artillery pieces that function as a single tactical unit, usually comprising 8 guns, commanded by 1 Major, 3 Captains, 6 Subalterns and with gunners and other ranks operating the guns.

BDE. Brigade. A military unit consisting of two or more combat battalions or regiments and associated support units. It is smaller than a Division and is commanded by a Brigadier.

BIVVY A simple shelter or tent

BLIGHTY A slang term for Britain.

BLITZ A sustained aerial attack: a heavy air raid intended to obliterate a target.

BOOTBLACK Someone who cleans shoes, usually in the street.

BREWED UP A direct hit – blown up

BULLY (beef) Tinned corn beef

CALIBRATION Standardisation of a measuring instrument, checking against an accurate standard to determine any deviation.

C.B. Counter Battery (Fire). The locating and silencing of hostile guns.

CCRA Commander Corps Royal Artillery.

CENSORSHIP To remove objectionable material from a play, film or letter, considered to be a threat to national security.

CHELMSFORD County town of Essex, 32 miles from London, and 32 miles from Colchester.

C. in C. Commander in Chief

C.I.G.S. Chief of the Imperial General Staff.

CIVVY BILLET Temporary accommodation for service personnel in a private home.

Cmd. Command

C.O. Commanding Officer

C.O. 2 Second in Command

COMPANY A unit of soldiers, usually consisting of two or more platoons.

CORPS A military unit, which carries out specialised duties.

CORVETTE An armed naval escort vessel, smaller than a destroyer.

D.C.M. Distinguished Conduct Medal

DE-BUSSING A military term meaning the unloading of troops and equipment.

D.F. Divisional Front.

DIVISION A self-contained military unit, capable of sustained operations, including a headquarters, and two or more brigades.

DRAFT (Military) – to send a soldier somewhere for duty, or to carry out a particular task.

DUFF A heavy suet pudding, steamed or boiled in a cloth.

FALL IN To join or form an organised rank.

FFW Fitted for wireless.

FIELD REGIMENT (Royal Artillery) Comprising 2, 3 or 4 Batteries and a Head Quarters. (111 Field Regiment had 3 Batteries.) The Commanding Officer had the rank of Lieutenant Colonel.

FOO Forward Observation Officer

FUS. Fusilier. Soldiers from certain regiments, who historically were armed with a 'fusi' or a light musket.

GAITER A strip of fabric covering the leg from instep to knee

Gnr. Gunner

G.O.C. General Officer in Command

Gps. Groups

GREAT BENTLEY, COLCHESTER A village situated midway between Colchester and Clacton-on-Sea, in Essex.

GUIDE BRIDGE 4¾ miles east of Piccadilly, Manchester, on the Glossop line. Operational today.

HALKIRK, CAITHNESS Halkirk is situated to the north of Caithness, the northernmost county of Great Britain.

H.B. Hostile Battery. (Enemy)

H.D. (51) – Fifty First Highland Division.

HELIOS – plural of helio, which is a shortened version of heliograph (Helio + Graph) = sun-writer in the Greek language. It is a mirrored communication device for sending messages in code by flashing reflected sun's rays to a distant station.

H.F. Harassing Fire

H.M.T. His Majesty's Troop Ship

H.Q. Head Quarters

H.Q.R.A. Head Quarters Royal Artillery

IND. DIV. (4) Fourth Indian Division

INFANTRY or INF Foot soldiers, trained to fight on foot. Also a unit of such soldiers making up a regiment.

ITC Infantry Training Company

JERRY Slang for German soldier.

K.D.G. Kings Dragoon Guards

KINGSTOWN AERODROME Situated 2 miles north of Carlisle, opened in the 1930's and formerly known as R.A.F. Kingstown.

KOSCIUSZKO Troop Ship that transported Charles Robinson from Durban to Egypt in Sept. 1942.

L.A.D. Light Aid Detachment. This unit carried out 'deeper' repairs and maintenance that were beyond the scope of the regular regimental engineers.

LEAGUER Camp, especially of a besieging army.

LINES Positioned formation of troops, weapons, or fortification, positioned in a place.

L.O. Liaison Officer

LUFTWAFFE German Air Force.

MACADAM Named after John Louden Macadam: 1756 – 1836 A Scotsman who developed better road building by laying a bed of broken stones, followed by a layer of smaller stones, weighing no more than 6 ounces each. Later a top layer of tar was added as cars began to run on the roads.

M.C. Military Cross. In recognition of an act or acts of exemplary gallantry during active operations against the enemy on land.

M.E.F. Middle East Forces

M.E.T. Mechanised Enemy Transport. (Enemy vehicles.)

M.G. Machine Gun

M.M. Military Medal. Awarded for acts of gallantry and devotion to duty under fire.

MORTAR A cannon with a relatively short and wide barrel, used for firing shells at a high angle over a short distance.

M.T. Motor Transport.

NAAFI Navy, Army and Air Force Institute. Founded by the Government in 1921, to provide café's, canteens, shops, etc for the armed forces.

NCO Non-commissioned officer

No.1 I.T. Coy: Number One Infantry Training Company

Obs. Observation.

O.O. Operation Orders

O.P. Observation Post

O/R. OTHER RANKS (None officers)

PHONETIC ALPHABET International radiotelephony spelling alphabet: "Alpha, Bravo, Charlie" used a more primitive form in 1943, with some different words, but the principle was still the same before being internationally standardized in the 1950s

PLATOON A subdivision of a company of soldiers, usually led by a lieutenant and consisting of two or three sections or squads of ten to twelve people.

P.M. Prime Minister

P.O. Postal order.

QUARTERMASTER SGT. The sergeant in charge of army equipment.

R.A. Royal Artillery.

Rds. Rounds

R.E. Royal Engineers.

REC. COY. Recovery Company

RECCE. To reconnoitre or explore an area to gather information about terrain or enemy positions.

REGIMENTAL WAR DIARIES Written by a senior officer in each Regiment detailing daily events.

REVEILLE A bugle or trumpet call, usually at sunrise to wake service personnel.

REXINE The trade mark name for a company manufacturing artificial leather cloth fabric. It was one quarter of the price of natural leather, and was used in the manufacture of padded dash boards and doors in the motor car industry. It was also used in book binding.

R.H.Q. Regimental Headquarters

ROMMEL Erwin. Commander in Chief of the German Desert Army: the Afrika Korps.

R.p.g. Rounds per gun.

R.S.M. Regimental Sergeant Major

RT. HON. Right Honourable

RTR Royal Tank Regiment.

R.W.F. Royal Welsh Fusiliers

SCHEME Training scheme.

SECTION COMMANDER Officer appointed to supervise a section of two guns.

SHRAPNEL An artillery shell, designed to explode before impact, producing a shower of metal balls and fragments. Named after General Henry Shrapnel British Artillery Officer (1761- 1842)

SILLOTH A coastal town situated on the Solway Firth.

SGT. MAJOR A non-commissioned officer, and enlisted soldier rising to a high-ranking position.

STAND TO To take up position in readiness for military action.

STATIC Relating to, or caused by, electrical interference.

STONK A quick, defensive artillery concentration according to a pre-arranged pattern.

STUKA Short for Sturzkampfflugzeug, translated from the German as: "diving combat aircraft".

SUBALTERN General term for a commissioned officer below the rank of Captain. In Royal Artillery terms a subaltern was a Lieutenant or a 2nd Lieutenant.

SUP. (Or SP). – Support.

TAC. H.Q. Tactical Headquarters. Situated on the front line during battle.

TGT. or Tgt. Target.

THETFORD A market town situated between Norwich and London

TIFFIN A light meal, usually at lunch time.

TRAM LINES & SETS Tram lines and sets of cobblestones set in the road.

TROOP, TR. or TP. A unit of soldiers that forms a subdivision of an artillery battery comprising 4 guns, and is about the size of a platoon.

WADI A mainly dry steep-sided water course, unless there has been recent heavy rain.

X CORPS Armoured Divisions.

XXX CORPS Infantry Divisions